Kids on Earth

Kids on Earth

The Learning Potential of 5 Billion Minds

HOWARD BLUMENTHAL
ROBERT C. PIANTA

HARVARD EDUCATION PRESS
CAMBRIDGE, MASSACHUSETTS

Paperback ISBN 9798895570333

Library of Congress Cataloging-in-Publication Data is on file.

Published by Harvard Education Press,
an imprint of the Harvard Education Publishing Group

Harvard Education Press
8 Story Street
Cambridge, MA 02138

Cover Design: Abigail Coyle
Cover Image: world map by Yana Lesnick via Shutterstock; student portraits © Media Learning, Inc., used by permission.

The typefaces in this book are A Garamond Pro.

This book is dedicated to children and teenagers all over the world,
and to the adults who make a difference in their lives.
When you see a child or teenager in this book,
you're seeing part of a Kids on Earth video interview.
Our thanks to the hundreds of children who have been interviewed so far
as part of the Kids on Earth project.
To watch them in action, visit www.kidsonearth.org.
We are also grateful to the hundreds of parents, teachers, school
administrators, university researchers, government officials, and friends
who made these interviews possible, and who shared their many ideas
about school today and in the future.
Thank you, everyone.

Contents

About the Book's Title

Kids on Earth began, and continues, as a global project. Hundreds of children and teenagers from dozens of countries have told us about their lives, what they want and need to learn, and their plans for the future. To watch these video interviews, visit www.kidsonearth.org.

Photographs in this book are still frames from the interviews. Parents and guardians, and "kids" over eighteen years old, have granted permission for use of this material in connection with Kids on Earth projects.

Generally, they express a very optimistic view of their own future, and their own desire and ability to learn. As authors, we have placed children and teenagers at the center of our own ideas about learning in the twenty-first century. We begin by defining terms.

Kids—A "kid" is a person living under adult supervision or control, as young as an infant, as old as a teenager, and sometimes into their twenties.

on Earth—This planet is home to more than 8 billion people, and about 20 percent of them are kids. For every ten kids on Earth, six live in Asia, two live in Africa, one lives in Europe, and one lives in the Americas. About one in one hundred live in Australia and Oceania.

Learning—The process of acquiring and connecting ideas and skills that are personally meaningful and worth remembering.

Potential—As humans continue to make progress, imagine what the healthiest, wealthiest, best connected, most literate, and longest living generation of humans in the history of the world can do! The healthiest, wealthiest, best connected, most literate, longest living generation of humans in the history of the world are among us. Imagine what they will do!

5 Billion—Nearly five billion "kids" growing up during the first half of this century.

Minds—Every kid, every human, possesses a means to learn, believe, know, and understand. The mind is constantly evolving, growing, trimming, remembering, forgetting, associating, dissociating, and redefining what it means to be alive. School is only one factor affecting what human beings learn, believe, know, and understand. Learning begins before birth. Humans learn for a lifetime.

INTRODUCTION

This is a book about growing up and learning in the twenty-first century. It is written to address the interests and needs of nearly five billion children and teenagers attending primary and secondary public school worldwide between now and 2050.[1] By then, the earth's population will approach ten billion people.[2] In short, this book is about educating half the people on Earth.

What do they need to know? Does everybody need to know the same things, or is there greater value in diversity of knowledge? Are learning, school, and education more or less synonymous, or are they learning in many different ways? What do Kids on Earth need to learn, know, and understand?

The lives of people growing up in the twenty-first century are very different from the lives of people who grew up in the twentieth century. A long and healthy life is now a reasonable expectation.[3] They are growing up amid a global consumer economy, a productive workforce, many career options, a larger middle class,[4] and what could be the end of widespread extreme poverty.[5] With notable exceptions, individual rights and freedoms are more rule than exception. Many young people now grow up in relative safety, without the economic necessity of working to support their family. They possess the time and resources to focus on their interests, their education, and their future. They make decisions based on abundant information and sophisticated reasoning. They enjoy more points of connection with people in other cultures and other countries than any past generation. Most are aware of existential threats related to peace and prosperity, clean air, food and water, mental and physical health, and economic stability. In part, school has been responsible for this progress.

More than half the people in the world can access abundant information on almost any subject via the internet (some cannot, but not for much longer). Roughly 1.4 billion students currently attend primary and secondary school, but preschool is being added to the universal mix, and secondary enrollment is increasing, so nearly two billion students will attend school in the 2030s.

Children and teenagers growing up in the twenty-first century require education aligned with their lives. Care for the planet and one another requires modern thinking. School remains a useful local gathering place, but the current structure of public education has run its course. It requires rethinking and reworking. To facilitate that process, this book offers a conceptual basis for a significant transformation, and a practical framework based on fresh thinking by students, teachers, parents, and other learning experts.

Mostly, this book is about children and teenagers, what they want and need to survive and thrive, what adults can do for them, and the ways school and community might help.

GROWING UP IN THE TWENTY-FIRST CENTURY

Children and teenagers have changed. A twentieth-century conception no longer applies. In 2021, UNICEF and Gallup surveyed young people aged fifteen to twenty-four and adults aged forty-plus—more than twenty-one thousand people in twenty-one countries. The survey confirms significant generational differences.

> Young people are almost twice as likely as older people to say they identify most with being part of the world, as opposed to feeling primarily part of their local community or country.[6]
>
> Overall . . . young people embody the spirit of the 21st century more readily than their older counterparts. Young people are more active and savvy users of digital technology than members of their parents' generation. They are quicker to see its benefits and more at ease with its risks, even as they too voice serious concerns.[7]
>
> When children have agency—the personal capacity to act and make free and informed choices to pursue a specific goal—it empowers them to actively participate in and engage with the world around them.[8]
>
> Young people are optimistic about the future and recognize the progress that has been made, including in key areas of children's lives. Yet they are not complacent. Young people recognize both the benefits from, and the risks associated with, their increasingly digital lives.[9]
>
> They are not just accepting of changed norms; they also demand greater tolerance and pluralism, including in the realm of LGBTQ+ rights. . . . This group has only known a highly digitized, interconnected, and more pluralistic world.[10]

The challenge now is to listen to these views on childhood and the world—and meet young people's clear-eyed optimism with action.[11]

THE BIGGER PICTURE

Powerful forces are reshaping daily life and resetting priorities. Ideas rarely discussed in the twentieth century are now top of mind. Driven by identity, agency, social justice, global awareness, unstable political systems, technology, and more, today's children and teenagers define childhood and adolescence in ways that were inconceivable when their parents and teachers grew up.

Children and teenagers watched as seven million people died in the COVID-19 pandemic, and nearly seven hundred million people were infected. Many hospitals were unable to care for the sick; loved ones died. Since the beginning of the HIV epidemic, forty million people have died, and eighty-five million have been infected, including one in twenty-five African adults.[12] Some students in the US are afraid to go to school because they might get shot by a former student with an assault rifle; the palpable sense of danger is amplified by shooter response preparedness drills in K–12 classrooms.[13] Children and teenagers study details of war in Ukraine and elsewhere through a ceaseless multiplatform flow of news coverage never before experienced on Earth. There are floods and extreme heat, and enormous wildfires, but no concerted action by adults to put aside fossil fuels to mitigate climate change. Young people are skeptical, fearful, and dealing with serious mental health concerns—with good reason. As they observe twenty-first century adults in action, many do not see the path to stability, safety, peace, wisdom, or economic success. They hope school will provide the answers they need.

There is much more to know now than there was in the 1990s, and many more sources of information, too. About half the people in the world share what they believe and know via the internet and social media, but the pool is polluted by disinformation, old information, and misleading and incomplete information. With uncertain editorial oversight and few trusted gatekeepers, as well as artificial intelligence (AI) generating stories, confirmation of accurate and relevant information is difficult for everyone—and especially challenging for children and teenagers because they possess less experience and thinner context. Diversity of ideas is valuable, but intermingled beliefs, opinions, knowledge, and contexts require clear thinking. Precise, accurate answers are hard to find. There is scant reason to believe technology's progress will be regulated or made safe for use by children and teenagers. In theory, children, teenagers, and everyone else could figure out what to believe on their own, but school offers at least the potential of an honest broker, an institution where young people can learn the skills they require to sort sense from nonsense. What they learn, they will probably rely on for a lifetime.

Children and teenagers are increasingly aware of the world of nations and cultures. They assess possible futures by considering college, careers, and perhaps life in other countries. To educate young people solely for life in their own countries is short-sighted and limiting. Media provides a global view. School falls short when it does not do the same.

SCHOOL

School now competes to be the primary source of learning; media and the internet are well funded, ubiquitous, agile competitors. School is open weekdays, six–eight hours daily, but closed half the days of the year. When school is closed, everyone learns on their own, albeit without school's standards for quality, integrity, and rigor.

Unfortunately, and probably by design, school resists change. It employs a legacy model based on dissemination, memorization, and testing. Mostly, school ignores twenty-first century cognitive science, contemporary understanding of human behavior, and scenario planning to examine possible futures. Many students, teachers, and parents recognize the need for change. Many are frustrated.

A century ago, when contemporary public school took shape, there were fewer people on Earth (approximately two billion in 1925, compared with eight-plus billion today).[14] In most countries, poverty was rampant, child mortality was high, longevity was low, food and other resources were limited, and expectations were lean. One in two children died before their fifth birthday. Many children did not finish primary school. Most teenagers did not attend secondary school.

Most of today's children and teenagers will live seventy, eighty, ninety years—twice as long as children growing up a hundred years ago. In most countries and cultures, boys *and girls* attend school, regardless of their economic and social situation. Nearly all the world's children—more than 90 percent—attend primary school.[15] About 80 percent attend lower secondary, and about 60 percent attend upper secondary school.

By and large, regional and national efforts to increase school enrollment have succeeded. In 1970, nearly half the world (43 percent) was illiterate. Today, 86 percent of people on Earth read and write (though not always very well).[16] In many communities, public education has been a success—but this is not true everywhere.

Contemporary realities place more pressure on public school than it was designed to bear. People growing up in the twenty-first century possess confidence and potential far beyond the dreams and capacities of their parents and grandparents. We are raising the healthiest, wealthiest, most connected humans in the history of the world. Their curiosity runs wide and deep. They make use of every available resource for learning because their future requires vast, diverse, and modern skills and knowledge. School has not kept up with their intellectual and social development, the transformed world in which they live, or their imagination.

> Quick anecdote. My oldest daughter was in kindergarten. She drew a picture of a purple leprechaun and got an unsatisfactory grade. When I saw this, I went in to the teacher and said, "I don't understand. She made the leprechaun purple. What was wrong with that?" Teacher said, "Leprechauns are green." I said, "Leprechauns aren't real, you know."
>
> —Dr. Mary Jo Podgurski,
> President and Founder, the Academy for Adolescent Health

Too often, students experience school as a rigid setting in which imagination and divergent perspectives are stifled. The material they are told to learn or understand is often experienced as irrelevant to their lives and without clear purpose or utility.

> Sometimes, I think about just leaving the public school system and starting a small school. But that's not the solution. It doesn't solve the problem, and it doesn't help very many students, either.
>
> —Dr. Herbert Monroe,
> Superintendent, Surry County Public Schools, North Carolina, US

Alternative schools and alternative programs within traditional schools are available, but they remain special cases, relatively uncommon in the marketplace. Their typical organizing principle: diversity of individual student interests and experiences. Students develop ideas, implement them as individuals and in small groups, interact with the community, and develop experience and wisdom that may prove useful in the future. Alternative models are used in private schools or charter schools but not at scale in most public schools.

The purpose, design, structure, and operation of public schools has not changed with the times. As a result, school experiences serious, widespread problems with attendance, discipline, motivation, academic performance, and mental health among both students and teachers. These problems are related to what is taught, why, and how. The best efforts, hard work, and dedication of so many students, teachers, principals, specialists, volunteers, parents, and community members could be so much more productive with an up-to-date model for learning in school and a tighter connection with learning not associated with formal schooling.

Despite many extraordinary examples all over the world of what school could be, there is no clear direction, no plan, no common framework for productive, locally relevant, globally useful learning. In this book, we propose a scalable framework for local reinvention that captures contemporary realities.

One more top-down design to modernize school is not helpful. After thirty-plus years of investment and practice, reform based on standards and extensive testing has produced little improvement because it is misaligned with current realities and high-likelihood futures. The current model—teachers prepare lessons to disseminate lists of facts and skills children and teenagers must remember in order to pass tests—has outlived its usefulness. Although certain basic skills and knowledge may be acquired this way, the top-down model is poorly suited to the diversity essential in twenty-first-century learning.

In a previous work, author Bob Pianta pointed out that

> evidence is abundant that deep, authentic, and accelerated learning starts with students—their experiences, goals, and ambitions—and focuses on topics relevant to their lives. . . . Effective teaching starts with recognizing and understanding students' perspectives on their learning and guides students toward new and deeper knowledge and more sophisticated skills. Standards define what adults believe is important to learn and follow a model of teacher-driven instruction in large groups. Is it surprising then that nearly every single study of student motivation shows them starting to disengage around fourth grade, a decline that shows up even earlier and more seriously for students from historically marginalized backgrounds or who have struggled to learn basic skills in prior years? Yet, every student craves learning when it is relevant—given a challenge they care about,

children and youth display high levels of motivation, engagement, and sophistication.[17]

As long as public school has existed, there have been urgent calls for reform. Contemporary arguments focus on inequity, economic and social justice, AI, and the need to address climate change, public health, student access to their mobile phones, and quality and quantity of teachers. In the US, culture wars generate heat around book banning, critical race theory, and values-based lessons.

Unlike many books about growing up and learning, this book does not attempt to reinvent school from the top down. It does not focus on incremental adjustments or local workarounds to satisfy government requirements. Instead, this book deals with economic, social, political, public health, behavioral, technological, local, and global realities.

A TWENTY-FIRST-CENTURY FRAMEWORK

A new framework must address each individual learner's unique interests, life situation, and future pursuits in the midst of rapid global transformation. The key idea: Focus on the individual. The operating theory is not based on mass education, but on fresh thinking about how young people learn:

- **Learning Is Personal.** Learning is a lifelong process involving curiosity, play, gathering and evaluating knowledge, fun, connecting ideas and adding new and discarding other ones, gaining skills, refining understanding, and building relationships based on each individual's unique interests, life situation, and goals. Identity emerges as each person cultivates their own patterns, experimenting and adjusting fit, not only through childhood and adolescence but for a lifetime.
- **Learning Is Relational.** Learning arises from and is deeply intertwined with relationships with others. It starts in the womb and is always "on." The mutual interactions and responses of individuals, a kind of "serve and return." It organizes attention, emotion, thinking, and behavior. Through interactions, relationships come to encompass, support, and shape interests and motivations. Relationships present novelty and risk. They often support sustained engagement that produces a shift in an individual's capacity to understand, and act adaptively in their world, resulting in real and powerful learning.

- **Learning Is Active.** Learning requires personal engagement in ideas that matter to the individual learner, ideas that are relevant and filled with purpose. Learning should invite discovery, exploration, and risk-taking. It should take place in a safe and supportive learning environment, generally free from stress and distraction. It's best when this takes place in connection with other people with similar interests.

As presented, the new framework is not intended to generate or support incremental changes to a stubborn status quo. Instead, it is a conceptual basis for public school based on the interests and needs of people living in a rapidly changing world. Our intention is to advance discussions and to start on the path to local implementation.

KIDS ON EARTH

Confidence in this approach grows from several sources. There is abundant local activity across countries, cultures, and communities that demonstrates positive impact. Our conversations with children, teenagers, parents, educators, and other adults in seventy-five countries have been remarkably consistent in their criticism of the current approach, and their interest in a new philosophy and a practical new framework. The philosophy is based on the way children, teenagers, teachers, and adults learn—except when they are in school.

One precipitating activity for this change comes from hundreds of one-on-one interviews conducted by author Howard Blumenthal with children and teenagers from diverse backgrounds and of various ages in Bulgaria, England, Brazil, Paraguay, India, Ghana, Uganda, Egypt, South Korea, Puerto Rico, Mauritius, Kentucky, Pennsylvania, and dozens of other places. These videos can be seen on the video platform, *Kids on Earth.*[18]

For example, Jonathan, sixteen years old, from England, is nonverbal and immobile. He asked to tell his story on *Kids on Earth* to focus adult attention on his literacy campaign for overlooked students. Jonathan explained that adults do not often listen to ideas from children and teenagers about learning, school, or education.

As *Kids on Earth* interviews were conducted in schools, some teachers and principals were surprised by their students' ideas. Many principals and head teachers admitted they had never asked their own students questions about their experience of learning in and outside of school, or their individual plans for the future. Often, students explained that adults "told them what to do" but "never really listen."

A parallel project, *Reinventing School*, an hour-long video interview series, featured school principals, award-winning teachers, authors, university researchers, superintendents, and government leaders, often with students in the same video conversations as peers.[19] Most guests—adults, children, and teenagers—explained that school is structured from the top down, that the wants and needs of individual students could not be easily addressed within the current structure. While acknowledging that every student is unique, the interviewees' capacity to discuss a modern framework for school and learning was limited. Instead, some described virtues of progressive private schools, home schools, and clever teachers.

THE 21ST CENTURY LEARNING PROJECT

Working with #Learning Planet, the Jena Declaration for Sustainability, UNESCO, and various NGOs, Howard was surprised to find similar frustrations in Africa, South America, Europe, the Middle East, Australia, and many parts of North America. Well aware of developments in technology, media, the internet, artificial intelligence, globalization, gender and identity, diversity, mindfulness, climate change, public health, personal growth, and human progress, the authors found nearly all of these topics to be front of mind for educators and students but lacking in practice in public schools. Education systems seemed too rigid, too inflexible, too fixed in their ways to accommodate the transformations that define life and progress in the twenty-first century.

Howard is neither a traditional educator nor an academic researcher. Gathering information from conversations with people of all ages throughout the world, he was curious about the intellectual capital, insights, research, and relationships a major university could provide.

Enter Bob Pianta, then completing fifteen years of service as dean of the School of Education and Human Development at the University of Virginia (UVA), and returning to his role as a professor. Bob's long experience in psychology and education, his involvement in a wide array of traditional and future-facing research projects, and his willingness to engage in the envisioning of possible futures proved a constructive counterbalance to Howard's enthusiasm and worldview.

They established the 21st Century Learning Project at UVA to articulate a reasonable path forward for the world's public school students learning in and out of public school between today and 2050. Working with faculty, graduate students, and local middle school and high school students, particularly in Virginia's Charlottesville Lab School, the authors saw a framework and path begin to emerge, providing the basis for this book and related work.

EVERY HUMAN LEARNS DIFFERENTLY

Many of the people who make decisions for today's twenty-first-century students were born in the 1980s and 1990s. Since that time, the world has added thirty-three new countries.[20] Our planet's human population has doubled from about four billion to over eight billion.[21]

Maybe you knew that. Most people don't. Maybe you forgot. Maybe these ideas aren't important to you. Maybe you were busy learning about something else. We're not going to ask you to name the fifteen countries that became independent when the USSR broke up, or what year East and West Germany became, simply, Germany. We're not going to ask because it doesn't matter whether you know the answers. If you're curious, you can look it up. You know lots of other things. We're glad you do. Otherwise, everyone would know the same things, and that wouldn't be interesting at all.

You are unique, an individual with distinct knowledge, beliefs, and interests. Just like every other person on the planet. For you, and for everybody else, learning is personal.

And, lest we forget . . . learning is natural. School is not.

CHAPTER 1

Growing Up

The number of people in the world is increasing: approaching ten billion by 2050 or so, eleven billion by about 2085. Overall, population growth is not due to new babies. Instead, it's because today's grandparents and parents, and children, are living longer. The number of children and teenagers is not increasing.

In 1950, just after World War II, 40 percent of the world's population was under eighteen. Many government and nonprofit organizations focused on the education and well-being of young people. Looking ahead to 2050, kids will represent about 20 percent of the world's population—and half that growth will be in Africa. As Africa becomes the youngest continent on Earth, Europe and North America, and parts of Asia (such as Japan) will shift their social and economic focus to people over sixty years old.

Below, compare the number of people who are sixty and older in figure 1.1: World Population 1950 and 2050.[1] The difference is profound.

People aged sixty-plus require far more care and social services than national budgets currently allow. Thanks to better health care, people live longer, extend-

FIGURE 1.1 World population in 1950 and 2050

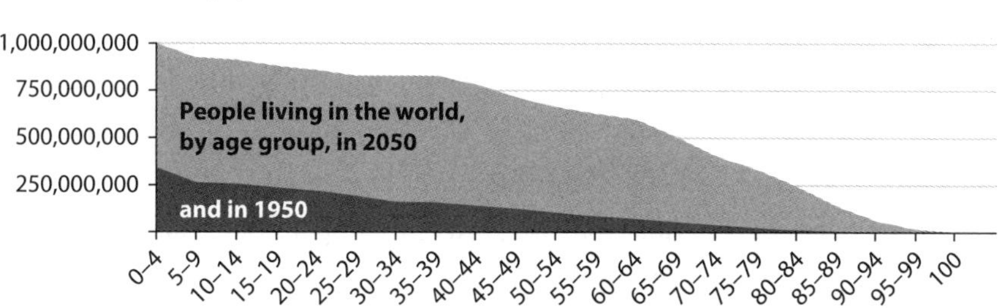

ing their years of productive employment. Many will require postretirement income. With the trend toward more seniors and fewer young people, governments will be reluctant to invest in new schools and services for younger people. Instead, they will prioritize facilities and services for seniors to keep them healthy, happy (they vote, kids don't), and out of poverty.

None of this will make life easier for people growing up in the twenty-first century.

GROWING UP DIFFERENT

Within a wide range of physical, mental, and emotional characteristics, every human being develops differently. Even within a group of same-age, same-background children, there may be big differences. Variation in human development is the rule, not the exception. For example, it's not unusual to find five-year-old boys and girls as short as thirty-nine inches and as tall as forty-seven inches.[2] A 100-pound teenage girl and a 200-pound teenage boy might be same-age best friends (both are within average range).[3]

Every child and teenager's body, mind, relationships, interests, capabilities, life situation, and plans for the future are unique. It's easy to understand why. Genetics, culture, family experience, economics, and epoch intermingle with social, physical, cognitive, moral, and ethical factors, and available resources—and more. It is unreasonable to assume that every person of a certain age or from a certain background will behave, think, or learn in a particular way. To do so is prejudicial. And yet, people of all ages make assumptions about popularity, physical attractiveness, friendship, capacity, and intelligence based on unreasonable categorizations and standards.

Just yesterday, more than 350,000 human beings were born. Almost all of them will grow up to attend school and build their own life—unlike any other human life on this planet.[4]

Family and Friends

In nearly all cultures and societies, family is the foundational building block of human development. Family provides food, clothing, shelter, companionship, guidance, instruction, and—usually—close personal relationships, and so much more.

Family nurtures behavior, values, expectations, responsibility, and more. This drives sense of self and plans for the future.

When I was a baby, I was a really shy kid. My mom and my dad taught me to become confident. To talk to others. And to be brave! . . . When I was a kid, I would spend a lot of my time with my mom. I trusted her. I was a really picky eater. I don't know why. I would just eat what my mom cooked. If others cooked, I would say, "I don't want it!" Our relationship is [still] strong. Even if I don't say anything, my mom will understand me, like, what's on my mind. She's taught me a lot of things—like being kind to others. . . . Now, a lot of my friends talk using curse words, rude words. I don't use those kinds of words because of my parents and what they taught me.

—Nadine, 14, Badung, Indonesia

Kids grow up in families of many shapes and sizes. About half grow up in households with two married parents—one male, one female—with one or more siblings sharing both parents. About a third grow up with one birth parent, same-gender parents, siblings who do not share parents, or with relatives, such as grandparents.[5] A much smaller number live with parents who are not blood relatives, or with an adopted or foster family, a constructed family, and/or no blood relatives at home. According to its 2021 census, almost half of Australians had a parent born overseas, most often from India.[6]

Family is the locus and source of many formative developmental processes—attachment, language, cognitive functions, physical growth. The connection between family and school supports academic learning, cognitive development, and social-emotional learning. By extension, families are building blocks of communities as parents learn from one another and share some responsibilities. When children talk about growing up, they talk about their interactions with people who live nearby.

I am a Buddhist. My Buddhist belief is made up of different communities. We have meetings. We do prayers. We also have storytelling. People tell their stories. . . . These programs are really nice. One of the things I like most is to be happy. I like when people see me being happy. I try to be nice with people so people are happy when I am happy.

—Larisa, 11, São Paolo, Brazil

I like to go to my friends' houses. I like to talk to them. What makes me most happy is to be with them, to laugh with them. Very important! My friends are strange but they are cool. I have a friend who likes to read, but not the same books I like to read. I have another friend who likes music and wants to become a musician someday. My other best friend—there are three—is really interested in culture. We talk a lot about our futures and what we'd like to do. When I tell them that I like to read and write about crime, and I want someday to work with that, some of them think it's cool, some of them think I'm crazy, yea. They think, okay, *why*?

—Catarina, 13, São Paulo, Brazil

ATTACHMENT

Human development is deeply rooted in our relationships. We rely on the care, kindness, and friendship of others. Without their love and attention, we fail to thrive. Beginning in (or before) infancy, humans pay close attention to their families and their caregivers' responses. We constantly assess, querying to ascertain safety and security. When interacting with a caregiver, are the responses predictable, well-timed, comfortable and loving? Or are they unpredictable, harsh, disconnected from cues—misreading an infant's state or needs? These interactions lay down the tracks of identity. They raise deeper questions that resonate through childhood, adolescence, and throughout adulthood. How do others perceive me? Am I worthy of care? Do I trust the other person? Can I and should I count on that person? Is our relationship safe, healthy, happy, and productive? Am I too independent—or not independent enough? Should I reach out to others for attachment my provider does not offer?

Each of us seeks a safe haven, attachment that feels secure yet flexible, grounded yet free. As humans grow, secure attachment remains paramount. Relationships and learning are intertwined and inseparable. Without successful relationships, learning is difficult.

Attachment is connected to friendship, love, self-worth, and more. It is an essential aspect of life and happiness for babies and young children, and everybody else. Attachment plays a major role in the health of seniors as well as their longevity. As young children pretend, mimic behaviors, role-play, tell stories and do so many silly things, they begin to understand attachment through play. Amid the laughter, tears, frustrations, and joy, they develop hypotheses, conduct experiments, and refine their understanding. They build knowledge about themselves, their relationships, and how things work.

CHILDREN AT PLAY

> Babies don't launch themselves into the world of strange people and objects from the abyss—they do what every smart explorer does—they establish a base camp. The flip side to a baby's intrepid exploration is her sense of a safe haven.[7]
>
> —Susan Engel,
> *The Hungry Mind: The Originals of Curiosity in Childhood*

If the baby feels insecure, there will be fussing, fitful behavior that disrupts curiosity and play.[8]

Babies are drawn to novelty, constantly gathering new information, and connecting ideas. "By the time they are nine weeks old, they [babies] will look only briefly at an image they have been shown before, and then turn to look at something new."[9] "By the time they are twenty-four months, they . . . try to figure out the link between two different actions (for instance, the link between piling the blocks up high and seeing the blocks tumble.)"[10]

Babies use all their senses—tasting, touching, listening, sight, and smell. They put their hands on things. They make noises. As they grow, they watch, wander, climb, collect objects, and make connections. Sometimes there's a purpose, or a temporary smudge of a purpose, but rolling down a hill or banging on a frying pan is purpose enough. They're playing and learning at the same time—the difference is inconsequential. If it doesn't work, try again later. Forget about it. Maybe stick with it. Do it a different way. Share. Make a new friend. There are few rules, but there are many insights and lessons that we carry through childhood, adolescence, and adulthood.

> I love to play Hula-Hoop and I love to play basketball. I play basketball every day, and twice a week, I do Hula-Hoop also. When I was little, around five or six, my aunt, she gave me a Hula-Hoop to play with. So I learned to play with it. . . . After a few months, I was really good. You can do it on your waist and you can do it on your hands. Your elbow. Your neck. Legs. There are different variations.

> You can get it from your legs to your hands. It's really not an India thing. Very less people in India do Hula-Hoop. Mostly it happens in America and Europe. Other girls asked me how to do it. So I asked them to come to my house and I showed them how.
>
> —Ashmita, 10, New Delhi, India

Play doesn't require structure, toys, or custom-built environments. Sticks, sand (especially wet sand), or mud are fine. So is a cardboard box. Puppets are more than six thousand years old, but they're still useful when pretending to be somebody else. Marbles date back to Ancient Egypt, Greece, and Rome. More than five thousand years ago, kids played with spinning tops in what's now Iraq. More than three thousand years ago, Chinese kids (and adults) flew kites.[11] Before anyone figured out how to make a ball, kids kicked around animal heads (still do).

A researcher could make this case: *Any object can be a toy, and all toys are tools for learning.* For example, a spinning top introduces sophisticated concepts in physics including force, friction, potential energy, kinetic energy, precession (related to wobbling), gravity, and angular momentum.[12] Playing with a top involves learning to spin it longer, straighter, and with greater control.[13] Most children don't care about scientific phenomena or underlying mathematical calculations. Through play, they learn all these things, but analysis takes the fun out of it.

When a child is having fun, the child *might* spend more time and energy on an activity. Sometimes, play increases the child's understanding, control, ease, and desire to do more. Sometimes, play increases curiosity and collaboration—"What if we try *this*?" Dominoes are lined up, precisely, on their edges, so one touch flips a long column and makes a wonderful sound; intersecting patterns add to the fun. When the child controls the experience, novelty and variation make play more engaging. When the child loses control, interest wanes.

It is not as if play has no structure. Sometimes, the structure (or set of rules) is made up ("*NO*! The *purple* one always goes on *TOP* of the red one!"). Sometimes, as with team sports, there are formal rules and structures. The critical factor is the child's buy-in.

STORIES AND STORYTELLING

Stories allow the child—anyone, really—to explain their version of the world in terms they understand and control. Storytelling is always subjective. (Despite claims of objectivity, even journalism is subjective because the storyteller determines which stories to tell, which characters and themes to include, what to exclude, what to explain, and how to tell the story.)

Often, storytelling is a form of verbal play, and as with play, there are no rules unless the storyteller deems them necessary. Characters may be versions of real people in the child's life, or abstractions of those people, or imagined. A story may reflect a vivid imagination, a cry for help, an inventive combination of ideas (a talking, red-haired elephant who wears sparkly sneakers and has potty issues). A story need not be fixed in permanent form or fashion. Retold stories may include new details, new characters, new roles for old characters. The storyteller makes the rules.

Telling the truth is less important than making mom laugh. Half-truths, backstories, utter nonsense, exaggeration, leaving out details—these tools are used by every storyteller, including bestselling authors, teenagers, and young children (parents do this, too—and watch out for grandparents!) Stories may evaporate. They may hang around for years.

Rarely do two children tell the same story in the same way. Each storyteller brings their own world view, role, and unique imagination into storytelling. Every person who watches or listens to a story interprets meaning in their own way. Even with the global sharing of stories, the dominant natural force is variability, not uniformity.

In every culture, making up and sharing stories is part of growing up. It's the way humans cultivate beliefs, knowledge, and culture. Stories are powerful ways to connect ideas—and connected ideas make learning possible. Humans are more likely to remember interesting stories than facts and figures—an aspect of learning schools often forget. In many stories, music, characters, and comedy are critically important. That's why Disney and *Sesame Street* make media the way they do.

PERSONAL CONNECTIONS

Ask a child to make a list of everyone they know. Then, ask another. Even if the children are siblings, or best buddies, their lists will be different because their lives are different.

Who merits a position on the list? Beyond family and friends, the answer depends on who takes the time to notice the child. It could be a bus driver or a dentist or a person who works at a store. A particular teacher or relative might make one child's list but not the other. As children grow into adolescence, their lists diverge because their interactions with people are based on their personal interests and experiences. As young people participate in formal and informal networks (both in the real world and the digital world), they meet new people and build new affiliations.

Over time, lists change. Quantity, quality, and frequency of interactions affect relationships. Some grow, some fade. Individual identity, group identity, and shared interests develop on these pathways. Social media affects relationships. One friend becomes vegan, another takes up skateboarding, another draws manga and watches anime. Each personal connection leads to new relationships, new connections, more shared interests, more explorations, and more differences between people.

SCHOOL ADDS COMPLEXITY

Before children start school, people in their networks are self-selected. School introduces a new factor: people who were not intentionally selected, such as classmates. Schools conglomerate people who live nearby, regardless of the connection between them. Young people are aware of diversity. They're curious. They ask one another questions about heritage, family customs, strange smells, other unfamiliar ideas. With new friendship comes exposure and experimentation. Again, this adds to diversity and variability.

School becomes a laboratory for social experiments. Some friendships can be trusted, others fall apart; some are resurrected or remain shaky. There is kindness. There are bullies. During middle school, behaviors intensify, and many young teenagers require emotional support. The variety of issues and each individual's response further distinguishes each teenager's life.

Broadly, school serves three purposes: supervision of children (so parents can pursue other activities), social interaction (kids interact with one another), and academic training (kids learn). The core idea: a safe place where many children and teenagers are supervised by adults who help them learn. Participation in activities outside of school further distinguishes one child or teenager from another. Religious organization youth groups and local sports leagues are among many examples. And remember, all of this is taking place as every child and every teenager is figuring out who they are and their role in the world.

[In my religious school], they teach us about God and Jesus. We learn the many ways to give people advice, people who lack hope. So I try to give hope to them. Some people have issues. Like, in our country, people take it like they are bewitched. People believe in small gods. They [offer] their sacrifices . . . it's called witchcraft. It's a kind of religion in Africa: an African tradition. Some people don't believe in God. So we help them ask for gifts, for life, for rewards. I am a Christian, so I do not believe in small gods, so [mine] is a different religion. God has different names, such as Allah for the Muslims, but they are all God. Different religions are related to each one's mindset. It comes from parents. If my parent is a Muslim, the family follows those traditions. You cannot decide for your own self. But if I want to become a Muslim, I can, because it is my right to do so. I can decide [to follow] any religion I want.

—John, 18, Kampala, Uganda

DIGITAL CONNECTIONS

For more than fifty years, kids have played computer games, but the paradigm changed in the early 2000s when mobile telephones became personal communication devices. It is now possible to share ideas, images, texts, stories, videos, and other material all over the world, instantly. This increases the number of people in any network, further multiplying diversification. Today, growing up requires digital awareness.

I use my phone to keep in touch with my family. I don't carry my phone everywhere because we're not allowed it at school. [Otherwise,] everyone would be on their phones all the time and not learning anything interesting. It seems a little strange that we're not allowed to use it at school, but it is safe. There are lots of things like cyberbullying, things that could happen that are dangerous to children. I am very careful online. If someone posted a video [that was bad], I would show my parents first, I would report it, and I would block that person, too. You should also be very careful about posting things online because it spreads very far and it spreads very fast. [And] don't give out personal information [such as] passwords.

—Erin, 12, Southport, England

Growing up in a digital world opens new possibilities. One example is a digital twin—an interactive playmate, study buddy, new friend, ideal storyteller, companion, doppelgänger, lover, abuser, and who knows what. This is becoming as much a part of growing up as teddy bears and comfy blankies.

A digital buddy could remember everything about its human's life. They could make friends with other digital beings, which might complicate the lives of their humans.

Ask a well-informed teacher about a deep sea blob sculpin and there may not be much of a response. Ask an AI learning buddy the same question—a buddy attuned to your personality, sense of humor, thirst for imagery, and curiosity—and you're likely to see a *Psychrolutes phrictus*, zombie worm, Sloane's viperfish, and giant isopod. These extraordinary creatures are even cooler than dinosaurs (collect all 3,465 species!).

GOING TO SCHOOL

When it's in session—about half the days of the year—school occupies about six hours a day for more than half the kids on Earth. Ideally, children sleep about ten hours a day, and teenagers need just a bit less. The remaining eight hours a day—fourteen hours when school is not in session—are available for everything else. How much of those eight–fourteen hours a day are devoted to learning? That's a silly question, because kids learn all the time.

Usually, preschool and early elementary school are fun. Some lessons may be challenging, but learning to read, learning about numbers, and learning to get along are usually happy experiences. So is making sense of basic science, history, geography, all sorts of stuff, really. Everything is new and—mostly—interesting. There's a lightness about primary school. Teachers tend to be flexible and supportive; social and relational learning are valued. Students and teachers are usually united in their pursuit of successful learning. Nobody wants to grow up stupid or ignorant—so students pay attention in primary school, in part, as a kind of insurance.

Most secondary students make an honest effort to pay attention and care, but much of the material is perceived as boring, irrelevant, and useless. Gradually, they lose traction.

> Sometimes, I'm super interested in whatever is being said, and I could just sit for hours listening. But sometimes, you know, I feel bad, but I'm just not that inter-

ested in it, and I just can't keep focused on what is being said to me over a long period of time. I feel like I have to sit there. If I left, I would feel like I was doing something wrong. I think I would feel SO bad! And I don't want to be disrespectful to anyone. But it drains me.

—Melina, 14, Kobe, Japan

At the time in human development when students' thinking becomes more personal and identity coalesces, the "space" of school narrows. Given school's general disregard for individual interests, students begin to withdraw. Some doodle, distract their neighbors, try to make others laugh, pretend to pay attention, or engage in covert nonsense. Maybe that's better than acknowledging that their curiosity and creativity are melting away by the minute. It's a function of being asked/invited to learn material that the learner experiences as irrelevant.

The teacher drones on about "the meaning of a *function*—a rule that gives a variable a value based on its relationship to another variable (2x = y)."[14] Students read aloud, "I have seen tempests when the scolding winds Have rived the knotty oaks, and I have seen Th' ambitious ocean swell and rage and foam To be exalted with the threat'ning clouds; But never till tonight, never till now, Did I go through a tempest dropping fire."[15]

Attention levels run low. Students find the material irrelevant, and many (thanks to the pandemic and closures) express their dissatisfaction through disinterest and chronic absenteeism. Relationships are reduced to a common interest in the end of the classroom session. For teachers with the best of intentions and extraordinary skill and talent, keeping 15, 20, 30, or 35 students fully engaged in standardized material is a formidable challenge. For most of the students, the relevance of functions or a notable soliloquy from Shakespeare's *Julius Caesar* are just too far from what they want to know and feel they need to know. And they cannot escape. They cannot choose to learn anything else. This causes them to question the whole system, their trust in the teacher, and more. Why is everyone devoting their time to these ideas? Does my teacher actually care about any of this? Who decided we needed to learn this? Can anybody unmake that decision?

LIFE AND LEARNING

This pyramid (figure 1.2) took shape as early secondary students in Virginia's Charlottesville Lab School discussed learning in school within the context of their lives.

FIGURE 1.2

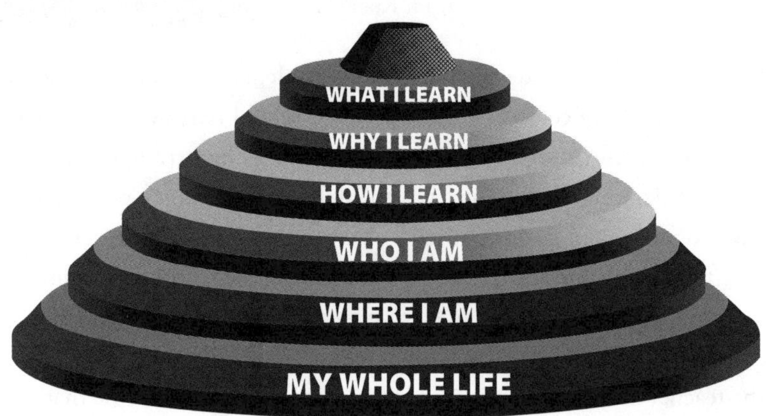

My Whole Life

The differences between one life and another are not the stuff of headlines. Instead, they are a rough sketch: sharing a noisy room with a pair of siblings without enough space, an upset stomach, saving money to buy a bike, a beloved aunt whose health is failing, a souring romance, a computer that doesn't work, plans to become a YouTuber, several rainy days in a row. Kids spend lots of time thinking about the future, but that future might be next Saturday.

> Hi, my name's Tilly. I like the name because it pretty much suits me, and what I look like. It takes about a half hour to get to Liverpool. There's Liverpool One, that has lots of shops there. I like all the toy shops. There's always something I want to buy there. My favorite shop is Smiggle, a stationery shop. It has bags, pencil cases, sharpeners. I got my ears pierced in Claire's. I was pretty scared, but once it happened, I felt fine. My mum had her ears pierced so it made me want it. Sometimes, people get it done in weird places, like on the nose, or here [eyebrow], in the tongue and stuff like that. But I'm not really comfortable with tattoos. It's kind of painful when you get that done.

I know that because my Nanna has lots of tattoos. I'm not really that into them. People are just different. You just do it if you feel like it.

—Tilly, 8, Southport, England

I'm thinking about all the animals in the sea. There are interesting kinds of fish, jellyfish, things like that. I will study in Slovenia and maybe in some other countries. I will get a job in Slovenia, and I will travel around the world. As a marine biologist, I can work in a lab, or in a marine biological station [on the sea].

—Martin, 10, Piran, Slovenia

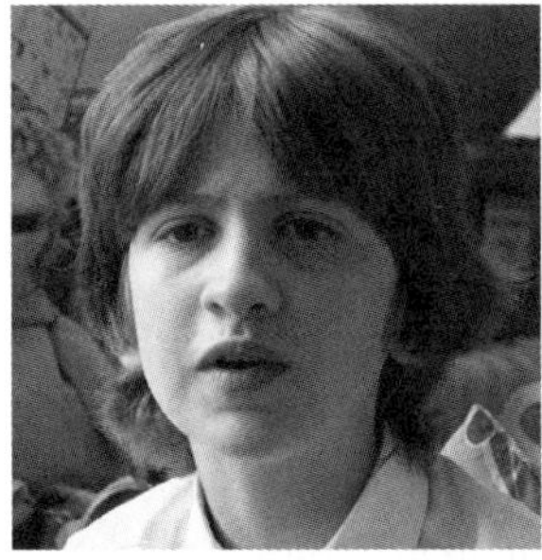

For my career, I'm planning to be maybe someone like Damon Albarn, the brainchild behind Gorillaz who partners with other artists and makes music that cannot be pointed at any genre, really. Gorillaz is a virtual band. They reject false icons. I'm planning to become a music producer, so I won't be L. A. Reid, but I'll probably be more likely to produce the music, then go on tours. I play piano, trumpet, drums, and guitar. I practice quite a lot, really. I'm hoping to build it from there. I've got big plans to become a musician. I'm the adrenaline junkie of music. I do it for the kicks!

—Dylan, 11, Southport, England

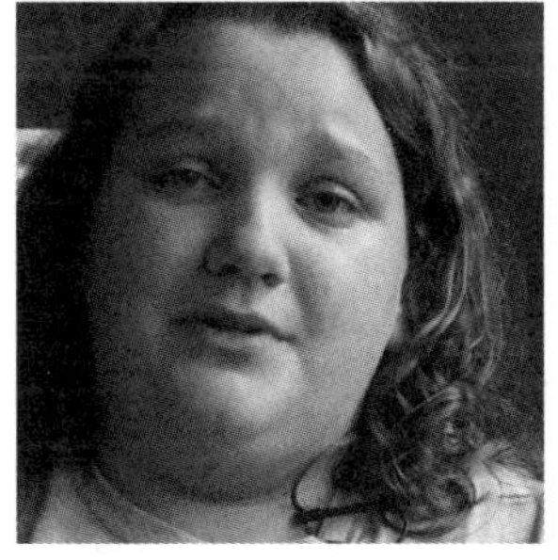

I live in the Appalachian Mountains. We use the mountains for our coal, lumber. . . . We mine the coal for . . . electricity. Miners work underground and they drill out the coal. My dad, you never know whether he's going to come home at night because he works in the coal mines. Every day, I wait and I pray that dad's coming home. Sometimes, we talk about it. He says, when it's his time to go, it's his time to go. I say, "I know." And I know.

—Jaylee, 13, Neon, Kentucky, US

I live in a trailer, there's three bedrooms, two bathrooms. We have a patio, a deck and a pool. A trailer is a step up from an apartment. When I was a baby, I lived

in the same room, never moved rooms, same house, same colors, everything the same. My mother is a nurse. My dad is a coal miner. He comes with coal dust all over himself. He works from three A.M. until like eight at night. He works six days a week. We only see each other on Sunday. He works all the time to make us a better life. . . . He's fun. He's a very good artist. I love him so much. He's a great dad, so supportive. Sometimes people pay him to do art. I don't think my dad would make as much money doing art as he does working as a coal miner. . . . It does worry me that he's in the coal mine. He could have a heart attack, a seizure, a stroke. Something could fall on him. I cope with it because he's wearing all these protective clothes. He used to smoke; that damaged his lungs. And he does coal mining, which makes it worse. Sometimes, the inside of his lungs is black. There's like [dark] popcorn all around [inside the lungs]. It's already making him not breathe. It makes it hard for the heart to pump enough blood. There's not enough oxygen. That will cause heart problems, lung problems, he won't be able to run as fast, be able to keep up. There's a lot of stuff to worry about because you don't know what's going to happen. So you have to stop and think about what will make life better. Say I become a pharmacist. I would make six dollars an hour, and I can pay for all his doctor bills. I'm repaying him. . . . I want to help people. I want to make medicine. So when I help people, I could give them medicine that will help cure their body. Like with my dad. You know, he's got lung problems. I might become one of those pharmacists that research stuff to make new medicines which will cure that disease or any other disease. Help people. Cure all the diseases in the world.

—Tori, 12, Neon, Kentucky, US

Where I Am

With a 2021 population of 6.2 million people, Toronto is Canada's largest urban area. Montreal is in second place with 4.3 million. Vancouver is third with 2.6 million. Quebec City, Winnipeg, and Hamilton each come in at about 800,00. Charlottetown, Prince Edward Island has 79,000 people; Sainte-Marie, Quebec, 13,000.[16] These places are very different from one another, but they are all places where kids grow up.

About 6,000 children and teenagers live in Moose Jaw, the fourth largest city in Canada's Saskatchewan province.[17] That's enough to fill five high schools and fifteen elementary schools. Most students are of European descent, but about

7 percent are Indigenous (Cree, Assiniboine, and mixed-race Métis, the first settlers). Another 7 percent come from Asia (in 2001, it was ~1.5 percent; the Asian population is slowly increasing).

Moose Jaw supports an active 2SLGBTQ+ community. (2S abbreviates "two spirits"—"An English term used to broadly capture concepts traditional to many Indigenous cultures . . . to indicate a person whose gender identity, spiritual identity, and/or sexual orientation comprises both male and female spirits.")[18]

With just 35,000 people, Moose Jaw is a small Canadian city. It is not without crime—it typically ranks as roughly the fortieth most crime-ridden city in Canada—but personal safety is not a primary concern.[19] It's easy enough for many Moose Jaw residents to reach much larger places. Regina is two hours east with about eight times as many people. It offers more and better shopping, a university, annual music and arts festivals, and a Canadian Football League team. Saskatoon is two hours north with more than 250,000 people. Edmonton is six to seven hours west, with 1.3 million people, a big science museum, an enormous shopping mall, the Oilers pro hockey team, and a large performing arts center. Drive six to seven hours east and there's Winnipeg, with 750,000 people, three performing arts centers, and several pro hockey teams.

A hundred years ago, these communities were isolated. Still, Moose Jaw is surrounded by open land and small rural communities, big lakes, parkland, and mines. Rural broadband lags, but advocate groups are making progress. In 2022, for example, SaskTel agreed to invest "an additional $100 million in its Rural Fibre Initiative to expand SaskTel infiNETTM Service to over 80 more towns and villages throughout the province . . . connecting tens of thousands of rural households to SaskTel's fibre optic broadband network. . . . Speeds reaching close to a gigabit per second [allow] subscribers to surf, stream and share . . . at incredible speeds."[20]

Details like these determine how young people in Moose Jaw spend their time, what they observe, and what people they meet. Children and teenagers who grow up in Guangzhou, China, or Manaus, Brazil, or Rovaniemi, Finland don't experience the same things, and as a result, they don't know the same things. Where I Am is a defining characteristic and a key differentiator.

Where I Am exists at the intersection of physical, mental, emotional, and spiritual space. Sense of place may be experienced differently, even by two children with similar backgrounds living and studying in close proximity. Where I Am exists in the mind. I feel comfortable in this place, but *that* place feels creepy! Many young people live a life of urban or rural poverty. Some live in the midst of war or other violence. Naturally, every human wants to be in a place where they feel they belong.

> When I complete my studies, I will not be able to find a job. I am not going to stay in Greece. To be honest, I don't like it here. Greece is a great place for holidays, but I can't find anyone like me. I have a different culture from them. My mother raised me differently. My opinion doesn't match anyone's. They are so closed minded. They can't accept anything different. I'm nonbinary. Nobody accepts me. No one! My mother says, "Okay, that's some personal information for you, but don't tell the others." Sorry, but if they cannot accept me, why do I live here? How can I be myself? I want to be myself. I don't like to pretend. I don't know where I want to go, but I want to travel to find someplace that treats me better. . . . Here in Greece, the way the school works, how we treat each other . . . I feel that I'm in a different universe or something. The internet!—it's the answer for everything!! (*Laughing*) So I looked up different countries and how their laws are, how everything works. I'm trying to do what I love now so I will be okay with myself . . . there will be a way for me to get out of here.
>
> —Rosa, 16, Athens, Greece

Several years ago, a well-intended field trip for low income (mostly Black) secondary students in Philadelphia clarified the importance of place. They visited an upscale (mostly white) high school in the suburbs. Teachers hoped the groups of students would develop common interests, friendships, and an ongoing exchange. On the bus ride back to the city, more than a few kids expressed a common opinion: "We are so *f***ed*." For the first time, they saw where they were clearly.

Data supporting their discovery and its implications is not hard to find. *The Opportunity Atlas*, published by Harvard University's Opportunity Insights Institute and the US Census Bureau, builds on work done since 2014. Briefly, "Children's lives are shaped by the neighborhood they grow up in."

Further detail: "Social mobility is about more than just earnings. Recognizing this, *The Opportunity Atlas* provides information on key indicators such as marriage patterns, college attendance rates, fertility rates, and incarceration rates.

As with income, we find very sharp differences in children's outcomes on these other measures as well."[21] The work involves nuance to capture conditions often obvious to the people who live there—"Neighborhoods are not unidimensional: experiences within those neighborhoods vary by racial and ethnic group, and by gender."[22]

Who I Am

Who I Am is always a work in progress. With bodies changing, minds developing, and relationships taking shape, young people are constantly in the midst of change—and so are their peers.

Figuring out Who I Am is a natural process, but each of us learns by experimenting and exploring. Sometimes this goes well—it's wonderful to discover new friends and new possibilities. Sometimes it goes badly, as young people do rotten things to get attention, push against boundaries, get into trouble, and make choices contrary to their best interests. Some teenagers try to remain invisible. Some struggle with mental health and hurt themselves or others. Each of us learns in our own way—choice of clothes or hair style or makeup, public persona, choice of companions, passion for sports, games, or other activities, and, if a child or teenager is lucky, the design of a personal space, such as a bedroom or a tabletop work/play space. Along the way, there's plenty of problem-solving (with some pretty crazy problems).

Everyone deals with behaviors and inclinations that may be difficult to manage or understand. Friends and family can help, but every situation and relationship is unique. Sometimes, it's difficult to recognize a potentially serious issue. Most people are not prepared to do so because they don't know much about the mind or the body. Some rely on the internet, without sufficient training or context.

Who I Am is often affected by Who *You* Are. Each of us is affected by friends, family, people we observe and follow, and people don't like us. Who I Am requires looking in a mirror to try to figure out what others see. Everybody exists in their internal world and also in the external one.

Friends move away. Brothers and sisters are born. Family members get sick. Some die. Parents separate and sometimes remarry. Everything may seem unpredictable. When difficulties become multidimensional, life becomes more difficult to manage. Peer interaction helps, especially when parents don't say or do the right things, or don't seem to understand.

Growing up takes place during the same years as primary and secondary school. Often, school and life compete for attention. Sometimes, school is put aside because a friend or family member is in need, or because the student cannot handle the stress of school and daily existence. Sometimes, school provides the necessary combination of peer interaction, academic learning, and adult intervention.

Hey! Growing up is hard!! When school interferes with larger problems, students become upset about school. This dissonance grows from a sense that school is uncaring and unresponsive to the most important aspects of growing up. That's not okay.

How I Learn

Everyone is motivated to learn, but we are all motivated to learn different things. Some things we learn because they are interesting. Some things we learn to make personal progress and eventually earn money. We learn to help others. We observe. We get ideas from friends. We watch videos. We experiment. We make use of every available resource, recognizing that resource distribution is inequitable—so we're resourceful. We rely on others—especially adults with resources and experience that kids do not possess.

At first, in school, the teacher seems to be in charge. With reading and arithmetic, mass education usually works so well, there is no reason to question authority. By third, fourth, perhaps fifth grade, How I Learn in school begins to unravel. The teacher begins to disseminate large amounts of information via lectures, textbooks, and testing. By now, it's clear the teacher is not in charge—that other (mostly unseen) adults control learning. Moving from primary to secondary school, students gain self-confidence, gain control over executive functions, build on a powerful base of experience, and develop a deeper connection with their personal interests. As school follows the old model, demanding everyone learn the same things in the same ways, student interest wanes. By de-emphasizing individual student interests and motivation, and overemphasizing what seems to be an endless list of must-learn items produced by mostly unseen and unknown adults, much of school follows a playbook that is contrary to How I Learn.

Why I Learn

When posed as a question—Why do you learn?—young children often include the phrase, "So I can . . ." in the answer. For example, "So I can read" or "So I can use the computer" or "So I am allowed to feed the dog myself." Their answers are clear and practical. Success is within reach. Some answers include an aspirational "someday," as in, "Someday, I want to run in a marathon like my mom" or "Someday, I want to design cars." In all cases, learning, whether in or outside of school, is intended to produce a personally meaningful, relevant, useful result

> This school has really kept me with an open mind and educated me about the things that are actually happening in the world. It's given me a lot more to think about, and a lot more to act on. I want to work in activism, and I'm a singer, and I love writing songs, so I want to write songs that bring attention to the environment.
>
> —Indigo, 13, Lismore, Australia

Why I Learn is driven by curiosity, the desire to learn more. Often, learning is motivated by a practical need. Practical—or situational—learning is usually associated with solving, or helping to solve, a problem. An animal is in distress, so a human assesses the situation, considers possible remedies, scans available resources, takes action, and evaluates the outcome.

Walking in the woods and trying to understand why tree limbs grow in many directions (but mostly up) may not involve practical learning, nor does wondering why two people are attracted to (or dislike) one another or why chocolate tastes so good. Pursuing curiosity just feels good. That is, Why I Learn does not require a specific answer. "Because" is just fine. Learning for joy is fine, too.

Once again, school operates in a way that is contrary to why most people learn. Much of what school offers is not particularly practical and does not cultivate joy. Instead, Why I Learn is reduced to "because you insisted."

When somebody, anybody, insists, "You need to learn this!"—unless it's a matter of personal safety or survival—learning usually falls outside the natural cycle of Why I Learn. Retention becomes unlikely. A steady diet of "You must learn this!" becomes unpleasant, and after a while, promotes inattention. When "You must learn this" is associated with too many ideas to learn in school, required homework, and mandatory testing, there's little space for joy, and good reason for stress. When teachers and students lack control over their time and attention, the situation becomes worse because it runs contrary to Why I Learn. Forcing students to learn in school causes many of them to watch the clock and pray class will end soon.

And yet, human flourishing, the well-being of people and the planet, has become a core organizing principle for twenty-first-century learning.

What I Learn

Learning begins early. The dangers of fire, water, vehicles, rats, crocodiles, and poisonous snakes must be learned. Some plants can kill you. Be careful around people with guns, knives, and other weapons. Stay away from people who are sick and contagious. Don't go near rushing water or a flood because you could drown. Don't go near vehicles in motion, even if they are moving slowly; the driver may not see you. If your skin is a certain color, you must learn how to behave, especially when law enforcement officers are nearby; otherwise, they may harm you or the people you love.

There is so much to learn at home and in the community: observing and mimicking adults as they prepare food, clean clothes, sweep away dirt, deal with insect pests, shop, protect the household from rough weather, deal with people, figure out what to do if a toilet won't flush or a pot is boiling over or somebody has an accident.

Children want to share their ideas, ask coherent questions, understand others. They want to read and write, build vocabulary, understand and manipulate numbers, and comprehend how the world works. They want to master fundamentals—essential skills that allow them to learn just about anything. They look forward to going to school to learn all of this and more.

As with Why I Learn, those fundamentals are mastered early at home, at school, in the community, and by watching television/videos. A child can borrow a library book about dinosaurs and try to understand it without much help from siblings, teachers, or other adults. It turns out, there are lots of books about dinosaurs, lots of websites, too. It's easy to learn more, and fun to discover what else there is to learn. Why aren't there any dinosaurs in the zoo? What happened to them? Did they live at the same time as cavemen? Were there any women or girls in prehistoric times? (And if yes, why isn't everyone called a cave person?)

What I Learn is determined by curiosity and our need to make connections between one idea and another. Why learn about malaria and dengue fever but not HIV/AIDS? Why do people in Brazil mostly speak Portuguese when most other people in South America speak Spanish? Why is their language still called Portuguese when only ten million people live in Portugal but two hundred million people live in Brazil?

Growing Up Aware—and Concerned

> I like helping others, and in the future I want to become a midwife. To assist mothers during that time of giving birth. I will go to university and [follow] that course. There are too few doctors. Some parents were dying in the process. The midwife is the medical professional in the room. I want to help people who are scared. I want to be a midwife in Uganda so I can help my fellow Ugandans. Yes, I want to move and see the world, maybe America, India, Canada, and get more experiences from other countries. I [will] bring [knowledge] back to Uganda. I want to come back so I can build my country.
>
> —Eseza, 18, Kampala, Uganda

In sub-Saharan Africa, and especially in South Africa, children and teenagers are aware of the impact of HIV/AIDS because they know people who died or who take medicine to control the disease.[23] Similarly, young people in Asia, Europe, and North America understood what peak COVID-19 was, and the messy adult pandemic response.[24] Many were deeply concerned about the availability of vaccines, masks, and hospital beds, people with compromised immune systems, social isolation, six-foot distancing, and much more. With widespread news coverage, many children and teenagers were as well-informed as adults. They worry because adults do not seem to be in control. They understand what climate change is because they see wildfires and hear about extreme heat and melting glaciers.

The gap between what children and teenagers know and what adults know is collapsing.

On July 11, 2023, *The New York Times* reported frightening local stories about climate change: "Torrential rainfall and widespread flooding wreaked havoc in the river valleys and mountain towns . . . ravaging communities . . . in New York and Vermont," "Lethal landslides . . . and roads knee-deep in water . . . in India," "More than 61,000 people died because of last year's brutal summer heat waves across Europe," "Hilltop collapses into canyon after epic storms lash Los Angeles county," "Soaring temperatures baking the desert Southwest [US] are not only strikingly high but also unusually persistent," and "Extreme weather fueled by climate change is the new normal." On the next day, headlines included "Floods Expose Failure to Meet Climate Threat," and "Unusually Heavy Rain Brings Floods and Landslides in Japan."

When kids cannot go outside because the air quality is dangerous or because it's too hot, too cold, too wet, or too risky, they experience transformation directly. When their families discuss climate migration because it may not be safe to remain at home, these stories become very real. That's happening more and more often—as is the sense that things are not going to be okay.

Growing up in the twenty-first century means thinking about the unthinkable. Young people are concerned about having enough food to eat and water to drink. They know climate disasters can kill crops and destroy the roads vehicles need to deliver food and supplies. What if the planet becomes so hot that the plants and animals needed for food die off or morph into things humans cannot eat? In 2019, Chennai, India—that country's sixth largest city—started running out of water. Every day, they trucked in ten million liters of water. "People stood in lines for hours to fill containers, water tankers were hijacked, and violence erupted in some neighborhoods."[25]

> Most people are leaving because West Virginia is dying. We have nothing here. I like it here, but it's not a good place to live because of all the homeless people. Your house could be broken into. We have a lot of drugs around here. Kids are involved when parents don't make good choices. Kids get pregnant early. People start on drugs in high school or middle school because they feel stressed out because their parents make them feel they're not welcome at home. This is a problem that grows. To break the cycle, I would start with homeless people and help them get jobs, more opportunities. They need to stop the cycle and stop doing drugs. They can say, "I don't need help." Actually, you do! I think it's a family responsibility. People do drugs, people cut themselves, because they feel there's nothing to life. We need to stand up and say, "YOU NEED HELP!!"
>
> —Lyric Lee, 13, South Charleston, West Virginia, US

If adults are not going to take action—which seems clear—then today's children and teenagers need to learn a lot about these problems so they can solve them (or, at least, mitigate potential damage) themselves. And they must act quickly—which is why many are frustrated by school's insistence on teaching so much useless material and wasting time and valuable resources on twentieth-century education.

As journalists and researchers document serious widespread mental health issues—particularly depression, anxiety, and a sense of hopelessness—among young people, there is a strong suspicion that adults have failed and will not turn things around. When children and teenagers observe government in action and political gridlock, they sense that adult leaders are "only in it for themselves" (a frequent refrain from teenagers everywhere), and that "nobody cares about people like me" (also common, in those words). When they say, "School is a prison," they are not just referring to rules restricting their freedom and movement, they are expressing frustration with their inability to control their own lives.

ACCEPTING RESPONSIBILITY

Many students realize that education is inequitable, that their postal code, their skin color, and the poverty level of their parents and communities dictate the shape of their lives. They sense that their ability to learn—and their teachers' effectiveness—means more to their future success than those often-cited postal codes or advanced technology.[26]

> My goal is to be a doctor because I'm seeing problems. People go to hospitals, but doctors are lacking in Uganda. Until I become a doctor, I have to go to school so I have enough material I can use so I am perfect to be a doctor with everything needed. The universities in Uganda . . . for me, I can't afford that. But if I could meet some person, any person [to pay for my future education] . . . I wish to go to outside countries for university studies. If I am employed there, I can stay. If they decide for me to come back, I have to come back.
>
> —Stephen, 14, Wakiso, Uganda

Fair treatment, equal opportunity, equity, and justice are still somewhat new ideas. Well into the twentieth century, and into the twenty-first, women, people with darker skin, people with disabilities, Indigenous people, immigrants, and many children and teenagers were (and are) denied rights. In many places, for hundreds of years, they were exploited, required to work under nasty conditions for very low wages that were sometimes not paid at all. They were excluded from opportunity. None of this was fair, but this was how much of the world worked.

During the past twenty-five to fifty years, progress has been unevenly distributed. Today, in twenty-nine countries, women cannot legally head their households. In ninety-eight countries, companies are not required to provide equal pay for equal work for men and women.[27] In some countries, twenty-first-century progress has been blunted by repressive, incapable, or misguided regimes.

The United Nations Sustainable Development Goals (UN SDGs) identify seventeen areas in which equity requires significant improvement. These include poverty, hunger, good health and well-being, quality education, gender equality, clean water and sanitation, affordable and clean energy, decent work and economic growth, climate action, and more.[28] For many children and teenagers in many parts of the world, these concerns define growing up.

CELEBRATING DIFFERENCE

Many of today's countries and cultures were built by disrespecting, abusing, killing, and destroying people and their cultures. Day after day, in full view of the world's children, the pattern continues in Ukraine/Russia, Israel/Gaza, and in Afghanistan, Burkina Faso, Myanmar, Haiti, Iran, Iraq, Lebanon, Libya, Mali, Niger, North Korea, Somalia, South Sudan, Sudan, Syria, and several Mexican states.[29] And elsewhere.

About 3 percent of the people on Earth live outside their home country; the number of migrants has remained stable since 1960. As the world's population increased from about two billion to about eight billion people—a fourfold increase—the migrant population also increased fourfold, but not more. That's because most people want to live near their families.[30] What has changed is the mix of countries sending emigrants, some of the receiving countries, and some of the reasons why people migrate. Economic opportunity and personal safety are established reasons. Climate migration is becoming a factor—but only in specific locations. What has also changed is the current (but predictable) wave of demographic shifts, notably in Canada, Australia, Saudi Arabia, New Zealand, Kazakhstan, Gabon, Cote d'Ivoire, Oman, the US, Libya, Sweden, Germany, and French Guyana.

In many places, fear, hatred, and rumors about the damage immigrants cause enflame frightening prejudice, woefully inadequate human services, flagrant abuse, exclusion from economic opportunity, and other unconscionable actions.

Many immigrant families share these stories. Today, there are more people from more places. Progress depends on their ability to cooperate and collaborate, not waste precious time and resources fighting.

When a family moves to a new place, they are most likely to find housing near others with a similar background (word of mouth and social services tend to cluster people in neighborhoods). The difference today: There's more interaction between cultures. It's easier to get around, and many schools are less segregated. There are more opportunities to cross paths with people from other cultures. Growing up in the twenty-first century, particularly in a busy urban or suburban environment, means making friends from Egypt and the Dominican Republic, South Korea and South Africa, the Philippines and Ghana, Panama and Serbia (and meeting a fair number of mixed families with parents from more than one country). It means learning words and customs, visiting one another's home and tasting new foods, asking one another about unfamiliar religions. Respect comes naturally—kids tend to get along unless they are instructed not to. Prejudice and hatred are taught, but more and more twenty-first-century children and teenagers don't want to learn anything like that. They do not want to live like their parents or grandparents. They want to be treated fairly, and they want to treat other people fairly. There are enough resources for everyone. They want to live in peace.

Nobody Knows My Story

The Philippines has become one of the largest source countries for new US immigrants. More than two million people from the Philippines now live in the US.[31] A Filipino child new to the US might reasonably assume that everyone in the US knows all about the Philippine-American War because everybody in the Philippines knows about it. That 1899 war is almost never mentioned in US schools.

It was a guerrilla war. Hundreds of thousands of Filipinos died from disease, famine, and atrocities. This happened just after the Spanish-American War, which is studied in US schools. Filipino patriots fought for independence, first from Spain, then from the US, but lost the war. The US annexed the Philippines—a forceable acquisition.

A child's family tree may reveal a great grandparent killed fighting for independence from the US. Some Filipino children wonder why so many Filipinos now live in the land of their oppressor. Should Filipino American history be learned only by children with Filipino heritage, or by everybody? Maybe just in and near Daly City, California, where one in three people are Filipino? Should every kid in California learn what happened in the Philippines more than a century ago because they interact with Filipino American kids today? Should every US student learn about this?

Many and perhaps most nations have invaded other nations, then buried those stories. Growing up means interacting with relatives and cultural groups who will never forget the atrocities, the insults, the inability to secure a job. In or out of school, growing up means learning how your family managed to get this far—sometimes, by choosing to forget.

Some Filipino children may prefer to learn about Italy or Argentina, or the mess that became the Spanish-American War in the first place.[32] There's nothing stopping those students from learning whatever they want to learn. They may or may not learn it in school, and learning in or out of school is easy to do—if the internet is available.

Everybody Knows My Story

A woman, now grown, recalls her middle school nickname: Swampy. It was not intended as a compliment. She's Korean, and she would bring kimchi (fermented cabbage and other vegetables) to lunch every day. Other kids hated the smell. They made fun of her and made her cry. Kids from other cultures tell similar stories.

Kids learn from their parents, their siblings, their neighbors. They build profiles of people from different cultures based on assumptions and limited information, then convince themselves they know the whole story. In the US, many Black and Latino teenagers know the routine—and they are very careful around law enforcement, school administrators, and even teachers who make assumptions about their lives.

Growing up in the twenty-first century does not shield children from prejudice. In fact, prejudice continues to determine which schools and school districts receive the resources they need. It continues to guide hiring and opportunity.

As twenty-first-century kids become more worldly and interact with more people from more places, there's an emerging belief system that growing up involves less prejudice and racial discrimination than in the past, but that is not true for everyone.

Yes, there is still racism here, in some places. People don't accept differences. They start to judge based on those differences. In my environment, I have never seen racism. But I am sure it exists. Judge people through their actions, by the way they deal with others, and by their honesty!

—Sthepany, 14, São Paolo, Brazil

Skin color, yes, that does affect my life. A lot. People don't like different. A lot of white people that live in my neighborhood, when they drive by, they scream [at me], "Make America great again" because I'm Black. When my parents grew up, there wasn't as much danger, there wasn't as much racism. Barack Obama was the first Black US President. He had . . . healthcare for families who were struggling. That really helped a lot of people. Civil rights means everybody should have the same rights as somebody else. It doesn't matter [about] your skin color, your religion, your sexuality, you should have the same rights as every other person. Whatever you were taught as a child, you are going to grow up having that mindset . . . but you can change your mindset! If you just keep going off the same perspective, you are not going to learn anything!

—Nevaeh, 12, Philadelphia, Pennsylvania, US

I think less people are racist now. Maybe a hundred years ago, no one liked people with darker skin, but now, a lot of people have come to Sweden knowing that being a racist is not okay.

—Molly, 12, Stockholm, Sweden

Fair Treatment for Everyone

I come from England, but my family comes from India. Many people come from other countries and they live here. And they speak different languages. I have friends who come from Poland, and they can speak Polish and English. And some of my friends come from Latvia as well. Everybody is allowed in this school. I am Hindi. I feel welcome here, even though I'm not Christian. Everyone treats me nicely. I treat them the same way back.

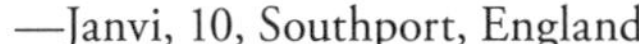

—Janvi, 10, Southport, England

"Fair" is a useful umbrella term children and teenagers often use when discussing equality, equity, equal opportunity, being kind to one another, healthcare for everyone, and the end of poverty, hunger, racism, and prejudice. There seems to be a shared sense of right and wrong, and a powerful desire to eradicate unreasonable thinking and unfair practices. It's easy for adults to dismiss notions of fairness as childish and unrealistic, but twenty-first-century children and teenagers consistently express very strong feelings about fair treatment for all. When combined with agency, fairness causes children and teenagers to speak out and fight for their rights, and to cultivate common cause.

> I tell my story, sometimes people dismiss it, but we can't ignore an army of stories. Maybe you can teach me: How do you assemble an army? When you are nonverbal [and nonmobile], you can't easily speak for yourself. How do you see the 21st Century Learning Project helping people with disabilities? Some educators go as far to say it's cruel to try to teach us literacy! They argue that you will never be literate, so why try? I argue if you don't try, you don't know. Denying literacy is a denial of the right to education. But I come across children who are surprising teachers all the time. I am a voice for the voiceless.
>
> —Jonathan, 17, Wiltshire, England

People, by Category

Taller, darker, smarter, more talented, a better friend—before school begins, humans compare ourselves to one another. We draw inferences, learn from mimicry, try on different roles, and learn. We generate analogies.

> The spotting of analogies pervades every moment of our thought's core. . . . Many are created to try to make sense of situations we face on a [large] scale. . . . The triggering of memories by analogy lies so close to what seems to be the essence of being human that it is hard to imagine what mental life would be without it.
>
> —Douglas Hofstadter and Emmanuel Sander

Categorizing people is common practice in school, at work, and in social situations. Systems, companies, and policies have been built on this creaky foundation. There are simply too many differences between individuals—too much variability—to assign credence to this approach. Every child and every teenager is a work in progress, dynamic, changing based on so many inputs and experiences every day. Schools famously rely on categorization; they deal with human variability and difference with labels and tests and groupings, and those decisions have a profound impact on a child or teenager's development and relationships. Kids also have a way of figuring things out on their own.

[JAYLIN:] We're twins. She's like the total opposite of me. She cheers for me when I play basketball. When I grow up, I want to be a professional motorsport racer.

[KAYLIN:] I would like to be a pediatric nurse and work in the nursery with the babies. . . . Here's what drives me crazy is that she looks like me! She's a smart aleck. I think I'm smarter than her.

[JAYLIN:] Yeah, she's definitely smarter than me. She's really good at reading and cheer. I'm really good at math and basketball.

[KAYLIN:] Once in fourth or fifth grade, we dressed up as each other, and one of our teachers didn't notice—until I talked.

—Jaylin (left) and Kaylin (right), 12, Fleming-Neon, Kentucky, US

Whether in *Kids on Earth* interviews or less formal conversations, we encounter a universal truth about children and teenagers. Any time we make an assumption or a comparison, we are wrong. Analogies and labels are so often off the mark, we don't even think about them. Every child, every teenager, and every adult is a unique human being, unlike any other.

Different People, Different Priorities

Growing up, every human follows their own path. Children evolve, teenagers evolve, everyone changes from day to day and year to year. Interests change. Some take root.

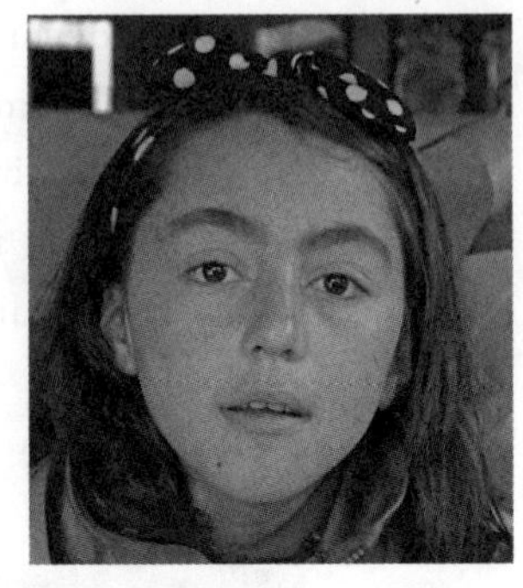

I would like to be a police officer because my father used to be one. You can save people, but it's dangerous, too. There are bad people, but you can arrest them. I think I could be very fast to run after a thief. I can be very strong. I can catch them! I would be worried about people with weapons. I don't want to shoot someone . . . but I would shoot someone [if they were threatening the life of another]. But I would feel bad, but I would still be a police officer after the shooting.

—Maite, 11, Valparaiso, Chile

I try to look decent at least half the time. People my age, they like to be on top of the latest fashion trends. They take [up to] an hour fixing their hair to make it look a certain way, or their makeup, their outfits. Right now, I'm only wearing mascara [no other makeup]. I have lighter hair . . . so my eyelashes are light. Mascara makes my eyes look bigger. Girls start wearing makeup around sixth grade. Boys in my school don't really wear makeup, but if I see a boy wearing makeup, that wouldn't be unusual; I've seen that on YouTube.

—Cecilia, 12, Richboro, Pennsylvania, US

Growing up, every young person is different. They want to learn different things for different reasons.

I want to be a pediatrician. I need to study a lot to find out what to do with a kid when they're sick, to know what that means. You need to learn a lot about people. I know there's the urinary tract here, the liver is here, there's a heart here and the heart beats but when it stops beating, the person dies. It's connected to the veins, and if they're cut and a lot of blood comes out, they could die. One time, my liver was enlarged so they had to do a sonogram. I could see everything inside. [I had an infection and they saved my life.] I want to live in Bulgaria and be a doctor.

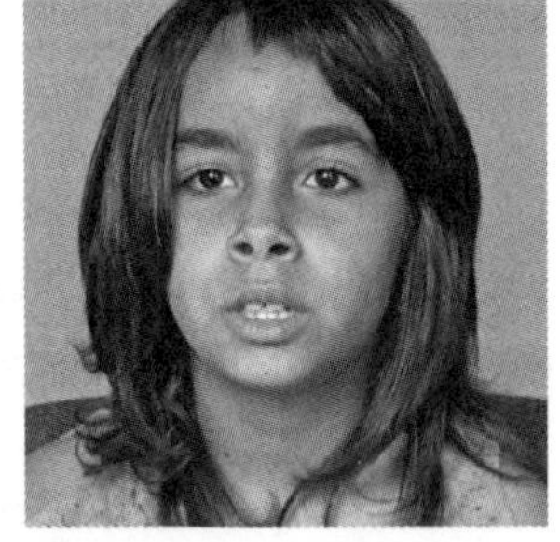

—Bozhidara, 7, Oriahovitsa, Bulgaria

CHAPTER 2

Learning

Golgi apparatus, lysosome, vacuole, vesicle, chloroplast, cytoplasm, endoplasmic reticulum. Maybe you learned these terms in school. Maybe you memorized them or did a project to make them more meaningful. Let's test your learning with a two-question quiz: (1) How are the above terms related? (2) What other items are missing from this list?

In high school biology class, you probably drew or made a 3D model of a *plant cell.* In addition to the above, it probably included a nucleus, ribosomes, mitochondria, peroxisome, and, of course, a cell wall and cell membrane. Score ten points if you can draw a diagram of a plant cell today. To check your work, follow this link.[1]

As you may know, the plant cell is the microscopic building block for food, clothing, and shelter. As coal, plant cells provide half of the world's electricity and much of its pollution. When there is a wildfire, plant cells are burning out of control. Plant cells become sneakers, furniture, perfumes, coffee, tea, automobile tires, paper, books, boats, pianos, guitars, and cigarettes. In the form of spices, plants were one reason Europeans colonized Asia. Just being around plants can calm the human mind and body and lower blood pressure. Plant cells reduce carbon dioxide in the air and convert it into oxygen.

What should every human know about plant cells? There is a lot that could be learned, but for nearly everyone, it's neither productive, possible, nor desirable to learn everything. Is it more useful for everyone to learn the same things about plant cells?

What should everybody know about climate change? A global phenomenon, climate change is experienced locally. A long-term phenomenon, its impact can be felt in a matter of seconds (a tornado) or days (storms and floods). About twenty thousand years ago, New York City and London didn't exist; their current locations were beneath deep sheets of ice.[2] Since then, the climate has changed. Today's wildfires in Canada and Australia, rising summer temperatures in Europe, melting glaciers, and increases in hurricane and tornado activity are all important, but are they equally important to everyone, everywhere?

Everything is important, but not to everyone, and usually, not at the same time. One friend wants to design electric vehicles, another wants to campaign against beef, and a third wants to become an eco–grief counselor. What must each of them know about climate change right now? Do they need to learn the same things or different things? If the answer is different things, your answer conflicts with the way children and teenagers are taught in school.

INTELLECTUAL LIVES OF CHILDREN

Human infants are naturally curious. Before birth, we begin to develop cognitive systems. Emerging from the womb, we gather enormous amounts of information about ourselves, people nearby, and the world around us. Babies identify gaps between what they know and what they would like to know. They ceaselessly test new hypotheses.[3]

> Six- or seven-month olds will systematically examine a new object with every sense they have at their command (including taste, of course). By a year or so, they will systemically vary the actions they perform on an object: they might tap a new toy car gently against the floor, listening to the sounds it makes, then try banging it loudly, and then try banging it against a soft sofa. By eighteen months, if you should give them an object with an unexpected property, like a can that makes a mooing noise, they will systematically test to see if it will do other unexpected things.[4]
>
> —Alison Gopnik, Andrew Meltzoff, Patricia Kuhl,
> *The Scientist in the Crib: What Early Learning Tells Us About the Mind*

Babies make decisions about what is interesting/uninteresting, safe/unsafe, desirable/undesirable, worth exploring, worth remembering. They communicate by making gestures and other nonverbal signals, and by making sounds. As young children acquire language, they ask questions to gather information.

> Adults are largely oblivious to the intellectual lives of young children. While children are busily gathering information, mulling things over, and speculating about the world, the adults around them are, for the most part, unaware of all of that mental activity. Watch and listen for twenty minutes in almost any school in the United States and it becomes clear that the educational system does not concern itself with children's intellectual lives.[5]
>
> —Susan Engel, *The Intellectual Lives of Children*

As each child makes decisions, they develop ideas unlike those in any other human mind. Each interaction contributes to identity, the result of vast amounts of input and a selection process based on relationships, culture, resources, language, and many other factors. They develop executive functions. What is executive function?

> The major components of executive functions include inhibitory control (the ability to control impulses); working memory (a type of short-term memory that involves temporarily storing and manipulating information); and cognitive flexibility, or shifting (the ability to switch between thinking about different topics). Each of these skills develops at different rates, with windows of growth and opportunity for intervention. . . . [Executive functions] can be substantially fostered or hindered by environmental factors including early childhood stress, family structure, and educational opportunities.[6]

Choices become more conscious, more unique to each individual's personality. Children gain control over their behavior, relationships, and desired path. A trusted guide—a teacher, parent, or friend—can ignite interest, amplify importance, and encourage curiosity.

Children happily obsess about collecting, finding patterns, and building relationships; they build, discard, pretend, have fun, stumble and cry, and wonder about things they don't understand. They may go deeper, go wider, move on, return later. Or not. Seemingly without reason. Later, reason may become clear. Or not. Teaching is structured, but in most domains, not much is linear, or predicable, about curiosity or learning.

Expertise

And yet, young people acquire skills and knowledge during predictable phases of their life (as toddlers, for example). Learning, however, rarely follows a fixed timeline. Each child makes connections unique to their own needs and their own ways of thinking: "Experts notice features and meaningful patterns of information not noticed by novices. Experts' knowledge cannot be reduced to sets of isolated facts or propositions, but instead, reflects contexts of applicability—that is, the knowledge is conditionalized on a set of circumstances. Experts are able to retrieve important parts of their knowledge with little attentional effort."[7]

Experts add to their knowledge in many ways. Some children and teenagers memorize lots of details (sports statistics) or watch a video over and over again until they know every word. They collect objects and arrange them in one way then another, decorate their spaces with ideas and images, dress and accessorize to become an idea's physical manifestation. In their way, children become experts.

"Experts' knowledge is connected and organized around important concepts; it is 'conditionalized' to specify the contexts in which it is applicable; it supports understanding and transfer (to other contexts) rather than only the ability to remember."[8]

> I'm learning on my own. There are no art classes at [my] school. I'm looking at lectures on YouTube. I am basically acquiring the skills myself. The school teaches me how to learn things. I take that skill to learn the field that I am interested in, which is graphic design. I learn by looking at the output, the designs of the students that came before me. . . . I can look at their work, I can copy their style. I get a lot of motivation by looking at the work of students who came before me, by looking at the work of the students who are better at design than me. Also, [my] G-School connects students with experts in various fields. We get to meet them. I show them my work, they give me a lot of feedback. This gives me the chance to grow, become better at creating my own design, and refine my own style.
>
> —Gyeong-eun, 17, Seoul, South Korea

Academics use the term *deeper learning* to describe sophisticated understanding and complex cognitive processing. Experts engaged in deeper learning are sensitive to novel ideas and patterns, and they are selective about their intake of information. In this way, experts greatly increase the quality and quantity of their knowledge, cultivate useful ideas, and ignore or discard irrelevant information.

As students mature, they develop expertise and identity. For many, school's rigidity becomes increasingly counterintuitive and frustrating. "Each learner develops a unique array of knowledge and cognitive resources in the course of life that are molded by the interplay of that [individual] learner's cultural, social, cognitive and biological contexts. Understanding the developmental, cultural and historical diversity of learners is central to understanding how people learn."[9]

Over time, each individual's network of ideas and experiences generates more internal synaptic connections, so each person's neural network becomes more complex, more capable of engaging in increasingly sophisticated information and problems, and more distinct from other people's networks. The learner becomes clearer about what they want to learn, what they will remember, and why. Learning becomes more intentional. These behaviors carry on for a lifetime.

In the presence of a supporting and challenging guide or teacher, learning expands and deepens. This is psychologist Lev Vygotsky's "zone of proximal development." When joined in a productive manner, learning becomes a series of building blocks that advance each individual's interplay with relationships, knowledge, capability, sense of self (identity), and the world. The foundation of those building blocks: Learning is personal, relational, and active.

Curiosity

Curiosity seems to drive learning, but "curiosity is such a basic component of our nature that we are nearly oblivious to its pervasiveness in our lives."[10] There is a lot of research about curiosity in creativity, learning, attention, motivation, basic human needs, perception, play, and animal behavior (curiosity is not exclusive to humans; dogs and worms are curious, too). Curiosity is not an academic area of study, but it can be.

Engel: "Curiosity begins as a feeling—a stirring, or a sense of mental unrest," but the term is difficult to define and the phenomenon is difficult to study.[11] She observes, "When our curiosity is aroused . . . we lean in to carefully observe. We touch, we smell, or listen. As we get older that moment of cognitive arousal may lead to a search through our thoughts or even through books [and the internet] for . . . information."[12]

Note the word choices: desire, satisfy, stirring, aroused. A connection between curiosity and dopamine seems likely. The brain's treatment of curiosity is pleasurable. Anticipation of sated curiosity is pleasurable, too. Research and experimentation powered by curiosity is pleasurable, too. Perhaps this is why "the more curious you are about something, the more likely you are to remember it."[13]

By design, humans pursue behaviors that release the compound known as dopamine, which is associated with our hard-wired reward system—if you are enjoying yourself, your brain releases dopamine. It's a good feeling, so your body wants to do more that is pleasurable so that it releases even more dopamine. Stanislas Dehaene, who directs an advanced brain imaging research center in France, explains, "Through the dopamine circuit, the satisfaction of our appetite to learn—or even the anticipation of that satisfaction—is deeply rewarding. Learning possesses intrinsic value for the nervous system. What we call curiosity is nothing more than the exploitation of that value."[14]

> When I was a kid, I asked my parents a question like, maybe, why is the sky blue, or why is my skin brown? I was always curious about things like that. My parents didn't really take it seriously. They say, "The sky became blue itself." It doesn't satisfy my curiosity. That's why I read books. Reading books, I know many things. Like why the sky is blue.
>
> —Nadine, 14, Badung, Indonesia

Engel: "Studies have shown again and again that when people want to know, they learn. Inciting children's curiosity is the best way to ensure that they will absorb and retain information. That sounds incredibly obvious [but] we know very little about what makes children more curious or less curious, under what circumstances curiosity can be encouraged, and how to build upon children's curiosity so they learn well."[15]

The addition of school, with its curriculum, structure, rigid schedules, lack of freedom, forced interactions, and abundance of information, is often problematic. Dehaene: "Children may lose their curiosity because they lack cognitive stimulation tailored to their needs. As learning progresses, the expected learning gain shrinks: the more we master a field, the more we reach the limit of what it can offer, we are less interested in it."[16]

Dehaene continues, "Students who struggle in school may wither away for the opposite reason. Metacognition remains the main culprit: after a while, they no longer have any reason to be curious because they have learned . . . that they do not succeed in learning." "Too many children lose all curiosity because they learn, at their own expense, to expect no reward from school."[17]

Role of Teachers and Other Adults

The fantasy image of unfettered children roaming freely, stopping to explore anything that captures their fancy is romantic but it's not the way curiosity or learning takes shape. Engel: "Inquiry does not bubble up simply because a child is intrinsically curious. Nor does it simply erupt when something in the environment is particularly intriguing. Whether the child has the impulse, day in and day out, to find out more, ebbs and flows as the result of adults who surround her."[18]

Relationships drive curiosity and engagement, which drive learning. Positive relationships generate energy, encouragement, stress relief, and (no surprise) more positive relationships.

Engel: "Smiling and encouraging children to explore are two of the ways that teachers influence children's curiosity. But as we know from a vast array of research . . . adults influence children in other ways as well. Children watch adults react to objects and events, listen to what adults say to other people, and they watch what adults do."[19]

In selecting teachers, schools often focus on natural intelligence, diligence, and disposition, but a teacher's curiosity or sense of humor may not be central concerns. Candidates who constantly learn and study new things, who see things from many different points of view, and who participate in community projects and pursue their own research are valuable indeed. They make connections so everybody learns more.[20]

Sensitivity and Selectivity

Sensitivity is related to sensory input, connecting perception with cognition ("all forms of knowing and awareness").[21] Within limited ranges, humans are capable of seeing, hearing, smelling, tasting, feeling, and perceiving the world. For example, humans hear sounds from 20 Hz to 20 kHz—roughly the lowest and highest notes produced by musical instruments—but we cannot, generally, hear sounds above or below that range. Dogs can't hear lower frequencies, but they can hear higher ones (hence, dog whistles).[22] Humans see from 380 nm to about 750 nm—violet to red on the visual spectrum.[23] Dogs see only blue and yellow, but they see in dim light better than humans do. Dogs also perceive motion ten to twenty times more clearly than humans.[24] Generally, the sensitivity of each human's senses is similar, but there are many individual differences.

Humans expand perception and improve sensitivity with inventions: corrective lenses, hearing aids, and public address systems among them. Advanced imaging has expanded our understanding of learning and the brain. For example, MRI is "a medical imaging technique that uses a magnetic field and computer-generated radio waves to create detailed images of the organs and tissues in[side] your body."[25]

Selectivity involves a series of decisions made before and after sensory input arrives in the brain. An infant can choose, or not, to eat or drink certain foods. By closing the eyes, a human can choose not to see. Still, much of selectivity is beyond our control.

> For more than a decade, my colleagues and I have been studying a form of invisibility known as inattentional blindness. In our best-known demonstration, we showed people a video and asked them to count how many times three basketball players wearing white shirts passed a ball. After about 30 seconds, a woman in a gorilla suit sauntered into the scene, faced the camera, thumped her chest, and walked away. Half the viewers missed her. In fact, some people looked right at the gorilla and did not see it.[26]
>
> —Daniel J. Simons, Beckman Institute for Advanced Science and Technology, University of Illinois at Champaign-Urbana

In fact, nearly all incoming information is ignored, discarded, or never processed because it's neither useful nor relevant. This survival mechanism is hardwired: Humans attend to what matters, and disregard what does not. These decisions are made very quickly, usually without any conscious thought at all. Relevance and utility are key determinants—if the material doesn't seem relevant or useful, the mind skips to the next thing. However, teachers (and other adults, and other students) can change that because humans are attracted to—more likely to pay attention to—interesting people (and animals), novelty, and a promise of safety and security.

Magsamen and Ross: "Many elements go into making experiences more salient for learning, among them novelty, humor, curiosity, attention level, creativity, motivation, environment, and the unique way your brain develops. Lifestyle factors also dictate how ready your brain is to receive and retain information, such as having enough sleep, a healthy diet, and hydration. . . . The arts create more salient experiences, triggering plasticity, neural connections, and greater understanding."[27]

When an interesting person offers interesting information, we pay attention until the information reveals its value. If we're intrigued, we may connect their new information to our existing information, attempting to learn more. If not, our attention fades. We see this in very young infants, so it's probably innate. It's easy to observe this behavior: Visit a classroom or almost any meeting in a conference room.

Sensitivity and selectivity are affected by "noise"—anything in a signal's path that impedes its progress from sender to receiver. For example, a room may be too dark, too bright, cold, hot, smelly; a chair may be uncomfortable; the learner may be hungry or thirsty or in need of a bathroom; the signal volume may be too low, extraneous sound may distract; and so on. Humans make accommodations for themselves when learning (or entertainment) offers value. When children and teenagers are fully engaged with a teacher who offers useful, relevant information in interesting ways, they do their best to overcome obstacles and pay attention. When school does not accommodate learners' needs, students are not likely to learn or will find other ways to do so.

ATTENTION

"She's really interested! Look at how she's paying attention!!"

Just outside on the patio, a family of deer nibbled on nearby bushes. The family's beagle was riveted by their every move and would not be distracted.

Some aspects of attention are hardwired. They are associated with safety and danger, food and water, and relationships. For other aspects, the observer makes a conscious decision to learn (improve, study, etc.) and determines the intensity of concentration and the depth, breadth, and duration of the experience.

> I would carry my big instrument, my euphonium, to a practice room in the music building on campus. I would find the best chair—posture matters when you're playing any instrument. I would set the tuner to B-flat—466.164 Hz, a half step up from A440 (the note that orchestras tune to). Then, I would close my eyes and play and hold that note over and over and over again. As I paid attention to my breath support, my posture, and intonation, I would envision two sound waves: my B-flat and the tuner's B-flat. Same note every time. I listened very carefully—so carefully, I could easily imagine two waveforms, and I tried, time after time after time, to consistently play a clean wave to get them to align perfectly, without wavering in and out. I tried to play and sustain a perfect B-flat—466.164 Hz—over and over again for hours. Nothing distracted me. It was almost a trancelike

> state. I paid complete attention to B-flat—nothing else in the world mattered. I did this with every playable note on my instrument. I did this day after day, night after night, because that's the way you learn to play a musical instrument at a high level.
>
> —Steve, 19, Pittsburgh, Pennsylvania, US

Researcher Mihaly Csikszentmihalyi interviewed athletes, musicians, and artists. He asked how they experienced optimal performance levels. "Optimal experience is something we make happen. . . . The best moments usually occur when a person's body or mind is stretched to its limits in a voluntary effort to accomplish something difficult and worthwhile."[28] Every time Steve worked hard for clean alignment with every note, he paid complete attention to the immediate task, undivided attention rooted in a powerful desire to learn.

UNDIVIDED ATTENTION

When they were developing the educational TV series *Sesame Street*, researchers measured individual preschoolers' second-by-second attention (to the TV screen showing a sample segment) and distraction (attention to anything else). They figured out how to attract and retain young children's attention—and explained their findings to the show's creative staff, which responded by designing the viewer experiences to minimize distraction.

Attracting and retaining attention on a massive scale is the superpower cultivated by social media, consumer advertising, political advertising, and network television. Every second counts—every image, every edit, everything is crafted to maximize impact. By commoditizing attention, consumer goods companies build successful brands, and political consultants persuade citizens to vote for their candidates. Social media creates algorithms that addict young people, often encouraging social comparisons, anxiety, fear, and depression. Working with abundant data, much of it gathered from the internet and processed through machine learning, marketers and social media companies have become very sophisticated in their manipulation of attention. Artificial intelligence and other new technologies increase their power and influence.[29]

Learning in school is much less sophisticated. School places the responsibility for attracting and retaining student attention on each individual teacher, but control over what is taught and why is beyond the teacher's control. Operating with limited flexibility and limited resources, each teacher must engage each student's attention for thousands of hours annually.

It's an unfair fight. Capturing and retaining the attention of fifteen or thirty students, each with a different level of interest and a different learning pace, requires seemingly endless hours of preparatory work, performance skills, clever delivery, a captivating sense of humor, personal interest in the material (real or feigned), and extraordinary classroom management skills. Despite the teacher's best efforts, some students won't care.

According to Magsamen and Ross:

> Your brain is expert at filtering out the inputs that it deems irrelevant and focusing its attention on what it believes to be pertinent. Something that is salient is important to us either practically or emotionally. . . . Things that create saliency indicate the release of neurotransmitters, like dopamine and norepinephrine, activating your synapses and increasing synaptic plasticity. This regulates memory formation. . . . The stronger the salient response, the stronger the synaptic plasticity because, at that moment, a number of cells are activated, releasing lots of neurochemicals, changing the synaptic connections. . . . This helps to change the synaptic circuit responsible for memory retention, making them long-lasting.[30]

MOTIVATION

As noted in *Psychology Today*: "Intrinsic motivation is the drive that comes purely from within, without any ostensible external rewards. You do it because it's inherently enjoyable, and not because of any anticipated reward, deadline, or outside pressure."[31]

Children play because they want to play, not because they are rewarded to do so. Extrinsic Motivation is useful to coax a child or teenager (or an adult) to try something new, or to try again. Typically, the gambit involves distraction from task—do this, you'll get that. "When you're extrinsically motivated, you're doing the behavior to gain an external reward."[32]

As Dehaene points out,

> Extrinsic motivation is any reason someone does work other than the joy of doing the work itself. Anything promised for completing the task or received as a result of completing the task are extrinsic motivators. An extrinsic motivator needs three elements to be successful, according to research by psychologist Victor Vroom: expectancy (believing that increased effort will lead to increased performance),

> instrumentality (believing that a better performance will be noticed and rewarded), and valence (wanting the reward that is promised).[33]

Extrinsic Motivation requires an effective reward structure, but rewards must be continuously upgraded to maintain motivation. Extrinsic Motivation is useful for specific classroom activities, notably test taking ("Get an A, you can paint your room purple"), but it's usually the wrong approach for comprehension and long-term memory.[34]

Extrinsic Motivation is aligned with mass education: Everyone learns the same things, whether they're interested on not, so they must be cajoled with grades and test scores. Managing learning on a massive scale via Extrinsic Motivation is exhausting (ask any teacher), expensive, and usually unsuccessful. When students fall asleep in school, or check out due to boredom, or complain, Extrinsic Motivation has failed. When applied repeatedly, it dulls the senses. "Children and teenagers who focus mainly on their own performance (such as gaining recognition or avoiding negative judgments) are less likely to seek challenges and persist than those who focus on learning itself."[35]

Intrinsic Motivation is aligned with individual learning, or what will shortly be identified as Personal Education. A student is internally motivated to pursue an interest, so the community and school support that activity. It is less complicated than Extrinsic Motivation and far less taxing.

Memory

By and large, school's approach is out of sync with twenty-first-century cognitive science.

Most incoming information is discarded and never finds its way into short-term memory. Information that survives is distributed to various parts of the brain for processing.

Dehaene: As neurons are activated, they begin a process of physical change that is learning: "They modify the strength of their interconnections . . . making it more likely that this set of neurons will fire in the future. Some synapses [connections between the neurons] become physically larger. . . . These changes are the physical basis for learning; collectively, they are the substrate [underlying layer] for memory."[36]

In these initial stages, everything happens very quickly: "The human brain can process entire images that the eye sees for as little as 13 milliseconds."[37] Once complete—"the memory remains dormant, unconscious but inscribed in the very anatomy of my neuronal circuits. In the future, thanks to those connections, an external clue . . . may suffice to produce a cascade of neuronal activity in the original circuit. This will restore a pattern of discharges similar to the moment the memory was made."[38]

"Memory involves reconstruction rather than retrieval of exact copies of encoded mental reproductions."[39] "Memories are not frozen in time; they are reconstructed anew each time a person recalls something, and the reconstruction takes into account current knowledge, expectations, and context. For this reason, memories are not fixed, but instead morph. and may omit details or include fabricated details."[40]

Generally, memorization of information is not an effective learning strategy. It should not be used in schools.

Nine Stages of Memory

1. The initial stage is *Prior Knowledge.* Every being is born with the memory of millions of years of evolution, and a deep understanding of nature. We possess our species' natural curiosity, attentiveness, sensitivity and selectivity, operating processes, emotions, and multigenerational trauma. When we enter preschool or kindergarten, we are not new to learning. As Dehaene noted, "Clearly, the blank slate conception of learning is wrong. Human babies are born with considerable core knowledge, a rich set of universal assumptions about the environment that they will later encounter. . . . Their brain circuits are well-organized at birth and give them strong intuitions in all sorts of domains: objects, people, time, space, numbers."[41]

2. *Attentiveness to Inputs* includes observation, inquiry, hypotheses, experimentation, exploration, and much more, but we remember a small portion of incoming information. We are more likely to remember what interests us, more likely to pay more attention to people who care about us. Magsamen and Ross: "New information is encoded by the hippocampus and then converted into long-term memories, which can be recalled years later. Learning involves clusters of neurons making new connections throughout the brain; the more you train those neurons

to fire together, the easier it becomes for a pathway to form and become strong, and this is why practice and repetition are keys to mastery."[42]

3. *Engagement* enhances information with action. Learning and memory are interwoven—driven by curiosity, personal interest, and intrinsic motivated motivation, often involving activities (collecting, drawing, exchanging information, etc.).

> Not having heard something is not as good as having heard it; having heard it is not as good as having seen it; having seen it is not as good as knowing it; knowing it is not as good as putting it into practice.[43]
>
> —Xun Kuang, Chinese Confucian philosopher (312–230 BCE)

4. Nonjudgmental, supportive *Correction* produces and supports reasonable memories. Learning involves a steady flow of errors and missteps. Unfortunately, in school there is less patience for this step and pressure not to make mistakes. This breaks the cycle of learning, so students become frustrated, think of themselves as stupid, disengage, make poor decisions, and do not learn effectively. Associating error correction with fear and negative consequences generates incomplete ideas, irrational memories, foolish decisions, and vulnerability.)

5. *Consolidation* requires sleep. It captures the day's events, moving memories for sensemaking (hence, dreams), contextualization, and ready access for reconstruction and revision. "Every night, our brain consolidates what it has learned during the day. This is one of the most important neuroscience discoveries of the last thirty years. While we sleep, the brain remains active; it runs a specific algorithm that replays important events it recorded during the previous day and gradually transfers them into a more efficient compartment of our memory."

Children require about ten hours of sleep every night; teenagers, about nine hours.[44] Sleep allows muscles and other organs to rest in preparation for the next active day. Sleep enables humans to make sense of what they are learning, to remember what the past day has taught. Without sufficient sleep, memories fail to take shape, connections are not constructed or are constructed improperly. Memory becomes less reliable. When students trade sleep for test preparation, they sacrifice clear thinking. When this is done repeatedly, confusion, disorientation, and poor cognitive performance creep in. Many students operate this way throughout secondary school. Some, into college.

"Sleep is not just a period of rest. It is an integral part of our learning algorithm, a privileged period during which our brain plays its models in a loop and enhances the experience of the day by a factor of ten to one hundred. Sleep and learning are strongly linked." According to the CDC, "6 out of 10 middle schoolers [and] 7 out of 10 high schoolers don't get enough sleep."[45] In many cultures, school's requirements and sufficient sleep at home are out of balance. The impact on learning is significant (insufficient sleep exerts negative impact on mental and physical health, growth and development, reason, relationships, and decision-making, too).

6. *Forgetting* is not a human failure. Instead, it's cleansing that frees the brain to process and store new information and generate productive connections. Developed in the 1880s, the Ebbinghaus Forgetting Curve mapped the scientist's ability "to remember using a list of nonsense syllables, which he attempted to recall after different lengths of time."[46] He found that memories weaken over time, that the biggest drop in retention happens shortly after learning, that it's easier to remember things that have meaning, that the way something is presented affects learning, and that how you feel affects how well you remember.[47]

If a learner isn't interested in what is being learned, roughly a third of the information is lost within the first fifteen to twenty minutes, about half is lost within the first hour, about two-thirds is lost within a day of exposure to the material, and about three-fourths is gone by the end of the second day. Then, forgetting slows down, but about four-fifths of the information is gone a month later.[48] It's easy for anyone, or any classroom, to construct a similar experiment.

7. *Rehearsal, Revision and Retention* can improve results, but only for specific items, not all memories. For example, a refresh ten to fifteen minutes after initial exposure seems to extend initial memory so that half is retained a day later; but a week later, only about one-fourth is retained, most of it lost by month's end. However, a second rehearsal twenty-four hours later improves results: After a week, half of the information is retained, and a month later, the loss is only about two-thirds. A subsequent rehearsal within the week offers more improvement: A month after the initial exposure, about half of the material is recalled.[49] This is the way human memory works. It's not the way school deals with memory and learning.

So you just go, read the book, try to memorize as much as you can, answer your quiz, and that's it, that's your education. You're just memorizing words. The next day, you don't even remember what you did. So I think you need to be knowing, not just memorizing. Understanding what you are reading so you can use it in your future [is much better] so you actually can depend upon what you are doing in school when you are an adult.

—Hazem, 14, Cairo, Egypt

8. *Automatization* is akin to *Consolidation*—the daily process of moving memories to permanent locations in the brain.

> Why is automatization so important? It frees up the cortex's resources. Remember that the parietal and prefrontal executive cortices act as a generic executive control network that imposes a cognitive bottleneck. It cannot multitask (so you can't, either). While our brain is focused on one task, all other conscious decisions are delayed or canceled. Thus, as a mental operation remains effortful, because it has not yet been automated by overlearning, it absorbs valuable executive attention resources and prevents us from focusing on anything else. Consolidation is essential because it makes our precious brain resources available for other purposes.[50]

When the brain faces a steady flow of largely irrelevant details—standard practice in school—curriculum and teaching impede learning.

9. *Recall and Retrieval* are related. "The initial perception . . . is generated by a subset of neurons firing together. Synchronous firing makes the neurons involved more likely to fire together in the future, a tendency known as *potentiation* [which] recreates the original experience. If the same neurons fire together often, they eventually become permanently sensitized to one another, so that if one fires, the others do [too]. This is . . . *long-term potentiation*."[51]

Hyphenating *re-collection* brings the word to life: A collection of potentiated neurons is re-activated. The "act of recollecting makes the [group of] neurons even more likely to fire again in the future, so repeatedly reconstructing an event makes it increasingly easy to recall."[52]

The opposite is true, too: If the original thought's neurons are not activated, the connection becomes dormant, and the memory fades. Testing learned within the past hour, or just days ago, reactivates those connections; testing weeks later does not.

Scholars express similar concerns. The editors of *How People Learn* write, "Textbooks are filled with facts that students are supposed to memorize, and most tests assess students' ability to remember the facts. . . . Research . . . clearly shows that usable knowledge is not the same as a mere list of disconnected facts."[53]

An Abundance of Information

Today, there is more information available than at any time in human history. Mike Shatzkin, thought leader in digital publishing, has commented that "we have gone from a world where nobody could effectively deliver a book without a publishing organization in 1990 to one where anybody can today."[54] He also noted "the choice of book titles has become so vast—going from about 500,000 titles in English three decades ago to about 20 million titles available through [leading book wholesaler] Ingram today."[55]

In 1980, there were twenty-eight US cable television networks.[56] By 2021, there were at least 124, but the number no longer matters.[57] With the exception of news and sports, viewer behavior has shifted away from scheduled programming to on-demand, anytime, anywhere viewing. In 2004, YouTube was a new company with no videos online. Twenty years later, YouTube is probably the world's largest website; its video library will soon exceed one billion videos.[58] YouTube is watched by about one in three people in the world. It is now the world's most popular tool for both entertainment and learning.

In December 1995, approximately fifteen million people used the internet (0.4 percent of the global population). By December 2005—ten years later—approximately one billion people (15.7 percent) did. In December 2015, the count was 3.4 billion (46.4 percent), and as of December 2022, it was up to 5.5 billion (69 percent).[59] As these numbers continue to increase, more users generate information, feeding and accelerating the cycle.

Increased communication capacity, and an increased ability to reach an audience, has transformed the way humans learn. From 1996 to 2020, the number of science and engineering research papers published in high-income economies doubled, and they increased nearly tenfold in higher-middle income economies. Among lower-middle income economies, research papers tripled.[60]

In an era already filled with more information, more ideas, more perspectives, more stories, more of everything, AI has begun to generate even more information. The quantity and quality of human connections grows very quickly because of the network effect. If there are five people on a network, then there are ten possible connections. If there are one thousand people, then there are a million possible connections. The growth is exponential.

> There is a person . . . and I would get to know them. And there is a person who is linked to that person. And there is a community linked to that person. And I can get access to the whole thing. I learn like that.
>
> —Kevin, 17, Seoul, South Korea

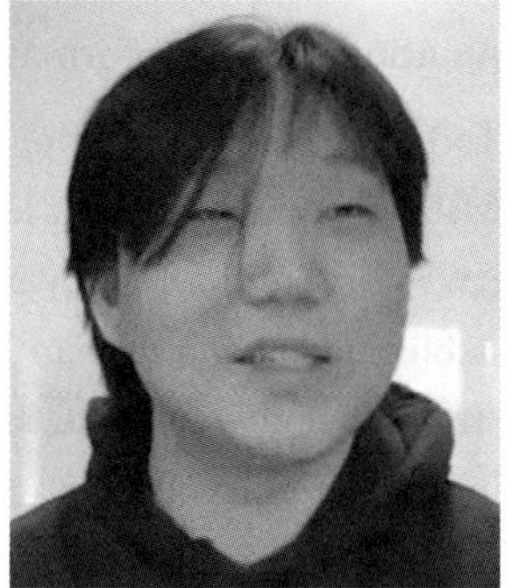

Data scientists and marketers have made good use of all these personal connections. School, not so much.

BUILDING A BETTER MIND

Dehaene:

> All research findings are remarkably convergent: *enriching the environment* of a young child helps her build a better brain. For instance, in children who are read bedtime stories every evening, the brain circuits for spoken language are stronger than in other toddlers—and the strengthened cortical pathways are precisely those that will later allow them to understand texts and formulate complex thoughts. . . . Exposing the developing brain to a stimulating environment allows it to keep more synapses, larger dendrites, and more flexible and redundant circuits . . . the blossoming of [young] brains depends in part on the richness of the stimulation they receive from the environment.[61]

Validation builds self-confidence, which increases *agency*—the sense that one's judgment and decisions are sound and reasonable. Self-confidence propels students to explore, experiment, excel, pursue mastery, and do things they've never done before. Validation of personal interest and curiosity, especially from a trusted adult, goes a long way toward encouraging a student to learn. Often, discouragement generates the opposite result.

Agency is enhanced through explicit or implicit permission. When a learner enjoys reasonable boundaries with unrestricted rights and privileges to think freely, pursue their own interests, and share, they thrive. When school restricts rights and privileges (which is standard practice) students conform, but agency is diminished.

Future-mindedness is a result of agency. Encouraged by exposure to a free flow of ideas, content, context, and new ways of thinking, learners imagine possible futures. Observing people who share their ideas (TED Talks are a good example), traveling to unfamiliar places, and interacting with people from other communities and cultures are powerful contributors to a sense of "maybe I could try that." Again, these choices are indications of each child's individual interests and plans for the future, each child's uniqueness. Vygotsky: "A primate can learn a great deal through training by using its mechanical and mental skills, but it cannot be made more intelligent, that is, it cannot be taught to solve a variety of more advanced problems independently. . . . Human learning presupposes a specific social nature and process by which children grow into the intellectual life of those around them."[62]

Pace

Everybody learns at their own pace. Some children and teenagers bring prior knowledge and well-practiced skills to learning. Some dawdle. Some diligently complete their work within the allotted time. Some deal with other issues. They are just not interested. In most any third grade classroom, there will be a small number of children who have finished reading a few *Harry Potter* volumes among other children who have not yet mastered kindergarten-level basic word recognition and phonetic skills. The same is true on a football pitch or in any other venue associated with growing up. There are myriad reasons why this is true: parental involvement, individual interests and capabilities, interactions with friends, fear, desire to succeed, curiosity, and lots more. Assumptions are pointless because every human is unique.

> My little sister, Kloe, was premature. She was born about five months early. She had brain blaze [brain bleeding] when she was born, which caused her to have cerebral palsy. She couldn't see well, so she's had three eye surgeries. She had braces for her feet. She still wears them now and she's six. And she's learning how to walk. And she learned how to sign. It's hard for Kloe to communicate with other kids when she can't speak. My family has learned sign language. I know the alphabet and some numbers, and words she knows like "eating" and "drinking."

Then there's words like "firefighter" that we don't even know, and Kloe would be signing them. We'd look it up and she'd be doing the correct [sign]. [We would ask her] how do you know that? She learned how to do it by herself. Kloe watches this show, it's called *Signing Time* and she watches it all the time! She wants to watch it at school! As soon as we get home, she goes straight to her iPad, and she goes to YouTube. She can find stuff very easily. Kloe just found *Signing Time* herself—one day, she was just watching YouTube and it popped up so she clicked on it. Now, she watches it all the time! She's a very smart kid!

—Karla, 12, Neon, Kentucky, US (signing "mom")

Kloe learns some things much faster than people around her. Her interest is intense because each new word increases her potential to communicate more clearly. Kloe is outpacing her sister, her classmates, her parents, and her teachers. Kloe knows the word for *firefighter*, but this is not useful if other people can't interpret the sign. This neither stops Kloe from learning nor slows her down.

If everybody learned the same things, everybody would know the visual sign for firefighter.[63] Must everyone must know the sign? How about people who rarely interact with a person who is hearing impaired? What if there's a fire?

Impediments to Learning

How many of today's children and teenagers face serious learning impediments? The answer depends on the definition of the term.

One useful source is the 2021 UNICEF report, *Seen, Counted, Included*.[64] It attempts to quantify the well-being and challenges of children with disabilities. It lists thirteen functional disabilities: seeing, hearing, mobility, self-care, communication/comprehension, learning, remembering, attention and concentrating, relationships, coping with change, controlling behavior, anxiety, and depression. Although results vary by income, gender, age, region, and other factors, the report estimates that about 250,000—one in ten—of the world's children and teenagers face disabilities.

Acknowledging the risk of some double counting and a high likelihood of under counting (unexamined, undiagnosed), add another one in eight children with a form of ADHD.[65]

According to a 2023 UNICEF report, one in six of the world's children and teenagers live in extreme poverty.[66] It is very difficult to overcome the many associated obstacles in order to learn, acquire significant knowledge, and attend to memory amid multidimensional poverty. Many more children and teenagers lack essential resources. In the US, about 16 percent of children live in poverty.[67] The global total is probably above 20 percent—that's one in five children! Adults: How can we allow this to be our global reality?

Adding in difficult social conditions at home, in the community, and in the country, and the percentage of children and teenagers who struggle with learning due to external conditions, the total number of disadvantaged young people is probably more than half of the total number of young people on Earth.

LEARNING DIFFERENT THINGS

Many, many years ago, Bulgaria was on Turkish slavery. The Turkish people killed many Bulgarian people. They kidnapped the Bulgarian children and made them Turkish soldiers. Then, those soldiers forgot about their families in Bulgaria and killed them. There were five hundred years under Turkish slavery, and it was very sad. There were many brave people. Russia helped Bulgaria to win in the war, and in 1878, Bulgaria was freed. Slavery started in 1396. About five hundred years. I think now Bulgaria is peaceful. Our nature is very beautiful. We can see many sides.

—Mitko, 12, Stara Zagora, Bulgaria

When the Portuguese came [to Brazil], they made arrangements so that the people fought among themselves. That was a strategy they used to win. I will give you an example of the symbol that I know that is like a Black Panther of that time. He was like The Guardian of capoeira. He had several moves, offense and defense, and was very good at martial arts. He defended very well. The landowner's gang pursued him, but he got away. He escaped into the jungle.

—Gabriel, 11, São Paulo, Brazil

> I think Ashoka was a great king. He traveled many places. He went down south, to Southeast Asia. He went to places like Malaysia and Thailand. You know how Bali has a very similar culture to India? Ashoka was the reason why! I've been to Bali. They told me that Ashoka conquered Bali. At one point in time, Ashoka would conquer and spread his religion. He decided to stop and let all of that go and follow Buddha, a man who seeks peace. For me, that's a huge mystery . . . why he just suddenly changed. It's very difficult to just let all of that go. He was a man with great power.
>
> —Abraham, 12, Gurugram, Haryana, India

Certainly, this information is relevant and personally interesting to Mitko, Gabriel, and Abraham, although perhaps not to one another. Being honest, most people categorize knowledge in roughly the same way:

- Ideas everybody must know
- Ideas most people should know
- Ideas many people should know
- Ideas some people should know
- Ideas a small number of people should know

In contemporary schooling, thousands of standards are stuffed into curriculum, delivered through instruction regulated by pacing guides, and evaluated in the most reductive form through mass testing. It's all based on a universal "everybody should know" strategy that doesn't make much sense in the real world.

LEARNING IN SCHOOL

More than a century ago, in many parts of the world, it became clear that most people ought to learn to read, master numbers, and develop certain scholastic skills and capabilities. Large numbers of public schools were organized to disseminate a very thin slice of human knowledge to very large numbers of people. School turned out to be a brilliant idea! Education has been, and remains, a major factor in human progress and economic development, and a human right, as articulated as UN Sustainable Development Goal #4: "Ensure inclusive and equitable quality education and promote lifelong learning opportunities for all."[68]

The World Bank adds,

> Education is . . . a powerful driver of development, and one of the strongest instruments for reducing poverty and improving health, gender equality, peace, and

stability. It delivers large, consistent returns in terms of income, and is the most important factor to ensure equity and inclusion. For individuals, education promotes employment, earnings, health, and poverty reduction. Globally, there is a 9 percent increase in hourly earnings for every extra year of schooling. For societies, it drives long-term economic growth, spurs innovation, strengthens institutions, and fosters social cohesion.[69]

Learning, school, and education are not synonyms. Learning continues to be robust, but school has lost traction, and education, as a system, struggles to provide the relevant knowledge, skills, capabilities, and support required for life in the twenty-first century.

I want to be a cosmologist. My father watches a lot of science [documentaries], so I know Stephen Hawking. Cosmologists basically study the creation of the world, the creation of the universe, and space. [As] we look by satellites, telescopes, we get to know more things. The Big Bang was an explosion that created the universe. There was no space, no time, no gravity, nothing. When it burst, everything was created. There was nothing outside of the Big Bang [including the molecules in my body]. There is no size of the universe. It is unlimited. There is no time [either]. I would like to be discovering new things.

—Dhruvika, 11, Gurugram, Haryana, India

Although Dhruvika spends many hours thinking about space, time, and cosmology, she doesn't do much of it in school. Instead, Dhruvika learns core subjects and minor ones, too. She is being trained to be a generalist, but she wants to become a specialist. Mostly, learning in primary and secondary school is not designed for specialists.

Adults decide what Dhruvika learns at school. Although Dhruvika attends a top-tier private school, her ability to learn what she deems important is not the guiding factor in her education.

I love space. I want to know more about space. I want to go to space. I want to find more life. I want to explore more planets. Other than Earth, which planets have life? People say that with all of the pollution, Earth has to end someday because of the damage that we are creating. If we have to evacuate, where else can we go and live? Where can we start a new life? I don't know about other people,

but I care!! I want to know answers to these questions. We have to find another planet so we can start a new life there!

—Trisha, 12, Gurugram, Haryana, India

How much time and attention should Trisha devote to her own exploration of space? On her own, or in school? Might her interest cause other students to spend more of their school hours learning about space, perhaps instead of something else on the curriculum? If students are allowed to learn based on their interests, school must change.

DECIDING WHAT MOST PEOPLE OUGHT TO KNOW

In 2015, Connecticut revised its social studies framework for primary and secondary students. This is common practice in US states and in many countries. Frameworks provide curriculum standards that become the basis for teachers' lesson plans and testing. Connecticut's K–12 social studies framework document is 145 pages long. The framework includes a thousand-plus big ideas, such as:

- "What causes regions of the country to interpret laws differently?"
- "How did indigenous peoples view the ownership of land?"
- "How did that view differ from the colonists?"
- "Why was there a lack of democracy in the Middle East prior to the Arab Spring?"[70]

Each question could generate a lively discussion with plenty of diverse opinions. Apparently, this was the intention of the forty members of Connecticut's clearly competent and dedicated Social Studies Frameworks Writing and Reviewing Team, including Stephen Armstrong of the Connecticut State Department of Education, John Tully of Central Connecticut State University, and Vanessa Diaz-Valencia of Hartford Public Schools, and "the many social studies educators who helped to review and approve this document."[71] These decision makers are mentioned by name for a reason. They are not shadowy figures; instead, they are real people who live and work in Connecticut, interact with real children, teenagers, teachers, and parents, and care about what is taught in their schools.

Connecticut's social studies framework is modern. It doesn't advocate memorization of long lists of names, dates, and places. Instead, it encourages deep thinking about big issues. Similar frameworks guide mathematics, science, language arts, and other subjects in Connecticut. Together, the frameworks outline nearly ten thousand ideas every student in Connecticut should know.

EFFICIENCY AND EFFECTIVENESS

> When I'm in school, bells which tell us the end of the class . . . I don't think that's a very good way to organize learning. If someone stops you when you are in the middle of writing something or researching, you don't really fully understand what you were doing. You don't get the full information. That's not good. When I am coding something, I would be in the middle of . . . making something work. The bell interrupting me would basically stop my mind there and tell me to stop, so next time I would not be as clear on what I was working on.
>
> —Shreyansh, 12, Gurugram, Haryana, India

Education is managed as an assembly line because more than a billion people reach the end point by their eighteenth birthday. With so much material to cover, operational efficiency is more important than learning.

EFFICIENCY AND EFFECTIVENESS

CHAPTER 3

Old School

> I feel the school system is based on ideas that are one hundred years old. . . . My parents are educated, so they can pass the knowledge to me. . . . Just talking to people, being observant, questioning, being curious, I think that's [how I gained] all of this knowledge about my own country. School teaches us history and dates, who's who in apartheid . . . but I think we need . . . a more hands-on approach in education. Just coming on a hike in Tsitsikamma National Park, I learn so much about the vegetation around the me, I can see effects of [2018's] drought.
>
> —Almaaz, 15, Johannesburg, South Africa

Like all children and teenagers, Almaaz learns in many different ways. Old School is just one of them.

Old School is a rigid system rooted in three core ideas: (1) everyone learns the same things, (2) adults determine what those things should be, and (3) the best way to determine whether students are learning those things is through testing and analysis of test results. Compare these with three ideas explored in the introduction: (1) learning is personal, (2) learning is relational, and (3) learning is active. These lists are not compatible. Learning is not going to change, so it's up to school to do so.

According to international education expert Pasi Sahlberg, "It has become clear everywhere that the schools we have today will not be able to provide opportunities to learn what is necessary in the future. . . . Indeed, education systems are facing twin challenges: how to change school so students may learn new types of knowledge and skills in an unpredictably changing world, and how to make that new learning possible for all young people regardless of their socioeconomic conditions."[1]

FAIR TREATMENT

If every student is unique, but Old School is based on standardized curriculum and practices, there is a disconnect. The bottom-up needs of the individual conflict with top-down dictates about what everybody ought to know. *Everybody* is a dangerous term because it endorses commonality but fails to recognize differences.

Matching standardized curriculum to serve each growing child and teenagers' needs, wants, and plans is nearly impossible. Far behind the front lines, a dizzying combination of adults interpret, promote, and politicize largely irrelevant test results to advance agendas that do little to correct misalignment. These adults include legislators, bureaucrats, curriculum and assessment companies, advocates, and even real estate agents (high test scores increase local home prices). In theory, a government framework could be the foundation of social justice in school and learning. In practice, the well-intentioned common denominator approach and standards-based reforms create stunning inequities.[2]

Many schools do everything they can to make sure every student, and teacher, is treated fairly, but the obstacles can be overwhelming. The system is not designed for fair treatment for every student. Accommodations and best intentions provide small-scale fixes, but fair treatment is challenging in Old School because students really are different from one another.

Three students sit in the same classroom. One can see and hear the teacher clearly. Another can see but not hear the teacher. Another can see and hear the teacher but cannot see the blackboard clearly. These students do not enjoy the same access to learning. The situation is *inequitable.*

Same students. They sit among twenty others. Every student's desk is equipped with a video monitor and headphones. The classroom now includes several video cameras and microphones. Tools are fairly distributed, but this *attempt at fair treatment* is overblown and unlikely to be effective.

Back to our three students. One has no issues. One now uses a hearing aid. Another wears eyeglasses. These students enjoy *a form of equality,* but now there's a fourth child in a wheelchair that cannot fit through the classroom door. Instead of a patchwork solution, the school redesigns the classroom, providing *fair treatment* for students and teachers.

Special education and accommodations for kids with disabilities may help "level the playing field" for equity, but when all kids are learning the same thing, the situation becomes inequitable because each student's circumstances set them up to learn different things—and yet, they are all required to learn the same things.

How about social justice for *what* the kids are learning? "The mission of the North Carolina State Board of Education is to use its constitutional authority to guard and maintain the right of a sound, basic education for every child in North Carolina Public Schools."[3] How does that work in practice? The 2021 edition of the *Quick Reference Guide for the North Carolina Standard Course of Study: Grade K* runs fifty-plus pages and sets priorities for every five-year-old. Should every North Carolina kindergartener learn the same things? At what age is a child respected and allowed to pursue their own path?

FIVE-DAY SUBJECTS

Time is money, so the amount of time devoted to each Old School subject is a reasonable proxy for financial investment. The very existence of each Old School subject suggests social and economic value that is far greater, and far more useful, than any other subjects that might be taught or learned. Dominant subjects—mathematics, science, social studies, and language arts—are functionally immune to questions about relevance, utility, time allocation, and effectiveness. Discussion and assessment are overdue.

Mathematics

For a dozen years during childhood and adolescence, mathematics is taught about forty minutes a day, five days each week, 180 days a year. That's a total of about six hundred hours of mathematics instruction per student. In the many countries we've visited or reviewed, Mathematics is one of the most taught Old School subjects.

Before kindergarten, most young children learn numbers, arithmetic, and some geometry through play, by watching videos, and from other people. Learning is informal, practical, and fun. In school, learning mathematics becomes formal, far more theoretical, and fun only for some students. In Australia,[4] year 3 students "recognize, model, represent and order numbers to at least 10,000 . . . represent money values . . . count the change." Year 6 students "identify and describe properties of prime, composite, square and triangular numbers . . . solve problems involving the addition and subtraction of fractions with the same or related denominators . . . and investigate combinations of translations, reflections and rotations with and without the use of digital technologies." Year 9 students apply "index laws to numerical expressions with integer indices and graph simple nonlinear relations with and without the use of digital technologies, and calculate the surface area and volume of cylinders . . . and deal with categorical variables."[5]

By Year 6, students face esoterica beyond a defensible standard of "everybody should know." The popular defense: mathematics is a holistic system of increasing complexity resulting in advanced knowledge that can elevate student skills, capacity, versatility, and self-confidence. Undoubtedly, this is true for some people, but not for most students who can easily find more productive uses for the time and effort that mathematics currently owns and controls. Similarly, some adults argue that advanced mathematics education increases the likelihood of academic success (in certain disciplines), but the same argument can be made for just about any subject.

No reasonable person would argue against students learning about numbers in school. The question is how much and what type(s) of skills and knowledge are relevant, necessary, and useful. Adding curriculum—perhaps coding, perhaps statistics—obscures the question. Most students will never require mathematics knowledge or skills beyond what's taught in primary school. Every student's path is unique, so there is no single answer. For students who pursue STEM careers, additional coursework and training are available in school and from many other sources. Calculators, spreadsheets, search engines (with instant calculation results), and AI greatly reduce the amount of process learning required for twenty-first-century students, but their availability has not reduced the number of school hours dedicated to mathematics.

In some schools, mathematics includes coding, robotics, data science, economics, game design, probability, statistics, and trend analysis. Perhaps these additions justify the large number of hours devoted to mathematics for some students, but these hours could be better deployed—by some and perhaps many students—in pursuit of other types of learning.

> I would want to be in New York and that career would be in the financial sector because I really enjoy math.
>
> —Teesha, 11, Port Louis, Mauritius

> Love doing math! I do math 24/7. I just love mathematics—figuring out problems, then seeing what I did wrong, and fixing them.
>
> —Jaylee, 13, Fleming-Neon, Kentucky, US

> Right now in math, we're learning about stuff that has to do with exponents and scientific notation. I like playing around with numbers. I think it's a subject I'm good at. When I grow up, I want to be an engineer.
>
> —Noah, 13, Richboro, Pennsylvania US

In the US, with its full-time workforce of about 165 million people (half the population), about three million people work in fields related to mathematics—more than a million are engineers. There are 1.5 million accountants and auditors, but AI will eliminate many of those jobs. Other roles employ fewer people: data scientists, operational research analysts, statisticians, and insurance actuaries, for example, with about 275,000 jobs.[6] On its own, mathematics is not a growing field. Computer science is growing, but math's relevance is fading because other skills and knowledge are becoming more valuable; for example, to become a full stack developer, knowledge of HTTP, HTML, CSS, JavaScript, internet security, databases, and APIs is useful.[7] The mathematical standard G.TS.3 from the Indiana Academic Standards for Geometry, "Explore properties of congruent and similar solids, including prisms, regular pyramids, cylinders, cones, and spheres, and use them to solve problems," is far less useful.[8]

Science

Old School's conception of science evolved when life was simpler before the internet. Children and teenagers are now aware of a very wide range of scientific pursuits and possible career paths. Why not oceanography, systems theory, electrical engineering, anthropology, climatology, mycology (fungi), biodiversity, therapeutic robotics, or 3D organ engineering?

Old School packages a very small slice of science, laden with facts to memorize, not horizons to explore. Essentially, it provides a survey of several scientific disciplines but pays scant attention to most of them. With this approach, even fascinating information becomes boring and difficult to remember: "At standard temperature and pressure, two atoms of [nitrogen] bond to form N_2, a colorless and odorless diatomic gas. N_2 forms about 78% of Earth's atmosphere, making it the most abundant uncombined element in air."[9]

Science class usually fails to address unknowns, exploration, and discovery—and that's the fun of it all. One student may be fascinated by the symbiotic relationship between coral and algae. Another may wonder about coral's varied colors. Another, the role of climate change, toxicity, and bleaching. Another: biodiversity. Another: crown-of-thorns starfish that eat, and destroy, coral.[10] Their curiosity drives their learning, but curiosity is not always easy to share or manage. Managing a biology lab with twenty different students dissecting twenty different animals and asking questions about each of them is nearly impossible. Unless—the teacher pivots from the person-who-knows-all to the person-who-guides students to learn. Students gain independence by doing research, handling dissection, creating video (or writing the report, or drawing the diagram), cleaning up, and safely disposing of carcasses. Or everybody can learn the same things in the same ways, whether they do or don't care about what's inside a dead frog.

Most people who become interested in science don't become professional scientists. Instead, they cultivate their own scientific literacy based on personal interests. Most amateur bakers (including serious and casual viewers of *The Great British Bake Off*) are becoming familiar with food science. They know which flour to use for which type of bread or cake, and they can explain their decision. They can explain why caster sugar is preferable, in some recipes, to granulated sugar.

They care because their choice of sugar is relevant to their interests. Shoving piles of scientific information into young brains is far less likely to generate a spark than experiential learning—visiting dinosaurs in a museum—and following the experience with student's choices of deep pursuits, for example. There are so many entry points, but they're easily obscured by school's incessant need to force everyone to learn the same things in the same ways. Still, there are solutions. Nature videos and documentaries make use of media's ability to visualize stories—and reveal ideas that are too fast, too slow, too small, or too large for classroom instruction (life inside a cell or on Mars). Students, and the world, benefit from a lifelong interest in science—school's job is to make some introductions and amplify that interest.

> Me, loving science, I think I'm going to be a veterinarian because you have to know animal biology, anatomy of a dog, a cat, any animal. Social studies? I don't really lean into that. How I become a veterinarian is, I go to high school for four

years, go to a college somewhere, do four years of that, go to Virginia—they have a veterinarian place down there, watch what she does, observe, and it should let me become a veterinarian. The pets I have around are a dachshund—his name is Julio. We had a firefighter [a dalmatian], he was skinny, it almost made me want to cry. Then we got Smokey. He's a mixed breed between a long-haired dachshund and a rat terrier. He's fuzzy and playful. Then, we've got a chihuahua named Oreo. He's old and grumpy. He's got cataracts in his eyes and a big bubble on his chin. Just makes me want to get through veterinary school faster and help him. You know he's gotta be hurting. I thought about treating wild animals at one point, maybe going to Africa because I've always wanted to travel around the world and see different cultures. So, I'd like to do that, too.

—Cruiser, 13, Neon, Kentucky, US

By far, the largest number of US jobs related to science are nurses (3.5 million), followed by doctors (about a million). Neither requires a broad-based survey of scientific knowledge; instead, they require extensive training in medical science. About a half-million people work as scientists in many specialties and subspecialties (zoologists, microbiologists, epidemiologists) and as technicians and support personnel. There are agricultural scientists, environmental scientists, materials scientists, food scientists—it's a very long list of distinct, often small, fields. So if you're not going to be a nurse or a doctor, science is a relatively small field.

Social Studies

Originally focused on history, geography, and civics/government, social studies now covers more territory: human rights, social justice, economics, media literacy, popular culture, sociology, culture, immigration, and their intersections. social studies is hobbled by "accountability systems [that place] social studies conspicuously lower in the hierarchy of academic achievement, [than] math, literacy, and science."[11] And, according to a 2018 report from the Council of Chief State Officers, "research consistently demonstrates that social studies receives the least amount of instructional time in the elementary grades when compared to the amount of time afforded to other core content areas."[12]

Today's students are the first generation of globally connected citizens. Often, they know more about specific topics than their teachers do—and teachers cannot be expected to keep up with each student's international interests. Social studies is also affected by misinformation, cultural differences, politics, and parents who may object to a teacher's handling of a particular issue.

Teaching students about Ukraine involves nearly thirty-five thousand years of human history. In the past, portions of Ukraine have been ruled by Mongols, Lithuania, Poland, and Russia. Its western region has been divided and made part of Poland, Romania, and Czechoslovakia.[13] In modern times, Russia has been trying to regain control over Ukraine. Since February 2022, more than eight million Ukrainians have been displaced within the country, and more than eight million more have left Ukraine, producing Europe's largest humanitarian crisis since World War II. More than three million Ukrainian refugees live in Poland; Russia has launched missiles from Belarus aimed at Ukraine; Bulgaria has supplied arms and ammunition to Russia. Moldova has a half-million Ukrainian refugees, and it's concerned about its relationship with Russia. Other issues include German reliance on Russian oil and Finland's NATO membership.[14] This is far too much to cover in a social studies unit on Ukraine, and another cause to question which information everyone must know, some people should know, and so on.

Children and teenagers are quick to point out that Ukraine is more than the history of its wars. It's family and social gatherings like *vechornytsi*—parties that originally celebrated the end of summer farming season.[15] It's *kutia*—a Christmas goodie with wheat groats, poppy seeds, and honey. It's *pysanky* eggs decorated at Easter time. It's *kolabasa*, and *borscht* with *smetana*, *pierogi*, and *salo*. It's weaving, lace making, wedding traditions, the football rivalry between FC Dynamo Kyiv and FC Shakhtar Donetsk, iconic embroidery on the *vyshyvanka,* and Sunday services in a Ukrainian Orthodox Church.[16] It's the long history of Ukrainian resistance and resilience and foreign domination. Mostly, it's love of family, friends, pride, and stories—all difficult to express in a prescribed social studies framework.

Every nation, every culture, every family has enough stories (and more than enough beliefs) to build their own social studies curriculum. With twenty-first-century prioritization of diversity and mutual respect, social studies in its present form is difficult to teach and learn.

> I will tell you about the Triple Alliance. It was a big war against Paraguay. It was Argentina [and Brazil and Uruguay] against us. We lost a lot of territory. We lost, in the fight, a lot of men, they died. It was a difficult time for Paraguay. After the war, there were more women [alive in Paraguay] than men. This happened in 1870. After that, the women had to rebuild the whole country. It was very tragic for us. We were wealthy before. And the country was [much] bigger. We lost, mostly, everything.[17]
>
> —Kiara, 14, Areguá, Paraguay

Even something as basic as soup can provide fundamental ideas about people and customs. Greenland's national dish is *suaasat*, a soup made from seal meat. Soups are pretty interesting. Why not a curriculum about soup (and soupy stews)? Ukraine's *borscht*, Greenland's *suaasat*, Spain's gazpacho, Brazil's feijoada, Japan's *nabeyaki udon*, Malaysia's *penang laksa*, Morocco's *harira*, Thailand's *tom yum*?[18] One entry point to Greek studies is *avgolemono*. Students can cook it themselves, or a community member or restaurant can take care of the lesson. Learning does not always require a teacher.

Oops—the list omitted *mansoor dal* and West African *egusi*,[19] and thousands of other soups. Gifty, age eleven, in Kumasi, Ghana, adds, "My favorite meal is *fufu* and light chicken soup. And sweets! Chocolate! Ice cream!! Strawberries!!!"

A formal social studies curriculum cannot cover everything, so it offers a weak representative sample—Britain's Parliament and Japan's National Diet become placeholders for legislatures all over the world. It's impossible to cover every Chinese dynasty or every African empire, so the Han and the Songhai must suffice—regardless of individual students' heritage or curiosity. The present system does not allow a student to study, for example, the major empires of Africa because they must study the British, Ottoman, Mongol, and Russian empires, plus the dates of most major wars and the history of the (European) Middle Ages.

Everything feels arbitrary—people outside the classroom making decisions about which history matters. The historical truth can be harsh, deeply divisive, soul crushing in its negativity. Is it wise for children and teenagers to learn the truth about their own country's past? The histories of the US, Germany, Japan,

Italy, Belgium, France, England, Turkey, and many other nations include horrors. They involve enemies—and some wounds take a long, long time to heal. When we interviewed teenagers in South Korea, they were skeptical about China because of abuses during World War II. Still, educating children is part of healing. But some or all children? Those whose families include terrorists or murderers and passive people who allowed devastation? Overall, the human story is of relentless domination by men. What should everybody learn about this?

> [In the US], in order to get elected to the House [of Representatives], it requires an absolutely ridiculous sum of money and access to capital that most people do not have . . . the representation of working-class people in Congress is extremely low. Women still only constitute 27 percent of our Congress. People of color, Latinas—there have only been, I don't know, two or three dozen Latinas who have been elected in [US] history.[20]
>
> —US Congresswoman Alexandria Ocasio-Cortez

The current system often fails to tell students what they probably ought to know.

> As of 1 January 2023, there are 31 countries where 34 women serve as Heads of State and/or Government. At the current rate, gender equality in the highest positions of power will not be reached for another 130 years.[21]
>
> —UN Women, the United Nations entity dedicated to gender equality and the empowerment of women

In theory, students learn curriculum-based social studies to become responsible citizens, but responsible citizens are easily persuaded to make self-destructive decisions on the basis of beliefs, not knowledge or reason. Examples include Brexit, widespread prejudice, income inequality, the US taxation of Social Security benefits, many and perhaps most wars, laws restricting voting rights, the choosing of leaders who harm their people (often claiming otherwise), unfathomable immigration policies, lousy access to health care and other services, poverty and homelessness, not voting in elections, and many more.

If the argument for extensive mass social studies education is employment, students will find declining careers. In the US, less than one-tenth of 1 percent of workers are employed as journalists (47,000; declining), economists (about 17,000), anthropologists and archaeologists (7,500), historians (3,300), sociologists (3,000), or geographers (1,600). At about 150,000, the largest number of people working in careers related to social studies may be . . . social studies teachers![22]

Language Arts

Language arts presents a different set of issues. Current curricula concentrate on reading and writing, which remains useful, but children and teenagers also communicate, process, and share ideas in many other ways. It's important to remember that the purpose of language arts instruction is to help students communicate in many different ways—with relevance and utility far beyond books alone.

Listening Language skills begin with listening, which provides a path to knowledge acquisition in each child's home language. Sounds are imitated and become speech. Listening combines aural perception with interpretation, attention, sensitivity to sounds, selectivity, decoding and processing signals, and connecting input to ideas stored in several areas of the brain. Each child develops their own vocabulary by connecting sounds to meaning, creating fascinating errors and misunderstandings on the way to building an idiosyncratic intellectual and emotional map. Always listening, each child and teenager's pace, observations, interpretation, interest, connections, and desire to respond is unique.

Listening is also a social skill. Attentive listening and demonstration of interest suggest compassion and personal connection. Being a good listener may come naturally, but most people benefit from listening instruction and practice. When children do not learn how to listen effectively, they miss verbal and nonverbal cues. Effective listening collects information from context, facial expression, eye movement, and body language. Poor listeners may not paraphrase, recap to confirm understanding, or provide appropriate, timely feedback. They may fail to convey the need for additional information. They may signal disinterest or disagreement. Listening is closely aligned with hearing, perception, and processing, and with behavior—as in "You are not hearing me."

Speaking

> Young children typically gain several new words a day, acquiring vocabulary at an "astonishing rate."[23] Yet by the time they start school, some children will have heard millions more words than others. The number of words a child has heard and can speak by the age of three is a predictor of later language development, so these early vocabulary gains are critically important.[24]
>
> —*The Reading Framework*, UK Department of Education

After a year of making sounds not easily recognized as words, most humans begin to express themselves and speak clearly. The National Institute on Deafness and Other Communication Disorders states, "Children vary in their development of speech and language skills. However, they follow a natural progression or timetable for mastering the skills of language."[25] By age one to two, most children can put together short statements and questions ("Where cookie?"). By two to three, they can point to objects and identify them for others by name, often in short sentences ("I want juice!"). By three to four, sentences contain more words, and descriptions are more complete ("I fell down and hurt my knee!"). By four to five, the child may be a competent storyteller.[26] Every child develops at a different pace, with varying skill, interest, vocabulary, vivacity, and so on. Caring adults and stimulation enhance the process, offering subsequent benefits in language skills and other competencies. Most of this takes place before primary school.

Mostly, Old School focuses on reading and writing but does not concentrate resources or instructional time on oral language or listening. Fundamentally, good oral language instruction is essential for good reading and writing skills, but oral language is not a focus of Old School instruction. This is unfortunate because speaking and listening are more common and more useful, and are essential for effective human interaction.

Writing Writing is an extension of speaking—but it involves symbols and rules unique to each culture. There are thousands of languages on Earth. Every written language must be taught and learned. Writing must be practiced, corrected, and internalized.

Truthfully, writing can be tedious. It requires concentration, few distractions, some inspiration, and sufficient time to prepare not only a first draft, but second, third, and preferably fourth drafts, too. Professional writers often struggle to get started, discard early attempts, and follow an uneven path to completion. The written piece, and the writer, often benefit from feedback, but feedback is not easy to accept or process—especially in school because time is limited, and due to social and emotional issues.

> First drafts are slow and develop clumsily because every sentence affects not only those before it but also those that follow.[27] Regardless of the writing project or its length, drafts 2, 3, and 4 take about as much time as [the] first draft.
>
> —John McPhee, writer, Pulitzer Prize winner,
> author (thirty-four books), prolific *New Yorker* essayist

Writing requires solitude, but a quiet place may be hard to find. Appropriate tools (pen, pencil, paper, writing surface) may not be available. Devices must be charged, connected, and deployed without distraction from social media. The mental and emotional space must feel free from judgment. A school classroom is not always the best place to write, but home may not be ideal either. If writing is a valuable skill, facilities must be available.

Artificial intelligence can provide a useful starting point and can solve tricky writing problems. In several ways, AI can be helpful in writing clearly through suggested language, review of what has been written, suggestions for rewrites, and more. Still, the point of writing instruction is the development of clear expression and critical thinking, not simply generating a paragraph for an assignment.

Reading Humans do not simply learn to read; we learn to decipher symbols, words, sentence structure, syntax, grammar, word order, and meaning. Without structured instruction and reinforcement, these symbols are impossible to decode:

私は公園で犬を散歩させた。
Я вигулював свою собаку в парку.
مشيت كلبي في الحديقة.
I walked my dog in the park.

(The languages are Japanese, Ukrainian, Arabic, and English.)

Learning to read begins well before kindergarten. New readers benefit from consistently successful techniques for reading and writing instruction. Students who learn from a phonics-based curriculum acquire and practice useful skills in *morphology* (internal structure of words), *phonology* (sound of words), *accidence* (inflection of words), and *semantics* (meaning and interpretation of words). They develop vocabulary and improve their spelling too. Learning to read cannot be absorbed through observation or balanced learning/whole-life reading. It requires the learner to "understand the relationships between sounds and letters, with daily lessons that build on each other in a systematic order. Plenty of evidence shows that children who receive systematic phonics instruction learn to read better and more rapidly than kids who don't."[28] Still, the top-down management of US education results in a 50 percent success because a phonics-based curriculum is not used everywhere.

Parents impact a child's interest in learning to read beginning at birth, when sounds and meanings are first connected, words and objects are associated, oral language and sound-making develop, conversations and exchanges of information and emotions begin to take place. Parents introduce children to books. Parents reading to, and with, their children adds layers and interweaves with other verbal skills. This becomes the foundation of reading; and more exposure to reading, at any age, improves proficiency, which encourages more reading. In primary school, there are two clear objectives: (1) make sure all students acquire and practice reading skills, and (2) cultivate students' interest in reading. In part, that's why many books for younger readers are funny, or fun.

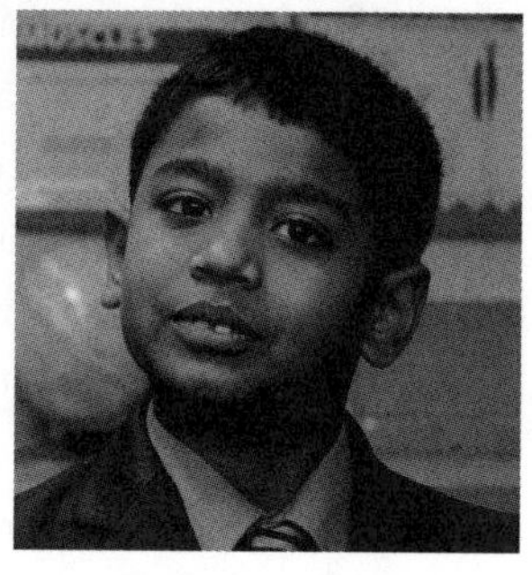

> I'm reading *Diary of a Wimpy Kid*, and some *Beast Quest* books.
>
> —Giyan, 8, Manchester, England

> I didn't like to read until, like, seventh grade, but then my younger sister told me about the *Harry Potter* series of books. I already watched the movie. I loved the movie, so I wanted to read the book. I think, then, I love to read, and I read a lot. My favorite author is Cassandra Clare. She wrote *Shadow Hunters*. My favorite book is *Vampire Academy*. It's about a vampire girl who has to save her boyfriend. The books I read came from other countries. I read their translatements [translations].
>
> —Marija Lara, 15, Ljubljana, Slovenia

In primary school, students are encouraged to read books that interest them. "Teachers should provide books likely to give the most pleasure, so that all pupils feel encouraged to put in the reading miles before they read more challenging books independently: sets of short, popular easy-read page-turners, hi-lo books, joke books, irreverent books—anything that helps to establish the reading habit." ("'Hi-lo' books provide high interest content at an easy reading level: histories of famous people, books about underwater life, biographies, semi-fictional stories based on real events and so on.")[29]

According to the UK government's *Reading Framework*,

> extensive international research shows that being a frequent reader is associated with a range of academic, social and emotional benefits. Far more than pleasure is at stake. Multiple studies suggest that enjoyment is associated with higher reading performance. The recent 2021 PIRLS data for England showed that the pupils who said they liked reading the most scored, on average, 34 points more than those who said they did not like reading. In effect, pupils who are reading regularly for enjoyment give themselves unofficial reading lessons, supporting their reading comprehension. . . . Further, pupils who read regularly report heightened levels of social and emotional wellbeing. For many, reading is a form of relaxation, a place to escape everyday challenges, a source of entertainment. Reading allows readers to adopt new perspectives, develop empathy and become more socially conscious.[30]

Reading requires more effort than speaking. If a book is interesting, a student may read the whole thing, but most written material is scanned, browsed, or read in part. We skim, and read parts of stories. Few adults read the 150,000 words in *The New York Times* daily print edition—the equivalent of two or three books. Everyone who reads is selective, but our school systems fail to teach a large proportion of students how to read; at least a third of the world's fourth grade students are not literate.[31]

According to author Rebecca Rolland, "We're thinking about teaching reading wrong . . . we're not following the science . . . we're not recognizing how much kids need conversations around books—talking about ideas, not just words on the page."[32]

Contemporary research links reading proficiency to many other benefits. "Reading benefits society, too, both economically and socially. Although estimates of the cost of low levels of literacy vary and the methods are often opaque, the costs to the UK are estimated to be very high."[33] In social terms, better reading might enhance opportunities for individuals to become more engaged politically, increase their tolerance, and become involved in their communities more effectively.[34]

The popular rapper, actor, author, and activist Common explains, "*Invisible Man* by Ralph Ellison. I read it in the sixth grade and it gave me the appetite to write. I loved what he was speaking up for and saying. It really impacted me as a young Black boy to want to be seen, heard and recognized, and his book made me feel seen and heard . . . It made me learn that through the music and art I do I can return the favor and make people feel seen and heard."[35]

Many students love reading as a richly personal experience. Reading is the most successful version of large-scale Personal Education devised so far. Quiet activity engages curiosity and imagination—and listening to someone reading aloud is also special. Each student chooses books based on their own interests, but most stay close to the pack. *Dragons Love Tacos* has been on *The New York Times* best seller list for 420-plus weeks because kids tend to buy and read the same books.[36] Through adolescence, students expand their range but remain loyal to the books and topics same-age friends are reading. Recent examples include: *I Am Not Your Perfect Mexican Daughter, Laughing at My Nightmare* (about disability), and *What Made Maddy Run: The Secret Struggles and Tragic Death of an All-American Teen.*[37] And, of course, reading and writing are still necessary for (most) social media.

Media If reading is so wonderful, why bother with other media? It's not an either-or argument—except in Old School. In comparison with mathematics (six hundred hours of instruction), how many hours should be allocated to listening, speaking, writing, and reading? How much time should be devoted to studying sounds, images, and interactive media? How much additional work should children and teenagers do at home?

How much time should be devoted to *making* media—which is often more time-consuming than, say, writing? Some stories can be told simply, but more complicated stories—fiction or nonfiction—require preparation and technical competence. A script, with multiple revisions, is often essential, along with site visits, props, costumes—and all of this must be planned, produced, and assembled. Access to resources, materials, and people, as well as transportation, group dynamics, clear goals, defanging conflict, and endless problem-solving affect every creative decision. Making media requires a lot of time and effort.

When students make media, they learn about subject matter and they learn about media development and production. They consider audience interest. Quickly, they realize school is not the best place to produce video. Production requires greater control and more flexibility than most schools can provide. And sometimes it rains on outdoor scenes. Or it snows. Logistics, opening and closing times, and control over shooting locations are tricky and require time, local cooperation, and relationship management. Many communities support a media-making group, useful for students who want to learn from others, borrow equipment, and perhaps develop a portfolio of their own work. This is possible in Old School, but other priorities conflict.

Podcasts are easier to make, but they require research, formatting, choice of voices, scripting, selection and editing of music, recording technology, audio editing, packaging, and a means of distribution. Students require sufficient time to go through all the steps—and make corrections when (not if) things do not work out. Graphic novels require a lot of time from the writer(s) and artist(s). Each medium is its own specialty—and some lead to employment. Should students learn to make media in school just as they learn to write? The answer is yes—but only for some students. Others will choose to learn, study, or pursue something else. There is no common denominator. Except one: AI will change the marketplace, the jobs, the necessary training, just about every production process.

"SPECIALS"—ONE TO TWO DAY SUBJECTS

The word *school* traces back to the Greek *scholē*, and a surprising meaning—*leisure*. In Greek culture, leisure allowed time for thinking and finding out. "Hence, leisure's connection to pursuit of knowledge, and eventually to a place of learning."[38]

In Old School, both teachers and students often encounter more freedom in specials. They may select what to study (Spanish or French), their form of expression (woodworking or art), their means of expression (a trumpet or a flute), whether to pursue a private or public pursuit (personal research or performing arts), their type of social interaction (individual, small group, large group), and whether to expand the time spent on the subject (extracurricular activities). In most cases, they may learn more from community or public activities (musical performance, art museum, Japanese restaurant, movies about other places, etc.) This is not, typically, what happens in five-day subjects.

Today, people of all ages choose to spend their time learning about foreign languages, computers/technology, art, music, and health/physical education, and in a library. Old School positions these pursuits as secondary to the five-day subjects. More kids want access to these things, but they are not getting it.

Foreign Languages

About one in twelve people in the US speak Spanish today. By 2050, one in four will speak Spanish.[39]

In the US state of New Mexico, one in two people speak Spanish today. Shall everyone in New Mexico learn to speak Spanish? How about everyone in the US? About one in thirty people in New Mexico speak a Navajo language; some speak Zuni, Tiwa, or Tewa.[40]

Should demographics determine which languages are learned in school? If the answer is yes, what about children and teenagers who speak other languages?

World language expert Dahlia Aguilar explains, "The goal is not just being bilingual. It's about being able to read, write, dream, and weave in more than one language. The U.S. eliminated hundreds of heritage languages through Colonialism. As a school focused on environmental sustainability, we learn biodiversity is health, it is wellness. We're teaching students that learning two languages is about that same health, that biodiversity."[41]

Exposure to a broad range of cultures and their languages sparks curiosity, but the opposite is also true. No coursework in Javanese or Turkish usually means little learning and discussion about Indonesia or Turkey in school. Regardless of their contribution to culture or history, most countries are invisible in Old School!

In the US, only about one in five students opt for foreign language classes.[42] About 70 percent of schools offer Spanish-language instruction, followed by French (about 12 percent) and German (3 percent). Other languages—such as Arabic, ASL, Chinese, Japanese, and Russian—are offered by a very small number of schools.[43]

Is it wise for schools to offer, and students to become familiar with, many different languages—or concentrate on just one or two? Is it valuable for a student to be able to write, speak, and translate to and from German, Korean, and Vietnamese—and to become familiar with sounds and letter forms?

Als ich mit meinem Hund in den Park ging, fand sie den Eisstand
und die freundliche Verkäuferin machte eine Eistüte—nur für sie
강아지와 함께 공원에 갔을 때 그녀는 아이스크림 가판대를 찾았고 친절한
상인은 그녀를 위해 아이스크림 콘을 만들었습니다
Khi tôi đi đến công viên với của mình, cô ấy tìm thấy quầy kem và người bán
hàng tốt bụng đã làm một cây kem ốc quế—chỉ dành cho cô ấy
When I went to the park with my dog, she found the ice cream stand,
and the friendly vendor made an ice cream cone—just for her.

A curious student wants to know whether it's okay to take a dog to a park in Busan, South Korea, or Hanoi, Vietnam? To explore whether the dog is likely to encounter a friendly ice cream vendor in parks in those places? Do people enjoy ice cream in those places? Do they have the same flavors as here, or different flavors? Does it taste like it does here, or does it taste different? Which flavors are popular? Now, it's off to the internet to learn about Trang Tien Ice Cream in Ha Noi, and matcha ice cream in Busan, look at their shop (and ice cream) pictures, and learn what else people in those places (and their dogs) eat. A learning adventure begins (and almost nobody is memorizing vocabulary lists or conjugating verbs).

> My dad's from Korea. My mom's Australian, but I was born in Hong Kong. [I am] a non-Chinese kid in a local school . . . where Cantonese is the main language. I can almost speak Chinese fluently, but I'm not very good at it. When I first went to the school, it was a bit hard, but as I have grown older, I'm not at that much of a disadvantage. My mom is the one who taught me Cantonese, but now I have surpassed her.
>
> —Sam, 10, Hong Kong

Gautami Shah, who has run Hindi language programs for several US universities, explained,

> We do not have to be perfect. It's not studying about language. It's about playing with it so you can make sense of it in your head. If someone was to ask me what is my first language, I would have no answer. I was brought up speaking four languages. One grandmother spoke in one language, the other in another, my mother in another language, [actually] my mother and my father in two mixed languages. I grew up in India, in Bombay [Mumbai]. The four languages are English, Hindi, Marathi, and Guajarti. Learning one language at a time, that's kind of outdated theory. It's theory that is coming from the Western world. And we are living in a very multilingual world! I can bet that most people, at some level, are multilingual.[44]

Although a minor Old School subject, instruction in world languages (formerly, foreign languages) takes big steps toward twenty-first-century ideas. Ali Moeller, University of Nebraska Distinguished Professor of World Language Education, takes the idea further:

> It's not difficult to learn a language because we now know from neuroscience how to do it better at a classroom level . . . to speak in the language, that we have to contextualize. For example, when we teach vocabulary, rather than giving English and then the target language, an image and the target language—called dual language, again a neuroscience concept—allows us to go right into short-term memory. If it's contextualized, language practice, where we use a story or context, we only need repetition seventeen times. If it's decontextualized like we used to teach it, [learning requires] over seventy times![45]

When learning a second language, Dr. Moeller continues,

> Plasticity is increased. Executive function is amazingly improved, [so] they can plan better. They become self-regulated learners. Neuroscience has now shown that . . . if you know another language, your chances of delaying Alzheimer's are 100 percent! Your neurons are actually restored and rejuvenated as a result of learning a language. The learning of another language encourages the rebuilding of parts of the brain. . . . Basically, there are synapses between the neurons, and there's a plasticity there. As we age, it becomes more solid. What world language is able to do, because it uses different parts of the brain, it allows it to regain some of its plasticity."[46]

English connects cultures, so many people, of all ages, use English to share ideas. Only about one in four people on Earth communicate in English, so it's not a universal language—at best, English is spoken or understood by two billion people.[47] Over time, people who speak English instead of their local language may be contributing to their native language's demise. In modern times (among many examples), this behavior nearly caused the death of Yiddish, once spoken, read, and written by millions of people, now understood by several tens of thousands (and undergoing a small revival thanks, in part, to the Yiddish Book Center, which celebrates and promotes Yiddish literature and culture).[48]

With nearly instant translation on digital devices, a person speaking Turkish can communicate with another speaking Swahili, so the perceived value of Old School foreign language instruction may fade. Students may take several years of French, but after the course is over, they often forget much of what they learned because they have little occasion to communicate in French. For many students, learning a foreign language in school is an interesting idea but does not produce useful long-term results. However, the newer world languages approach makes more sense in their increasingly diverse world.

Art

The perceived insignificance of Art instruction allows its teachers to operate under the radar. Making a collage is not treated with the same concern as remembering details about types of rocks or names of presidents, so teachers and students operate with greater freedom in Art than in most other classes.

Most public schools do not invest much in art programs. At best, there may be an art teacher or two, and a classroom with tools, supplies, and large tables and adequate lighting. (Often, "art on a cart" reduces art instruction to whatever supplies a part-time art teacher can wheel into an ordinary classroom). Students become familiar with materials, processes, techniques, safe practices, respect for one another's work, feedback and criticism, and cleaning up on their own—but most of time, they make art.

Art teachers lecture and show images, so students become familiar with many types of art—but these presentations are brief because students are anxious to make things. On classroom walls and in school hallways, students may see some ancient and modern art from China, colorful textiles from Ecuador, pottery from Maine, puppets from Indonesia, surrealism from Salvador Dalí, and modern work by Keith Haring and Amy Sherald.[49] And they participate in group discussions about graffiti, abstract art, still life, portraiture, and whether it's okay to paint the sky pink or yellow instead of blue.

> Oh, no, no, we haven't got an art class! I want, but we haven't! I learn at home. I have a book. It tells me what I have to do when I draw. I like to draw flowers and animals. Sometimes, I draw people. I draw from the internet or from the book. I want to do art when I grow up. I started when I was five. I drew everything. I draw almost every day, in my free time. I want to go to an art school. When I graduate, I want to go to another country [to] study [more]. I will come back to Bulgaria and open a school for art.
>
> —Kamelia, 13, Stara Zagora, Bulgaria

Total careers in art-related fields: more than five million—about twice the number in mathematics, science, and social studies combined. Many people also pursue art part-time and for fun. Art museums, awareness of advertising, and other forms of visual expression are now part of being human. But Old School does not devote much time, money, or energy to art.

Music

Music is one of school's most challenging subjects. It requires years of diligence, practice, and collaboration. The experience of learning music is very different from the experience of learning any of the five-day subjects. It begins as each student chooses their own instrument—with guidance from teachers, peers, family, and friends. This is a big decision. For most students, it involves a commitment to take care of the instrument, learn how it works, practice, and perform for other people. There is a commitment to teamwork, too.

Students must overcome frustration. It is difficult to get the right sounds to come out of a wooden box or a metal or plastic tube. Each student is encouraged to "stick with it," no matter how they sound or how much practice is required. Music requires learning a new language (aural and visual notation), memorization, synchronous collaboration, error correction, resilience, and dealing with the uneven progress of other students. Each young musician constantly self-assesses and receives feedback from the teacher and other students. Some are haunted by the possibility of having selected the wrong instrument—and having to start over, this time on flute, not violin.

In a student band or orchestra, every young musician must play the same music in the same way at the same time. If they don't, the music may sound awful. Music must be played at a certain pace, or tempo, often in unison with other people playing similar and different instruments, always with other inexperienced students. Unlike most other subjects learned in school, failure and error correction are routine—everybody makes mistakes and strives to improve. Students rely on adults for lessons and technique, but each student works on their own (and in small groups) to get it right.

Of course, in a garage band, the results are relaxed, and everyone is not playing to a written score. Kids gravitate to music as a form of self-expression, and they learn all sorts of valuable skills. And yet, there is a code of good conduct: Kids expect one another to practice, to know the songs, to listen to recordings, and to show up.

As with mathematics, progress is cumulative. It is not sufficient to learn to play a few notes or a few songs. As each student gains competence, individual and group engagement increases. Students begin to play together, sometimes forming their own band. As they do, they realize what they capable of accomplishing on their own. There isn't enough time to practice or rehearse in school, so they accommodate one another's afterschool and weekend schedules (they self-manage their schedules). When the music comes together, that's something special. Some students continue to play music for years after school ends. No other subject produces these results.

Building and sustaining a full-time, long-term career in music is challenging, but many people support themselves in other jobs and careers, playing music on the side because it's fun (and may bring in extra cash). In the US, fewer than 250,000 people work full-time in music.[50] Some lucky people who pursue music careers can become rich and famous; for some students, this is a motivator. Making and listening to music is part of human flourishing.

Library/Research

Some schools contain a library filled with books and other media materials. Many schools do not—but there may be a lending library in a hallway or a cabinet, or a book cart that travels between classrooms. Some communities support a community or public library; many do not. Some schools employ a full-time librarian to manage the library and to teach students how to find information and explore interests. In this environment, each student is treated as a patron—a curious, responsible individual with particular interests and capabilities. Each patron is expected to find their own way, but staff are available for guidance.

At its best, a library offers a satisfying combination of individual freedom and assistance from knowledgeable, caring adults—with no prejudgment and no testing. The library presents an opportunity to learn from small, colorful packages, well organized and numbered so every item can be easily found, with a professional librarian whose purpose is to help (and teach some research skills). If a desired book or other media is not available from one library, it can usually be found in another. In many regions, a librarian can access a list of other libraries' holdings, so almost everything a student may want or need is available. Libraries routinely exchange books to serve local patrons, offering access to many resources beyond the school itself. Remarkably, school libraries, and most community and public libraries, are operated free of charge, funded by local residents through taxation and donations—a wonderful model of community support for learning.

In the midst of concern about dis- and misinformation, the library provides a calming source of reason and accurate, up-to-date information. Librarians are constantly exposed to new material—as budgets allow, they are always buying new books and receiving donations. Library staff take pride in matching student needs with relevant material. Unfortunately, many libraries, particularly school libraries, are under resourced and poorly promoted.

Ploi Sripoom, a University of Virginia School of Education and Human Development student who grow up in Thailand, points out, “In some countries, including Thailand, libraries are often overlooked with barely any role in our lives. Libraries do exist in our schools but they play no role except physically exist.”

Most students treat their library books with respect. They borrow and return books and other materials, usually on time. Borrowing books feels like a privilege, so students learn to take responsibility. They keep materials in good shape for other students. Students read books in class and at home, on their own schedule.

In public and community libraries, children and teenagers learn alongside adults. Unfortunately, libraries are not available in every community, and opening hours are restricted. Public and community libraries are situated in neighborhoods. They are gathering places. With constant foot traffic and windows facing the outside, libraries are well-suited for community displays—local history timelines, murals, and public art. In regions where a stand-alone library is beyond reach, a mobile library can fill the gap. Mobile libraries—bookmobiles, for example—are an idea that’s more than a century old. In many neighborhoods, public libraries introduced immigrant children to books. Libraries on wheels were reintroduced in New York City in 2019.

About four out of five US public schools include a school library. About 105,000 US public or community libraries serve more than 336 million people—that is, one library for every 3,200 people in the US, but some people must travel to the nearest library. Many countries have fewer libraries per capita. Many require travel that may be difficult for kids and parents.

Most students do not learn in libraries with the intention of someday working in the industry, but they do learn valuable research skills. In the US, the field offers nearly a million careers in libraries and related fields, including librarians and library media specialists (140,000 jobs in the US), archivists, curators and museum workers (related, if not spot-on, 38,000), library technicians and assistants (162,000), noninternet publishing (over 100,000), and internet publishing (about 300,000[51]). In total, that’s more than mathematics or social studies jobs.

Computers/Technology

Old School is conflicted about technology’s role in learning. In many schools and classrooms, cell phones are considered a distraction, so students are not permitted to use them while learning. This is understandable because teachers must cover a certain amount of required curriculum, at a certain pace, but it's also crazy. A mobile device is a powerful computer that provides easy access to tools and information useful for classroom learning.

Many schools offer computer and/or technology classes, but curriculum varies from place to place. Some concentrate on basic skills, such as word processing or spreadsheets (which many children figure out on their own). Others encourage students to code and to experiment with AI and robotics. Learning requires planning, experimentation, hypotheses, failure, correction, revision, attention to feedback, creativity, critical thinking, and many other useful skills. A lot can be learned from peers and YouTube, and via experimentation.

> When I was in seventh class [grade], I thought there should be an app that told me what homework I had to do today. I didn't know, really, how to do it. That's how I started. Now, I've projects in education and health. In eighth class, I developed an app called Diabetes Doctor. My grandfather had diabetes. It's a very common disease in India. It led to solving other problems, like blood pressure and heart-related diseases. Looking at websites, I found the American Diabetes Association and there was information about reversing diabetes. That's how I got interested and developed an app so I know what steps I can take as someone with diabetes in my family background.
>
> —Hitarth, 18, Surat, Gujarat, India

Learning about, and gaining experience in, computers and technology provides students with meaningful exposure to a large, fast-growing industry with more than three million jobs including software developers, testers, systems analysts, video game designers, web developers, digital designers, information security analysts, data scientists, and database administrators.[52] For many students, this is a first step to a productive career.

Physical Education/Health

Although the health and wellness of the whole person are typically included in government mandates, local implementation is often less than comprehensive. Old School's "physical education" and "gym class" remain common.

Brett Fuller, curriculum specialist for health and physical education for the Milwaukee Public Schools in the US state of Wisconsin, points out: "If kids are not having fun, they're less likely to [be active] as they get older. . . . If you never learn to swim as a child, you're likely never going to learn to swim as an adult. If you never learn to ride a bike . . . that's why we are trying to expand biking programs in elementary schools. We are trying to teach the skills, knowledge, and hopefully develop the attitude to be physically well for a lifetime."[53]

In Old School, science covers anatomy, physiology, and some nutrition. Physical education encourages exercise and some aspects of fitness. Extracurricular sports go further, and the school nurse or family practitioner addresses immediate health concerns. Lacking integrated instruction, knowledge, beliefs, and interest in the human body vary widely. The result is ghastly: One in five US teenagers is obese; one in four for the Black or Hispanic kids.[54]

Mostly, Old School concentrates on movement—cardiovascular exercise—because most schools lack the time and resources for active instruction in nutrition and the facilities for strength training. Educators in this field usually lack the power, respect, and support to advance a more robust agenda. Mental and emotional health is beyond Old School's gamut, except when dealing with specific issues. And yet, there is a powerful connection between exercise, fitness, nutrition, wellness, and learning.

> Exercise improves learning on three levels: it optimizes your mind-set to improve alertness, attention, and motivation; it prepares and encourages nerve cells to bind to one another, which is the cellular basis for logging in new information; and, it spurs the development of new nerve cells in the hippocampus.[55]
>
> —John J. Ratey, MD, Clinical Associate Professor Psychiatry, Harvard Medical School
> Author, *SPARK: The Revolutionary New Science of Exercise and the Brain*

Based on extensive research and field tests, Dr. Ratey recommends fifteen minutes of exercise for every forty-five minutes of traditional classroom instruction. In schools that follow this regimen, Dr. Ratey sees significant, sustained improvement in student health, and significant, immediate, and long-term improvement in grades, test scores, and overall wellness. Regular daily exercise, throughout the school day, reinforces cognitive processing, regardless of the subject matter, and aids in short-term memory and long-term retention. Even a ten-minute walk between classes is helpful to clear the mind, reset, and prepare the brain before the next barrage of information is unleashed. Not only for students—for teachers, too.

Contemporary students need quiet, reasonably private places for individual contemplation, relaxing, healing, meditation, exercise, restful reinvigoration, or the likes of yoga. The Old School emphasis on everybody-plays competitive games does not address these needs.

Modest time and resource allocation for Health, Fitness, Wellness, and Nutrition is misaligned with widespread student interest, public health benefits, and potential employment. In the US (and throughout the world), this field is large and growing fast—supporting seven million careers including nurses, doctors, pharmacists, radiologists, physical and occupational therapists, dentists, veterinarians, exercise trainers, and more.[56]

OLD SCHOOL OUTCOMES

Is Old School effective? If the measure is completion of primary and secondary grades, the OECD average was 83 percent. The US rate completion rate was 87 percent, less for Black and Hispanic students (83 and 81 percent).[57] Completion of a tertiary education (including but not limited to earning a college degree) among people 25–34 finds Canada at 66 percent and Japan at 65 percent, considerably higher than the US at 51 percent or Germany at 36 percent. In many large countries with economic power, graduation rates are quite low: Mexico comes in at 27 percent, Brazil at 23 percent, and India at 21 percent. And these are among the countries of the Organization for Economic and Cooperative Development (OECD). [58] Globally, "according to Harvard University and the Asian Development Bank, around 6.7 of the world population has a college degree."[59]

If the measure is test results, the overall pattern of secondary school student performance on OECD's Programme for International Assessment (PISA) international scale shows a decline in the knowledge and skills "that are essential for full participation in modern societies, particularly in the core domains of reading, mathematics, and science."[60] Some countries improve, most do not, and many are making almost no progress (the trend began long before COVID's disruption). In the US, the National Assessment of Educational Progress (NAEP) for the 2023–2024 school year showed significant declines for fourth and eighth graders in both reading and math, continuing a prepandemic decline—despite very large investments to improve results.

Other Old School metrics are equally discouraging. Measured by absences and dropout rates and through surveys, student disengagement has increased during the past decade, again after accounting for pandemic disruption. Mental health concerns among students and teachers are gaining considerable attention—again, worldwide. According to a 2024 RAND survey, "59% [of teachers] say they experience frequent job-related stress."[61] In a 2022 survey by the National Education Association (NEA), a US teacher's union, "regardless of age or years teaching," a staggering 55 percent of educators were thinking about leaving the professional earlier than planned.[62] This is "regardless of age or years teaching." Enrollment in teacher preparation programs has declined dramatically.

Encouraged by teachers Ryoko Okamoto and Erin Noxon, students in Japan's Sagano High School in Kyoto were reluctant to schedule time for a *Kids on Earth* discussion because "they must spend every available minute studying for the big tests" and "they are reluctant to sacrifice an entire hour on anything that would not be tested."

Teacher and radio journalist Yerica Park describes an urgent situation in South Korea.[63] Dangerously high stress levels are associated with testing for admission to the most desirable colleges in South Korea (this is a significant national problem in many eastern Asian nations). According to the BBC: "The exam is considered crucial as it determines not only which university students can go to, but also their career paths. Both students and parents feel that it will directly impact their futures. . . . Parents begin preparing children for it from very young ages—usually around four—although there is also a significant percentage of children who start at two."[64] *The New York Times* says, "The test, notorious not just for its rigor, has also long kept the private education industry booming. So-called cram schools are typically filled with students until well past midnight, and the stakes that come with acing the CSAT have fueled an intense rat race among students to enter the nation's best universities. Hundreds of thousands of students sit for the nine-hour exam, typically held every November."[65]

Extreme rigidity and high-stakes testing affect each student's sense of self and emotional well-being. The cycle is difficult to break, in part because soft characteristics are more difficult to measure than, for example, GDP. The spectacular economic success of Japan and South Korea is built on this way of thinking.

(Japan is the world's third largest economy, South Korea is tenth.[66]) Still, the world is changing, and students in Japan and South Korea are gaining agency and independence along with the rest of the world. The internet (widely available in these countries) provides exposure to other ways of thinking and acting. There are grave concerns about population patterns in these countries—many seniors, fewer young people—along with serious questions about the interplay of national unity, mental health, sustainable productivity, lifelong learning, immigration patterns, and education systems.

> At my old school, I was really just a number. One thing that really annoyed me. I had a math teacher. I was in her room, basically every day for math, and she never knew my name. I was in that room every single day for a whole year! I got lost in the crowd. I felt the teacher didn't really feel the need to make the connection. You're never going to get the day back. You want to do something good with it. You don't want to waste a whole year at a school where you're not being treated well and you're not happy.
>
> —Jazmin, 14, Lismore, Australia

Old School is seriously out of touch with contemporary needs. It does not do a good job in preparing students to become our next generation of capable, knowledgeable, forward-thinking adults ready to solve the world's significant problems.

Things are not going well. The Old School model was designed for top-down education and employment in an era when life expectancy was much shorter, children and teenagers did as they were told, far fewer people attended school, and opportunity beyond the local region was largely unknown. Planning assumptions for the Old School model are no longer relevant. It is time to rethink the model.

Japan is the world's third largest economy; South Korea is tenth. Still, the world is changing, and students in Japan and South Korea are gaining agency and independence along with the rest of the world. The internet (widely available in these countries) provides exposure to other ways of thinking and acting. There are also concerns about population patterns in these countries—many among them young people—about serious questions about the interplay of national unity, mental health, sustainability, productivity, lifelong learning, immigration patterns, and education systems.

[illegible]

CHAPTER 4

New School

Old School is based on ideas far removed from the ways human beings learn, how they remember, and what they need to know to survive and thrive in the twenty-first century. See figure 4.1 for a general representation of Old School curriculum priorities.

FIGURE 4.1

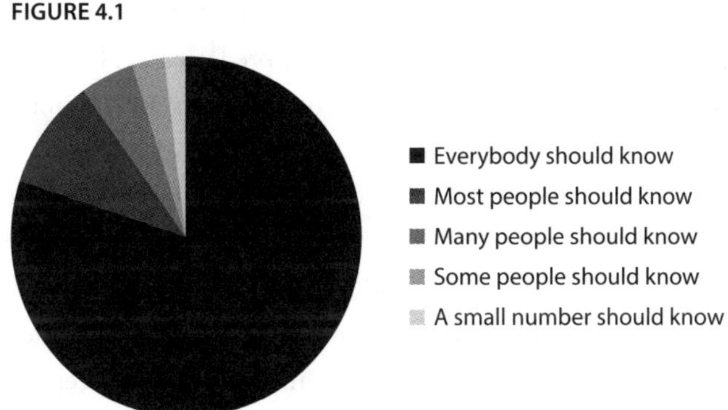

As early secondary students in Charlottesville, Virginia's Community Lab School explain, "Nobody likes to be told what to do!"

This model relies on compliance, oversimplification, and limited perspectives. For those in the dominant group, emphasis on status quo and a glorious past may be comforting, but the model fails other people because it does not represent their needs, interests, world views, or futures. However, the model is useful for the assimilation ("to take in and utilize as nourishment: to absorb into the system") of large numbers of immigrants, and was successfully used in the US for that purpose in the first half of the twentieth century.[1] Much used throughout history, the extreme version of this approach is now prominent in China's effort to indoctrinate Tibetan schoolchildren as Chinese citizens.[2]

MONOCULTURE

Sir Ken Robinson set forth a vision:

> We have to go from what is essentially an industrial model of education, a manufacturing model, which is based on linearity and conformity and batching people. We have to move to a model that is based more on principles of agriculture. We have to recognize that human flourishing is not a mechanical process; it's an organic process. And you cannot predict the outcome of human development. All you can do, like a farmer, is create conditions under which they will begin to flourish.[3]

In agriculture, the term *monoculture* refers to cultivation of a single crop, or single group of crops. This efficient, profitable way to operate very large farms relies on chemicals and destructive practices that deplete soil, damage soil fertility, and wreak havoc with other forms of life.[4] "Invasive (that is, non-natural) species sometimes thrive because there are no predators . . . but many invasive species destroy habitat, the places where other plants and animals naturally live."[5]

Commoditization of learning works against the happiness, productivity, and economic interest of every child, teenager, and adult. Learning the same things as everybody else is counterproductive and dangerous. It stifles original thought and innovation. Concentrating most student instruction across a small number of subjects that seemed to matter in the twentieth century impedes progress. Maybe contemporary students might benefit from a more balanced portfolio, something along these lines? A balanced portfolio would look more like figure 4.2.

This chapter describes a different approach to school, a New School approach to learning. We propose the elimination of many Old School mainstays and their replacement with broad and relevant Learning Categories, assessment freed from testing traps of the past, and full expression of individual differences among the world's young people (and beyond).

FIGURE 4.2

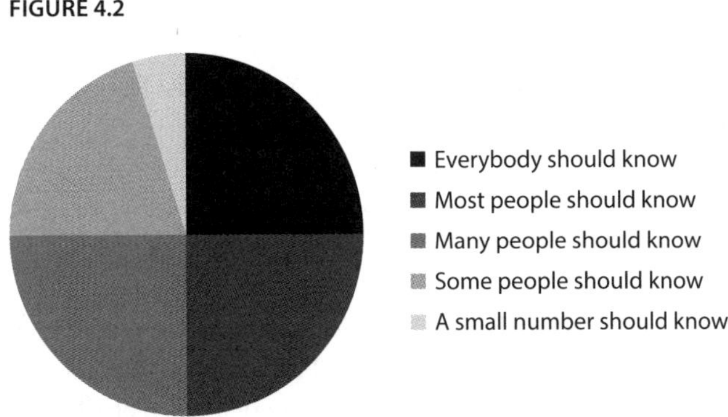

MONDAY MORNING IN OLD SCHOOL

> Before we start today, remember your League of Nations reports are due tomorrow (Tuesday), and the big World War I exam is Friday. So: After the League of Nations failed, countries tried again, this time with the United Nations. Last night, you read textbook pages 121–157, so you know about UN's founding, its history, its leaders, its six principal organs, its four pillars, and you've read the handouts about UNICEF and UNESCO. Today, we start on UNESCO's seventeen Sustainable Development Goals. We'll do eight SDGs today and the other nine tomorrow (Tuesday). Tonight, your homework is to summarize the eight goals we discuss today; you'll do the rest tomorrow night. Be sure to focus on SDG number one tonight—poverty. On Wednesday, we'll do NATO and other international treaty organizations; that test is Thursday. Let's begin with a question: What is poverty? . . .

The hurried pace and this excessive amount of information will not result in meaningful instruction, clear understanding, or learning. Instead, it's just a bunch of words, an overly ambitious list of things some adults decided kids needed to know. Everyone will be very busy this week.

MONDAY MORNING, NEW SCHOOL

> . . . This morning, we will start with the first UNESCO Sustainable Development Goal: Eliminate extreme poverty everywhere.
>
> Before we talk about poverty, let's talk about the United Nations. World War II is over. It was a horror. Nobody wanted anything like that to happen again. One in thirty-three people on Earth died. The US dropped two atomic bombs on cities in Japan and killed more than two hundred thousand civilians.[6]

The Germans wanted to kill all the Jewish people on Earth, plus gay men, Black people, people of mixed race, and the disabled.[7] In Russia, eleven million people died. More than a million died in China. WWII was the bloodiest conflict in the history of the world.[8]

For a peaceful future, nations needed an organization where they could work out problems. After a few failed attempts, the United Nations was born. Nobody knew exactly what the UN would do, but it turned out to be a good idea. The UN is a big organization with lots of parts. We're going to focus on one of them: the United Nations Educational, Scientific, and Cultural Organization, abbreviated UNESCO. If you're interested, I can help you learn more about the role of the UN in world peace, protecting human rights, and providing humanitarian aid, especially during emergencies . . .

. . . About twenty-five years ago, just as the twenty-first century was getting started, UNESCO made a list of eight really important things the world could do by 2015 and then revised the list so it included seventeen important things by 2030. They encouraged people all over the world to get involved, including students. Officially, that list is called the UNESCO Sustainable Development Goals. Everybody calls them the SDGs. The first SDG—the one we're going to talk about now—is "No Poverty." That is, "End poverty in all of its forms everywhere." You may decide to learn about some of the other SDGs on your own, and of course, I am here to help. Let's start with a question: "What is poverty? . . .

Instruction is focused. It does not attempt to cover everything. It is about depth of understanding, not breadth of familiarity with facts. The teacher provides foundational background so students can construct their own knowledge by asking questions. In New School, this is called a Fundamental. Based on what they know from observation, experience, and the media, students try to define the term *poverty.* "Not enough food" and "not enough money" seem too simple. The teacher explains "multidimensional poverty," which ignites a discussion about context. Students add homelessness, race prejudice, economic inequality, food deserts, unfair laws, water supply, access to health care, and the roles of government and NGOs. A bigger picture begins to take shape. When the teacher asks where poverty exists, students begin far from home, but further discussion migrates and becomes uncomfortably close to home. Students offer personal observations. For the teacher, this signals readiness to move from a Fundamental about extreme poverty to a wide variety of related (and unrelated) ideas to be explored, one-on-one and in small groups, through what we'll call Personal Education.

During these first twenty minutes, the teacher tells a story, then listens, then watches each student settle into greater depth. But not every student.

Some seem distracted, uninterested, at a loss, not engaged. They require immediate one-on-one attention from the teacher and some support from other students.

Some tell the teacher they need help—no shame in that, no embarrassment associated with not knowing what to do, being confused, uninterested, or just not getting it. Meanwhile, students talk to one another to refine and clarify their individual and small group projects. Some get started on their own. Some ideas deflate, so students help one another develop new ones because the teacher is busy. They learn from one another.

By the end of the hour (yes, a full hour, not forty-two minutes), students have compiled lots of ideas about poverty and homelessness in their home town, poverty in Ethiopia (related to drought and food shortages), multidimensional challenges faced by refugees, questions about how poverty is measured and why metrics are often inequitable, what a poor family can afford, social programs, and more. The diversity of their inquiries is impressive, sometimes naive or marginally coherent, but they have begun. Some will go further. Others will decide to learn something else, perhaps focusing on SDG 10–Gender Inequality, or the role of UNESCO or Doctors Without Borders. Not everybody needs to study extreme poverty.

Initial student–teacher conversations are check-ins: quick rundowns on the concept, next steps, and end product. Some conversations require more time—so students schedule longer conversations later the same day (using modern, student-centric scheduling software).

Nobody expects the teacher to know a lot about the UN, the SDGs, or global poverty. That's not the teacher's job. Instead, the teacher's job is engagement—making sure every student is interested in what they are learning. Students manage their own projects; teachers serve as guide, mentor, and resource expert. And because the teacher is working closely with every student, as an individual, the students most in need of help can be certain that their teacher will help them navigate the rough spots.

> When you want to do stuff, but people say that you can't . . . you try and do it harder and harder. And when you succeed, people will be amazed.
>
> —Amy, 8, Southport, England

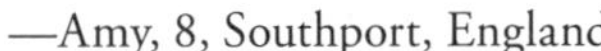

FUNDAMENTALS

Anchored in the ideas that learning is personal, relational, and active, New School fully embraces two big ideas:

- Children and teenagers should learn many, but not too many, Fundamentals.
- Children and teenagers should learn to think for themselves.

What, exactly, is a Fundamental? It is a set of facts, a story, a survey or overview, a context, skills, techniques, a process focused on specific learning needed by all, or almost all, students. It is well organized, well presented and concise, well chosen, interesting, and relevant. Mathematics is not a Fundamental, and neither is social studies. Instead, fractions and decimals are two Fundamentals, and the US Bill of Rights is a Fundamental. Think about it this way. If you had twenty minutes to explain fractions to a seven-year-old, what would you want them to know? And if you had twenty minutes to explain fractions to a fifteen-year-old, what would you hope they would remember several weeks later? Similarly, if you were faced with a room full of third graders, you probably wouldn't start with the idea of the first ten amendments; instead, you would help them understand the concept of personal rights, and why a country would make a list of those rights for everyone. And if the group was made up of eighteen-year-olds, you might concentrate on "the right to a speedy and public trial" for all criminal prosecutions.[9]

FUNDAMENTAL LAUNCH PADS

Fundamentals provide an entry point. A Fundamental introduces students to India as the world's most populous nation, the world's largest democracy, and the world's fastest growing national economy. India is composed of many ancient and modern cultures. That's more than enough to get started.

A community may decide that the James Webb Space Telescope will be a Fundamental in the Learning Category called Our Planet & Beyond. Why does the world need such a powerful telescope? This Fundamental, this path of inquiry, is intended to ignite individual student interest in the Big Bang, the early universe, astrophotography, galaxies, black holes, NASA, astronomy as a profession, light years, and more. No need for every student to learn all of this, certainly not as a Fundamental, but the Webb telescope is a good starting place.

Every Fundamental is a launch pad.

WHO DECIDES?

Some Fundamentals, such as learning how to read, will be carried from one school year to the next, but over time, some Fundamentals gain or lose currency. At various times, different communities, states, and nations prioritize different ideas. Who decides what every student, or most students, learn in school? Governments outsource these decisions to framework and curriculum committees. No reason to reinvent the whole structure—but pruning and updating are necessary.

In Old School, students are required to learn too much information, teachers are required to prepare far too many lessons, and students forget much of what is taught. New School provides students with a smaller amount of relevant, useful information. Every student learns a reasonable number of very important concepts—Fundamentals. They can explain what they are learning and why it matters. If every student learned—truly learned, internalized, and remembered one Fundamental per Learning Category per week of school—ten Fundamentals per week—that would be a wonderful starting point for Personal Education. Of course, every student will learn a lot more, but they will do so on their own terms, based on their own interests, not because unseen adults require them to do so. The youngest students require more Fundamental instruction, probably in Words & Stories, Numbers & Money, and Sounds & Images.

Who decides what to include in each school year's list of Fundamentals? Teachers, students, experts, community members, and government leaders. Working together for the common good, each bringing insights and priorities to the discussion at a local, regional, and national level. Developing the initial list of Fundamentals is intentionally challenging. After the first year, corrections and improvements will grow from collaboration among varied communities, best practices, and students' changing needs.

The process won't be perfect—it does not need to be. Even with a fairly fixed idea about what a given Fundamental might be—say, the solar system—variability from one teacher and school to the next would be common. One teacher may focus on planetary orbits, another on moons and other objects, another on visiting the planets, another on measurement. And that's okay.

In Old School, everybody learns the same things for the same reasons. In New School, everybody branches out from Fundamentals to learn different things for different reasons in Personal Education.

THE PATH FROM FUNDAMENTALS TO PERSONAL EDUCATION

Students in any given classroom know they are not the only classroom studying the UN SDGs, not the only students working on SDG number one—No Poverty. Many other classrooms will be doing the same thing. As students settle into their Personal Education topics, for a day, a week, a month, they can access work done by other students, share materials, and collaborate. A student learning about poverty in Botswana will find other students with similar interests, as well as experts, both in Botswana and elsewhere. Teachers coordinate efforts. Students gain self-confidence, and interact with new people.

School becomes more meaningful. Students do not spend long days in a well-intended intellectual prison. Their ideas are respected. Their work has value. They enjoy freedom. They are seen and heard. They contribute to global knowledge and understanding. They make mistakes, but they know error correction is part of learning. They make good use of adults as guides and for access to resources, but adults no longer tell them what to do.

Old School is not banished. It is reshaped. Essentials remain. The rest fades away because it is no longer useful. In fact, this is the way the human brain operates—shedding connections to become more efficient, more effective.

Personal Education

All learning is personal. There is no other way to learn, so *personalized learning* is not a meaningful term. *Personal Education*, which expands Fundamentals, is a defining component of New School.

Responsibility for learning shifts from teacher to student. This reset recognizes and values the contributions of each individual student in an authentic, meaningful way. Students are supported by teachers, parents, other students, and the community. As described in chapter 5, students share their learning to build global knowledge and understanding.

At least once each week, all students are introduced to a Fundamental in each Learning Category in an age-appropriate way. The Fundamental serves as a starting place for further exploration.

Often inspired by group work in a specific Learning Category, each Personal Education project takes shape. Each student works on their own or in small groups. Each project runs for an hour, perhaps as much as five or ten hours over several days or a week or two. The limitations are meaningful; it is easier for a student to stay on track if projects are clearly defined and doable. If a pursuit is especially interesting, or opens doors to other pursuits, the student can add a related project.

For example, the Fundamental might introduce clouds—types of clouds, how they are formed, why they look the way they do, how they can be used to forecast weather. One student may decide to learn more about cumulonimbus clouds—they are associated with lightning and big storms. After that's done, the student may jump to thunder, other big noises. Another student may be curious how artists depict clouds—El Greco's *View of Toledo*, Van Gogh's *Wheat Field with Cypresses* and J. M. W. Turner's *Sunrise with Sea Monsters* being good places to start.[10] Where to go next? Sea monsters! Not just any old monster: *Jörmungandr*, a terrifying monster from Norse mythology.

Yes, learning is supposed to be fun. It causes the release of dopamine, which is associated with pleasure. It activates neural activity. Yes, it feels like play—happy engagement with learning activities, with the material being learned and the process, and the people involved, is critical.

As each student develops and completes each Personal Education project, they publish their (digital and analog) "working papers," sources, and output. They are careful to tag everything so other students can learn from their work on El Greco, cumulonimbus clouds, clouds in art, and so on.

On occasion, a student will generate an extraordinary insight. Sometimes, a student will follow their idea into a dead end or into unexpected complexity—that's worth noting so others can learn from their missteps. Sometimes, the idea isn't very interesting, expected resources are not available, or the student struggles with completion. That's when the student asks for help—or the teacher takes notice and guides the student toward alternatives. Student-to-student mentoring is always encouraged, freeing the teacher to work with students who need more time. Mentors may package their help as projects of their own.

The teacher's job is to keep every student interested, well-resourced, and productive. More specifically, their job is to form a personal connection, a relationship, with every single student, to know their interests and goals and strengths. The teacher supports students' risk-taking and exploration, connects them with information and resources, and identifies skill or knowledge gaps that need special attention so each student can achieve their aims. And their job is to help students evaluate their progress.

Teachers require training and practice to do that—new approaches to professional development.

NEW SCHOOL'S LEARNING CATEGORIES

The etymology of *subject* is dreadful: "one under authority" and "to subject, literally, to throw under." And *subjecting* is associated with "one who is placed under authority or control;" *vassal* is related.[11] It's time to eliminate *subject* from education.

Figure 4.3 shows a version of New School Learning Categories. The term *Learning Category* is clear and nontoxic. The etymology of *category* is related to *affirm* and *gather*, *agora* and *aggregate*.[12] Below, we present a tool and a way of

FIGURE 4.3

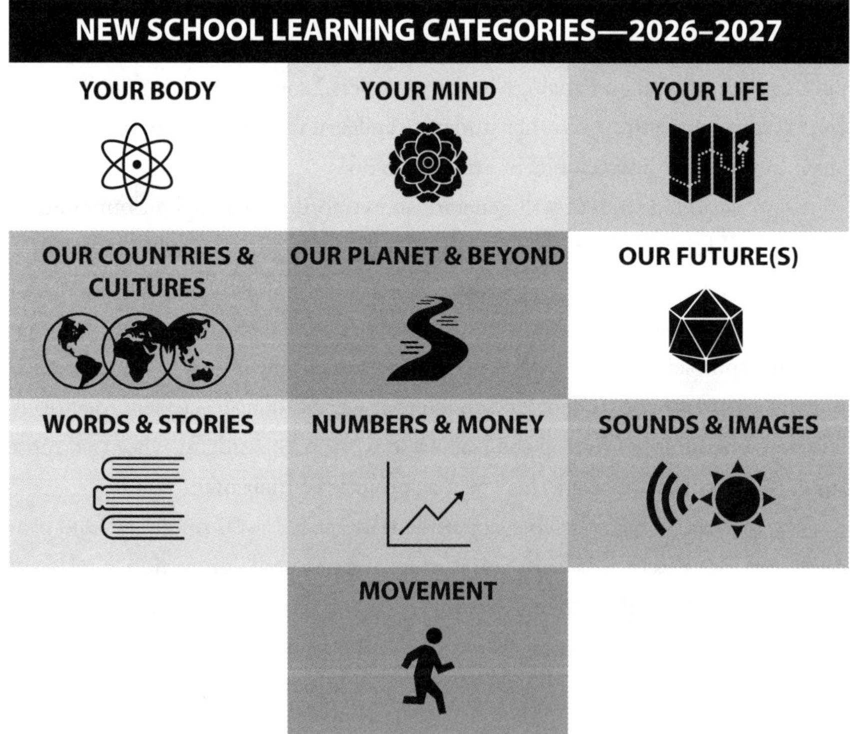

thinking, a workable set of ideas. Learning Categories are intended to initiate discussions among students, teachers, parents, government leaders, and researchers about the structure of school and the knowledge and skills students acquire. It is not a prescription, it is a working hypothesis to be explored and tested through experimentation, experience, shared results, and collaboration. Note the use of "Your" and "Our" to suggest both individual and shared learning experiences that resonate with students' lives.

Learning Category 1: Your Body

A human being is responsible for the care of their body—most body parts cannot be replaced. Each must last a lifetime—and a lifetime could be a hundred years.

Beginning in kindergarten, learning about Your Body would occupy at least one hour per week throughout every student's school career. If, at minimum, students studied Your Body for one hour per week, thirty-five weeks each year, for twelve years, they would have spent 420 hours of their lives learning about their bodies.

Within Your Body, Fundamentals may include: how the body grows, how a body's internal systems work together (circulatory, respiratory, digestive . . .), what can go wrong, keeping a body in optimum shape, and caring for other people's bodies. Personal Education continues the journey with students deciding what to learn, know, and share about brown eyes, toenails, sunburn, acne, ribs, armpits, teeth, and (of course) farting. They'll develop hypotheses about what happens when they do or don't exercise, eat a whole pizza, run as fast as they can on a very hot day, drink gallons of soda, touch their genitals, touch somebody else's genitals, sneeze, get a tattoo, break an arm, sleep too much, or stay up all night. Prompted by Fundamentals about physical growth from infancy to adulthood, and their own lives, they'll pursue questions about emotional growth, reproduction, growing hair, smelling stinky, and death. Students will learn to respect one another's curiosity, their right to know.

Children and teenagers are exposed to the same health news as adults. Children need to understand what is normal and not-so-normal. In New School, learning and talking about the human body becomes commonplace, not a cause for embarrassment. A conversation among prediabetic, overweight adolescent girls ought not be uncomfortable.

I know that a lot of my family has diabetes, and, I think, lung cancer? I went to the doctor. They told me I had premature diabetes (prediabetes). I realized that my mom was right about exercising. I realized I needed to do better. Here's what I know about diabetes. I know that you have to get, like, medicine and shoot into you. Oh! And you can also go into a diabetic coma, right? Some of my dad's friends have diabetes, and they black out sometimes when they're working. I really don't want that! I'm trying really hard! I think it's caused when you're overweighted. When you're over, like, two hundred (pounds) or something, it can cause your body to have diabetes. I think it has to do with sugar. Some people have to actually eat sugar in order to deal with diabetes. It's really dangerous! You have to realize it's important to take care of yourself.

—Janeen, 13, Philadelphia, Pennsylvania, US

A competent teacher could encourage the community to include type 2 diabetes on the next year's list of Fundamentals. That might be difficult, but Janeen could be guided to Personal Education about type 2 diabetes, and that could happen right away. Janeen would learn the facts, and she would find a path to learning more. Working collaboratively on a school-related research project, Janeen could access doctors, nutritionists, authors, behavioral experts, and learn. Government or philanthropic support might be available to her group. Right now, Janeen is trapped without the necessary medical advice, education, or access to knowledge. And she's frightened.

In New School, the teacher's role is to help Janeen learn about diabetes. The teacher's role is not to spend half the night brushing up on glucose and insulin and developing a lesson plan for a class filled with students who are, mostly, not likely to develop diabetes. Learning about type 2 diabetes is Janeen's job. The teacher is her guide and mentor.

Students who have studied Your Body for a dozen years—learning for themselves, learning from others, asking and answering meaningful questions—will be well positioned for employment in health, medicine, and social services. In low and low-middle income nations, eighteen million more health care workers are needed today, and that number is growing fast. (Think Africa and Asia.) Nine million more nurses and midwives are needed, too.[13]

As the global population increases from eight to more than ten billion, there will be many more jobs for opticians, therapists, geneticists, pharmacists, doctors, researchers, clinicians, and more. With New School, students can easily envision the connection between studying Your Body and working in related fields, and taking care of their own bodies, too. There are direct, immediate benefits from learning about Your Body by living every day. There is a clear connection between New School and real life.

Learning Category 2: Your Mind

We know a lot about the brain, and we're learning more every day. "The human brain weighs approximately 3 pounds. It is made up of billions of cells called neurons. Junctions between neurons, known as synapses, enable electrical and chemical messages to be transmitted from one neuron to the next in the brain, a process that underlies basic sensory functions, and that is critical to learning, memory, thought formation, and other cognitive activities."[14]

We know less about the mind, and the spirit, because there is no physical evidence of their existence, but that does not diminish their importance.

Fundamentals provide a first step toward deeper learning about Your Mind. There is so much to learn—and 450 hours of Fundamental learning about Your Mind is a good start. Studying the mind comes to life with personal relevance: my feelings, my emotions, my dreams, my fears, my imagination, my family, my grandparents, our shared characteristics, my anxiety, my friend's happiness, my grandmother's resilience. Growing up, kids think about their behaviors and try to figure things out on their own.

> I'm concerned because my dad and my grandpa were both a little bit, [well] pappa [grandfather] was mentally insane, and my dad was a little bit insane, too. I am not mentally insane, but I am very, very hyper, and I feel that kind of impacts on my happiness. I sometimes will get really, really mad. I'll go psychopathic and beat everything up. Everything around me. I don't want it to impact on me. I have a lot of video games, and I kind of spread them out. Some video games help me to just calm down. I have a racing game that I just love. It calms me down so much. I have a little brother and he's like a bull in a

> china shop. He is like a mad scientist and I'm like a bunch of buttons. He loves pressing them and getting me mad. He is a very tough kid, but when he makes me mad, I force out on him, I flash out on him. My mom knows how to deal with this very, very well. It's amazing how she does this—because she had this when she was little with her stepbrothers.
>
> —Aiydun, 12, Neon, Kentucky, US

Children and teenagers spend a lot of time thinking about who they are, what they think, why they think that way, what they believe, who to believe, how to behave, who they are becoming, and so much more. Each student benefits from a reasonable number of Fundamentals, then pursues Personal Education about topics that interest them during each day's flexible Personal Education hours. Each student acquires a customized understanding of theories of mind, family relationships, happiness, emotional wellness, mental illness, self-control, relaxation, anxiety, consequences, and more. They learn to think more clearly, to distinguish fact from fiction, knowledge from opinion. They explore the many forms of curiosity and creativity, and understand more about themselves and their potential. They may try to communicate with a family dog by developing a barking language (would not be the first). A teacher may lead them to articles in *Science* about the similarities of a dog's gaze at a human partner, a mother's gaze at her child, and the role of the chemical oxytocin in the process.[15]

Inspired by Your Mind, students will talk about what they think and why. If and when they don't understand, or go astray, their teacher will guide them. (There's no stopping people from exploring whatever interests them on the internet; the difference here is one-on-one support from trained educators.)

With so much emphasis on identity, agency, mental health, emotion, behavior, and ideas related to the mind, adults must address the scope of learning that students now require. Students have a deep, personal, and vested interest in identity and ideas related to the mind. For the most part, for most students, Old School keeps these topics out of scope. In a Personal Education experience, these topics are explored systematically and openly, enabling students to see themselves, their lives, their goals, and their relationships in a more complete way. For many students, New School ends the dark ages and brings Your Mind into the light.

Learning Category 3: Your Life

In Old School, each subject's boundaries are clear. In New School, boundaries are porous, and overlaps are intentional.

One way to think about Your Life is past, present, and future, but nobody's life runs in a straight line. We experience many pasts, multiple presents, uncountable futures. The past may be ten minutes ago, or in 1911, when a student's first known ancestors show up on a family tree.

What, exactly, is a "best" friend? Are friends from social media real friends? What does it mean to fall in love? How do I navigate a relationship with my mom's third husband and my second father? What is it to truly hate somebody—enough to do them harm? To deal with consequences of our own actions? To blame somebody else? Life is filled with relationships, but people change, and relationships change too. People move away. New ones move in. Stability varies. Parents lose jobs, transfer to other places. Sometimes, parents choose other partners. There are celebrations and disappointments, highs and lows, long periods with neither.

Your Life—everyone's life—contains so many questions. My family doesn't have enough money, what can I do to get more? How do you know whether a goal is worth achieving? The air quality is so bad, it's dangerous to play outside—can I convince my family to move? What happens when a friend begins to make bad decisions? What are the unwritten rules for Palestinian teenagers and law enforcement in this part of Berlin? Is it okay to lie so my friend doesn't go to jail? How do I get things back to normal? (What is normal?) Are angels real?

Aspects of current social-emotional learning (SEL) are candidates for Your Life (and Your Mind, which overlaps): taking care of yourself, identity, making good decisions, resilience, overcoming obstacles, happiness, sadness, adversity, contemplation, and more. Happiness could be a Fundamental. It's likely to be popular: Taught by psychology professor Laurie Santos, happiness has been the subject of one of Yale University's all-time most popular courses (teachers can enroll in a free online version[16]). Learned optimism, resilience, and self-awareness are also potential Fundamentals. Gaining useful work experience, making contacts, earning a living, getting along, spending more time outdoors, breaking bad habits—such as lying, stealing, bullying, fighting—are all good ideas for Your Life's Fundamentals.

In the US, nearly all causes of nonfatal emergency department visits for people under twenty-five result from unintentional falls, getting hit or struck by a foreign body, animal and insect bites, inhalation/suffocation, piercing and cutting, overexertion, and motor vehicle accidents.[17] In many countries, local chapters of the International Red Cross and Red Crescent offer training suitable for students. Perhaps first aid is a candidate for Fundamental status, not just once, but year after year.

Learning about setting goals, planning, making reasonable decisions, career paths, establishing and shedding certain habits, and playing a productive role in a local community—all of these are potential Fundamentals in this Learning Category, too.

Learning Category 4: Our Countries & Cultures

Your Body, Your Mind, and Your Life center on the individual student. The next three Learning Categories—Our Countries & Cultures, Our Planet & Beyond, and Our Futures—encourage students to think beyond their own lives.

Our Countries & Cultures means different things to different people. Most people learn about the world from sports (the Olympics), movies (*My Neighbor Totoro*), food (*injera*), music videos (Rema's "Calm Down"), books (*The Little Prince*), news (climate change), politics (Mexican President Claudia Scheinbawn), and more. We learn from family and friends who travel, do business in other countries, pursue higher education, and work in other places.

Students want to know where they came from, and what happened before they arrived. At home, they get pieces of their own stories, limited views through photographs and home videos. Most parents and families cannot pull together a comprehensive story. An organized approach within Your Life could be helpful.

> From the history, I know it's seven thousand years before Christians. This is one of the oldest cities in the world. You can find some things from the Stone Age era, the Roman Empire, the Byzantine Empire, the Ottoman Empire. Stara Zagora changed its name eight times because it was occupied by so many others.
>
> —Siyana, 12, Stara Zagora, Bulgaria

> I know some, because I am not very good about history. I know that Bulgaria was *occupied*! 1878 was the year [we became a nation]. The men who helped were many. I can talk about some. Vasily Levski.

Stefan Karadzha. Georgi Sava Rakovski. Hristo Botev. They are heroes to Bulgarian people. They emancipated us from Turkey. We needed to start a war with Turkey. Russia helped us. Macedonia, she helped, too. I know this. There is a TV channel called NOVA, and there are TV shows, a few about the life of heroes and peoples. I believe Bulgaria is safe now, but there aren't heroes to help us.

—Alexandra, 12, Stara Zagora, Bulgaria

There are streets to stroll, buildings, cafés, recipes that have been in the family and culture for decades, centuries. There are existing historical timelines, maps, and often written or oral histories. Bulgarians and Greeks debate about feta cheese (Bulgarian uses sheep's milk, Greek uses cow's milk, perhaps some goat milk, too). There are old family recipes, and if there's a good recipe on YouTube, flexibility too. Pride of place, global interaction, it's all part of learning about Our Countries & Cultures.

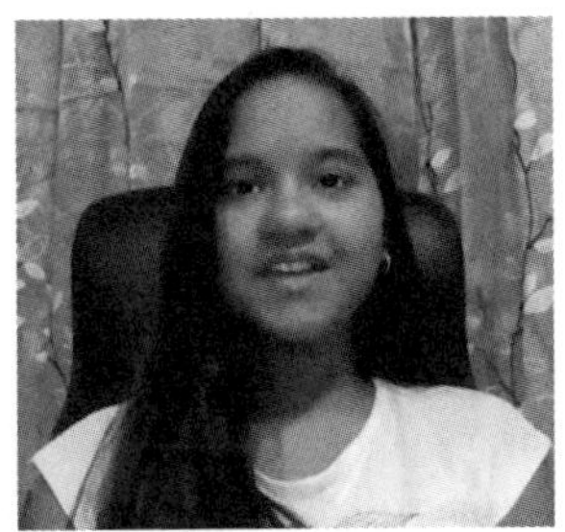

Back before it was an independent island, we had a lot of indentured laborers from Asia and slaves from multiple parts of Africa. When more generations came to be, that became a very diverse community. . . . Here, it's very diverse. You coexist with many communities, other cultures, and religions. That's one of the really good things about Mauritius. If I had grown up somewhere else, I would be very different.

—Teesha, 11, Port Louis, Mauritius

I speak French, English and sometimes Creole. My Creole is really bad. Creole is my mother language, my mother tongue. Before, I could only speak French, but now, it's mostly English for me. I have three friends from London. With them, I speak English, but I have other friends who speak French and English. But I hang out with a group of friends, and they're always all there, so we speak English so everybody can understand.

—Shailee, 10, Port Louis, Mauritius

Must every student in Mauritius know the island's history? What about students in nearby Rodrigues and Réunion? Do they need to know the story of Mauritius, their own islands, the Mascarene Islands (of which they are a part, too)? Nearby Indian Ocean islands? Madagascar is 734 miles away, and it has a very different culture. How much do they need to know Malagasy people?[18] To what extent does proximity determine what students know? Teesha, Shailee, and their parents tell us that Mauritius is a very interesting place, but it's a small place most people in the world know nothing about. In New School, some students may choose to learn about Mauritius and perhaps build new online relationships with friends like Shailee and Teesha. Already, Shailee has friends in London, and she would like to study abroad. Who determines what Shailee must or might want to know?

With more than two hundred countries and about six thousand languages in the world, and recognition that a single country often includes many cultures, potential learning is spectacular.[19]

> My mother is Swedish. My dad is from Syria. We lived in Syria. Growing up, I don't have mom. I didn't know much about my mother until I was nine years old. We came to Sweden. I met my mother. My mother is very kind. When I was in Syria, she took care of my sisters in Sweden. [When I arrived here], I didn't know Swedish. She helped me to learn. My father is Muslim and my mother is Christian. Muslim, we have one God, and a Prophet. In Christian, you have Father, the Son, and God. I go the church, sometimes, with my grandmother. I go the mosque with my father. My father told me I can choose my own religion, whether I want to be Christian or Muslim, or . . . it's my choice (I'm still deciding). In Christian, you have good things and not good things. In Muslim, you have the same. In Christian, if you curse at your mom, God will forgive you. In Muslim, you are not forgiven. In the morning when you go out, there are people causing trouble. Sometimes, when people start a fight, they call in their friends. The fight becomes bigger. Somebody was talking badly about my mother. I told him not to say bad things about my mother, but then, he waited outside school for me, to fight. I've been boxing for six years. He went down on the first punch. My father, he was a professional boxer. He taught me.
>
> —Khaled, 15, Stockholm, Sweden

Imagine going to school every day to tell the story of your people and to learn about the lives of new friends who live in northern Ontario while you're going to school in Peru—and finding out you're in the same time zone so you can actually talk, via Zoom, every day![20]

Fundamentals in Our Countries & Cultures take shape based on student, teacher and community, and government interests. Many stories involve colonization. People—ancestors—traveling across inconceivably vast oceans to trade, conquer, rescue, exploit, and more. Year after year, students collaborate, challenge one another, write reports, produce videos, interview one another, create pictures, make music, and attempt to explain the world to one another—but their output is rarely shared. With a central repository, students may assemble the largest repository of information about the world and its people in human history—their stories, pictures, maps, insights, interviews, projects, and far more than any museum collection could accommodate. It is possible today, and it can take shape in a remarkably short time. This new concept is described in detail in chapter 5.

Learning Category 5: Our Planet & Beyond

One Fundamental starting place is the story of Earth itself, beginning 4.5 billion years ago when it was mostly gas, and unimaginably hot—"the surface remained molten for hundreds of millions of years."[21]

Fundamentals could explain what's below (mantle, core) and above (clouds, moon, sun, stars, asteroids, galaxies, nebulae). Earth supports plant and animal life; humans have not identified another planet that supports life, but the search continues. There are so many types of animals and plants on Earth, and so many interdependencies. Lots of life forms are still to be discovered—especially in the deep oceans.

So much is still invisible, undetectable, unimagined, not plotted, and not understood. Improvements in digital imaging and other technologies continue to reveal more, but much of what is known is also unfathomable. Old School focuses on what humans already know. In New School, the focus expands to what humans want to know. Some of these ideas are categorized as supernatural phenomena—ideas not yet understood, perhaps unworthy of primary and secondary school study. New School removes that barrier and encourages students to explore.

Humans and their governments continue to make terrible decisions about life on Earth in order to maintain economies and industries. If students and teachers concentrate on climate science, they will know more about biodiversity loss, wildfires, atmospheric rivers, and the melting of glaciers, but problems will continue to worsen. Instead—and controversially in some sectors—students may focus on "coal, oil, and gas burned by humans [as] the primary cause [of climate change], followed by deforestation and intensive farming."[22]

Climate change is something students will probably explore every school year. Media is one source of information, but many students already know that media does not tell a complete story because of its involvement with industry and government. Students may decide that they need other ways to learn about climate. Some students might take an active interest and try to do something to change the current situation. For example, they might convince their families to stop eating beef, and demand that local stores and restaurants stop selling beef. Or they may decide to work for the government in public policy. They may become scientists.

"According to a Greenpeace Southeast Asia analysis of IQAir data, approximately 54,000 premature deaths in New Delhi were attributed to PM2.5 air pollution in the year 2020. This pollution also resulted in estimated economic losses of about USD 8.1 billion (INR 58,895 crore) for the same year."[23] Today's children and teenagers are right to be deeply concerned about the air they breathe, the water they drink, the food they eat, and more. They see adults not solving the problems. They see the problems getting worse. The only sensible thing to do is to begin solving these problems on their own. Otherwise, their personal and collective peril will accelerate and danger will become more formidable.

Air pollution, energy sources, climate change, and the exploration of alternative futures are not independent ideas. They are connected. Some kids already see the connections between these ideas and the idea of colonizing parts of the sky, mining asteroids, and owning parts of space.

> I don't think anyone owns space. I think it's okay to have like a space force to explore space, but not to own it. Humans own the world. It's their job to care after it and not to damage it. I think we're doing pretty bad looking after our planet. There's pollution always happening. People throwing rubbish into the sea. And plastic in the sea, which kills fishes. Humans must be careful and take care of the earth because, right now, that's our only place to live. If we damage Earth too much, we would have to go into spaceships to another planet. I think it's going to work out pretty bad. First of all, we won't have materials to build. Second, if we did, it would take a very long time. I think there might be life on Mars. I mean,

> there's only, like two droids on Mars to investigate. Out of the whole Mars, there might be some life on Mars. If we move to Mars, it is our fault—first, we destroyed Earth, and if there is life on Mars, which I believe there is, we would be taking away their planet.
>
> —Philip, 10, Southport, England

Today's students possess two remarkable advantages. They are located all over the world (nothing new), and the majority of them can communicate with one another (very new). As each student pursues many Personal Education projects each year, they can collect and share data, and offer observations (including sound and video files). Their geographic diversity makes it possible to learn locally—about oceans, shorelines, glaciers, air quality, climate and its impact on people and communities, and microscopic worlds in ways that were never practical before. They can observe and report on local climate change on a massive scale. With diligence, their widespread sharing of abundant information could be transformative.

Learning Category 6: Our Futures

Does the contemplation of migration to Mars or asteroid mining belong in Our Planet & Beyond or Our Futures? Just about anything in Our Futures will overlap with at least one other Learning Category. As with Your Life, Our Futures opens flexible learning time to reflect on, study, and learn about the rapid multidirectional change so much a part of growing up in the twenty-first century. Again, it fills a minimum of an hour each week, plus time that students allocate from Personal Education.

Our Futures investigations usually begin with "What do we know today about the world tomorrow?" Rarely is the answer "nothing" or "not much." There is always a place to begin.

Skills developed in Numbers & Money (below) are useful here—data gathering, sampling, geographic and cultural differences, identifying bias, asking data-based questions: How long has this been going on? How many people have been affected? Can I graph a long-term trend? Answering those requires students to think creatively and critically, and to make use of every available resource. Students develop hypotheses, challenge assumptions, and reach out to peers and experts all over the world.

Electric vehicles are likely to replace many vehicles powered by fossil fuel. This will require a different approach to the delivery of power for those vehicles and probably new designs for roads and highways. Students considering possible futures may stop to wonder where the electricity for those vehicles comes from. A Honda Civic weighs about 3,000 pounds (plus passengers and cargo). How much energy is required to move 3,500 pounds at 60 mph for 100 miles? How much wind energy would that vehicle generate while in motion? (An overlap with Numbers & Money.) How much solar energy could the car collect and store on a sunny day (or a dark cloudy day)? If wind and solar cannot adequately fuel the car, how would that energy be generated? When will that technology be available for use by large numbers of cars and trucks? In the meantime, would we use fossil fuels (like coal) to generate electricity to power electric vehicles?

These questions are not beyond the reach of many students, but the questions are not easy to answer. To answer them, students need to work together with other students, and with experts. Some of those people may live in different time zones. This may require early morning and late night Zoom conversations, which makes traditional local school schedules problematic. They will also navigate differences in language (Zoom becomes a universal translator). Imagine students in Bratislava, Slovakia taking charge of calculations, students in Aqaba, Jordan focused on solar energy for vehicles, and students in Georgetown, Guyana asking their moms—who work in the petroleum industry—for future-facing guidance. As students work on these problems, they publish their findings, share their ideas, and probably attract some media attention. Along the way, they build resumes and learning portfolios for higher education and employment opportunities, and perhaps solve some problems, too.

Not everything needs to be serious. What will kids in 2045 do for fun? Will it be possible to time travel? How about a weekend visit to Saturn?

Learning Category 7: Words & Stories

The next three Learning Categories—Words & Stories, Numbers & Money, and Sounds & Images—emphasize the importance of human communication, individual expression, and clear thinking.

With student engagement at the core, every New School student is encouraged to express their own ideas and learn from other students. Words & Stories imports reading and writing instruction from Old School and adds listening and speaking.

Learning to read and write requires concentrated attention every day in primary school. Similarly, initial instruction in arithmetic and basic money skills requires extra time in the primary grades. As students master the concepts and skills, the extra time is converted to create more Personal Education hours in the schedule.

In New School, one useful way to develop clear thinking is to write, show the work to others, collect feedback, and rewrite. At least once a week, every student writes a lucid paragraph, then a page, then several pages—and goes through this process. Good writing requires structure, careful selection of words to convey specific meanings, a credible argument in the form of a story, essay or some other form, and comprehension by the reader. New School recognizes that good writing requires sufficient time and a quiet place to write. Students may learn or brush up on specific writing techniques and practices through Fundamentals, but mostly they need the time to write—and in New School, they can spend several hours a day writing because half of each day's schedule is devoted to Personal Education.

In New School, teachers are always available. So are other student mentors. New School supports a rigorous approach to writing based on multiple drafts to develop high-level skills.

Hand-written drafts are fine—a good way to get started—but writing and rewriting is often easier with a computer. Drafts are more easily stored and shared. Students acquire discipline as they maintain each draft, date it, and file it for later use.

> I want to write stories about how women are now making a big leap. I think I have the skills, especially with so many [good] teachers in my area. I have built up the tenacity to do this. It's something I'm really passionate about. So many females have been getting involved in politics and sports. They've made international news. I remember a conversation with my brother who asked, "Well, what are you doing to be like them?" I started a club at my high school through a Girls Up organization. They're all about fighting for women's equality in any way possible, fighting the wage gap, getting involved in politics and education. We just want to be viewed as equals. I have so many classmates who are fighting the same fight I am. . . . I want to be a writer—a journalist.
>
> —Katie, 15, New Jersey, US

Reading elevates and expands vocabulary, demonstrates use of structure, and widens perspective, too. Students will refine their skills and comprehension if they read regularly—perhaps twenty to thirty minutes daily, without interruption. What to read? Student choice, with some guidance from peers, parents, and teachers. So, yes, there is homework in New School—a daily reading commitment.

Writing a good story comes easily to some people, but not everyone. Fortunately, there are many ways to learn to become a better storyteller—a useful Fundamental skill worth learning and improving over a thirteen-year school career. UNESCO Story Circles helps people tell their stories. They advise, for example, to "share simply and clearly, uphold positive intention, be authentic, be open to learning, and listen for understanding."[24] As the world becomes more diverse, students will find it helpful to express themselves in different languages. Along the way, they will learn to listen and to read what others are telling them.

Do we need or want a soft or hard mandate that requires every young teenager in every English-speaking country to read Jane Austen, *Animal Farm*, *A Tale of Two Cities*, *The Giver* and *The Crucible*? That's a Fundamental community decision. Is there a state-mandated reading list, organized by grade level? Probably not, but there might be a list of recommended books supported by promotion and free access at the public library, discussions, and special events to get everyone excited about reading. The term *required reading* almost always means that well-intentioned adults have decided what every student ought to learn. Sure, that's okay once in a while, but there are better ways to cultivate lifelong readers.

Words & Stories bridge oral traditions, so music, art, video, games, and other forms of media fit easily into this Learning Category. Journalism, poetry, and blogging reside here (and in other categories). So do rap music, movie scripts, comic books, graphic novels, social media, comedy, theater, and much more.

For most students, familiarity with a wide range of languages is useful. Languages connect to diverse ideas and cultures (also pursued in Our Countries & Cultures and Your Life). Over time, many students become familiar with Arabic, Chinese, Bengali, Hindi, Farsi, Hausa, indigenous languages, tribal languages, Spanish, French, Italian, and more. Some students will go further, looking at similarities and differences, as somewhat different forms of Arabic are spoken in Tunisia, Qatar, and Indonesia. Some students may develop fluency and literacy in Guaraní (a Paraguayan national language), translate lyrics from Dagbani (spoken and sung in Ghana) into French, and explore international sign languages. Technology can help: Duolingo is a popular app for practicing and building vocabulary, and Google Translate is one of many useful tools. As a community project, learning an unfamiliar language as a Fundamental for a week (or more) would be fun for everyone (children, teenagers, adults).

Learning Category 8: Numbers & Money

As with Words & Stories, in the early grades more time is allocated to Numbers & Money to assure sufficient instructional time and desired competence. Some Old School Mathematics curriculum is included here—mostly numbers and arithmetic—but Numbers & Money covers more territory. The underlying philosophy assumes a more modern shape, too.

The purpose of Numbers & Money is clear thinking and reasonable decision-making. Numbers are used for many purposes, including measurement. Money is primarily used to express value for value-based transactions, but money is such a ubiquitous part of daily life throughout the world, it has gained parity with numbers. In addition to practical day-to-day application, Numbers & Money may provide a career path. Fundamentals should provide what most students want and need to know, and Personal Education allows students who want or need to know more to learn based upon their specific objectives.

Thanks to Old School Mathematics, early Fundamentals are easily defined: arithmetic, fractions, decimals, and the rest. Secondary students benefit from familiarity with trends, data analysis, probability, statistics, and also aspects of logic, coding, and more. There will be debates: Which aspects of algebra and geometry must everybody know, and what could be studied individually and in small groups during Personal Education?

Regarding Money, every student could learn Fundamentals about earning, saving, spending, debt, consuming, budgets, supply and demand, wealth, poverty, the middle class, and something about running a small business. Fundamentals should differ from place to place and from one year to the next. Almost every important issue can be made more clear through the examination of data and analysis from multiple perspectives.

Widespread numeracy is achievable, especially if students sense personal relevance in learning about Numbers & Money.

Learning Category 9: Sounds & Images

Sounds & Images is New School's home for music, visual arts, and more. Most children happily sing, dance, and pound on a drum. They draw on any available surface, with any available tool. It comes naturally. Fundamentals add some training: There are many types of music instruments, and a clarinet sound like this; this is how to paint (without making a mess); when drawing a human face, eyes are halfway between the top of the head and the chin; it is possible to see into space and into microscopic worlds and beyond the visible spectrum.

Sounds & Images gives students the opportunity to explore the spectacular soundscape of life on Earth (and beyond): birdsong, the din of a construction site, humans shouting, dogs howling, cats meowing, an opera soprano at top of range and a basso profundo at bottom, the sound beneath the ocean, breezes across a field of flowers, sounds just above and below human sensitivity.

Night and day, the sky shows off, sometimes in vivid colors (the Northern-Lights). Human eyes cannot see infrared light, but we invented infrared photography to see what our eyes cannot. Stars and planets are far away, but we can see their long-ago images with telescopes (a connection to Our Planet & Beyond). Seeing the sky requires darkness, which may be inconvenient for school schedules and for students in light-polluted metropolitan areas, so schools must learn to be flexible with suitable times and places for learning.

It's not possible to see inside the body without opening it up, but digital imaging technology changes those rules. Speed confuses human perception, but photography can stop motion. On the maker side, stop-action allows inanimate objects to move as if they were alive. The image universe is full of wonderful surprises.

Each year, each community decides on its Fundamentals for every Learning Category, including Sounds & Images. The mix can be thrilling: Tokyo's giant illuminated signs, marching band acoustics, fireworks, local music of Indigenous people, making a sand mandala and blowing it away, being a rock star, painting each classroom a different color and studying everyone's reactions, and so much more. Some Fundamentals involve making things. In many communities, these activities exist, but they're only tangentially part of Old School. New School's approach widens everyone's view of learning, expands the idea of education, and attracts community involvement.

A musical theater production requires students to select a project, make creative decisions, decide who will do which job and play which role, design and paint scenery, light the stage, arrange the music, memorize singing and instrument parts, rehearse, and fill other roles. Students learn about Sounds & Images in practice through direct experience. They are hands-on with technology, storytelling, and performance. They participate in decision-making: Cut that song, recast that role. They perform for a real audience that laughs, applauds, or remains uncomfortably silent. Some students will learn what they need to know to begin a journey as a creative professional.

For centuries, scholars have studied Words & Stories and Numbers & Money. The study of Sounds & Images is a newer field, but that does not diminish its importance.

Learning Category 10: Movement

Students move their bodies to improve strength, agility, endurance, flexibility, balance, and fitness. Bodies stretch, walk, run, dance, do gymnastics, and compete. For at least an hour every day, every student is very active, in their own way. Engagement always involves a combination of fun and challenge, guided by teachers and other students.

In Your Body, students learn what muscles do. In Movement, muscles and other body parts learn by doing. Students move faster, smarter, more efficiently and effectively, more gracefully, with greater control. Fundamentals concentrate on the operation of the body in motion. Students become familiar with every muscle group, how it works, its role in the body, how it becomes stronger and more flexible, and how it repairs when injured. Students understand how strength, endurance, balance, flexibility, and a growing body all work together. Routines evolve over time. Personal safety and steady improvement are critical—staying healthy, avoiding injury, and the mental game are all part of learning. Students learn how to set, manage, and achieve goals based on their own lives and bodies. The objective: Through direct experience, students learn how to use their own body.

Unlike other Learning Categories, Movement becomes part of every student's daily schedule. This can be accomplished in fifteen-to-twenty-minute segments before school, in the morning, in the afternoon, and after school, for a total of about one hour of movement every day (including weekends, holidays, and vacations). Movement involves engagement with the outdoors, which becomes a community priority, especially for students moving without direct supervision. Fully 20 percent of New School's Learning Categories are devoted to learning about health and fitness.

A NEW SCHOOL STRUCTURE

For a century, Old School has followed a predictable structure, but there are other ways to design the experience of life in school.

For example, New School proposes ten Learning Categories in place of subjects. The scheduling can be different, too—hours, not forty-minute sessions. One hour per week per Learning Category, not daily doses of every major subject every day. In New School, ten of each week's twenty hours of instruction per week could be assigned to specific Learning Categories, and students could use the other ten to pursue Personal Education related to these Learning Categories or to other worthwhile pursuits. The exception: early primary grades, where more time is allocated to Fundamental instruction in Words & Stories and Numbers & Money. Again, these are examples of what could be done—a starting place for discussions—not instructions to operate any particular school.

Each student's connection to their learning is based on individual behavior (personal, relational, active)—that is, teachers do not organize their students' learning. They present Fundamentals, then help and guide their students to learn based on their interests during the many Personal Education hours. Early on, all students take responsibility for their own learning. Beginning in kindergarten, they accept responsibility along with freedom. They rely on and monitor one another. Teachers become less concerned about classroom management, discipline, and lousy behavior because students are engaged, or will soon be. Nobody is being forced to learn, not for long, anyway. Every student knows the teacher is available when things go sideways. Every student, every teacher, every school is supported by a community dedicated to providing support and resources. Everything is based on helping each individual student learn, not teaching what adults insist every student must know.

A BETTER ALTERNATIVE

All over the world, many types of private schools and public schools provide viable examples of alternative primary and secondary schooling. Mara Linaberger, who focuses on very small schools, describes her professional transition:

> I taught in an inner city school in Pittsburgh, Pennsylvania. I taught at this super creative elementary school, but as a teacher I could feel that my ability to do the kind of things that [microschools do] were being taken away from me . . . slowly. It was kind of like being the lobster in a pot of water and you turn the heat

> on and very slowly you come to realize that you're getting cooked. I got some more education and I [became] a teacher-trainer and then I went to work for a school district. When my job got eliminated, I started thinking about bringing back the one-room schoolhouses of the past but with all of the new modern things we have available: the technologies, the ability to communicate with other people all around the world, the ability to travel and all. This isn't new: I think a lot of people have the same ideas. There's something called the alternative education movement which has been around for a long time. People will know schools like the Montessori schools, the Waldorf schools, the Sudbury schools, the Democratic Free schools.[25]

Alternative schools offer lessons to build the much larger, scalable solutions suggested by New School. Small-scale solutions, perhaps shared by a handful—or even a hundred—schools are inspiring, but New School is concerned with large-scale transformation.

REMNANTS OF OLD SCHOOL IDEAS

Standards, testing, grades/report cards, and homework are defining features of Old School education. How do they fit into New School?

Standards evolve to become Fundamentals. They are developed from the bottom up by students, teachers and other adults, community members, and experts, and are revised for each new school year. There are far fewer Fundamentals than there were standards. The people who develop each year's Fundamentals are known by the students and their teachers, but they work in collaboration with government and with other school districts. As a result, each year's Fundamentals are based on best practices and shared ideas.

In New School, students and teachers assess students' individual progress during, not after, learning. This information is consistent with contemporary ideas about learning. In-line assessments can be used by students, teachers, and parents to reset, correct errors, and make adjustments. That is, there is little reason to study for, or pass, a test. With few exceptions (early literacy, basic arithmetic), it no longer makes sense to test students or to collect and analyze post-testing data. Old School's approach to assessment is the wrong tool to evaluate learning—mostly because it occurs so long after the learning has taken place.

How will each student's work be graded? Once each month, the student writes a one-page reflection and assessment of their work in each Learning Category, and the teacher does the same. They read one another's document and discuss it in person. They may annotate their own and one another's document. Then, the material is stored in Global Brain (see chapter 5), which uses AI to extract patterns and trends for students, teachers, and parents. There is no letter grade. Instead, there are one-on-one discussions about what has been learned, why, and how, the value of the work, ideas for improvement, and action plans. To provide feedback and to encourage local adult responsibility, students are asked to assess teachers, schools, and districts for review by government officials and the public.

Will there be homework? Teachers assigning (and grading) homework is a thing of the past, but students do have work to do: read for twenty to thirty minutes every day, and write something meaningful every week. Personal Education hours fill half the daily New School schedule, but some students, and some projects, require more or different approaches to time, or bespoke access to resources. If students want to learn more after school hours, that's always their choice.

Despite a very active media-making community, there is probably not enough media available for students to learn about Your Body, Your Mind (big need here), a wide range of countries and cultures, Our Futures, Money, Sounds & Images, and Movement. Adults, educators, creative professionals, governments, and NGOs can make more. Students can make more, too. The textbook industry may embrace new ideas about school and learning, too.

What about students who prefer to learn—and teachers who prefer to teach—in the Old School manner? For the waning number of adherents, New School's flexibility can generate something akin to Old School—without negative consequences.

OUTCOMES

As a student contemplates the end of secondary school, several paths come into view: (1) a job, (2) military or public service, and (3) higher education. Of course, there's also the option of doing nothing, or dreaming without a realistic plan, but for the moment, let's put those aside—but not completely. It is now possible, for example, to play video games at a very high level and to get paid as an esports champion, or to become a famous YouTuber, but (so far), those options expand on Not School, not New School.

Old School is designed as if most students move on to higher education, but in the US, a third do not.[26] Instead, they go to work, learn a trade, follow a passion, start a business, find a job to pay the bills, and declare independence. A small number go into public or military service.

Generally, students who opt for college do so because they believe higher education will lead to better opportunities, higher salaries, and social and professional connections. They believe the loss of several years of employment income, plus the cost of tuition and other expenses (which may exceed the cost of tuition), are worth the investment because of potential long-term return.

Greg Roberts, dean of undergraduate admissions at the University of Virginia, described a variety of inputs considered for student admission, including each student's unique package of activities outside of school and an evolving learning portfolio they may choose to share.[27] He also explained one of several trends affecting admissions: "[the] emergence of more local, regional, and national Community-Based Organizations (CBO) that help schools identify and recruit high achieving, low-income, first-generation, and underserved students."[28] Michael Mills, director of national fellowships and scholarships at SUNY Geneseo in western New York state in the US, works with students in need and students with unique opportunities. Grades and test scores are less meaningful than each student's combination of personal interests, accomplishments, capacity, capabilities, relationships, community connections, international awareness, demonstrated history of leadership and collaboration history, and their ability to develop scenarios for the future.[29]

Unfortunately, the link between a college degree and high-value long-term employment is becoming less reliable. There have always been more graduates in certain majors (psychology, for example) than available positions, but in other majors (nursing, for example), there are more openings than qualified candidates. Now, as more students opt for college, much of Africa (for example) does not offer the robust employment marketplace to absorb their knowledge and skills. As AI transforms jobs and careers, students may find that their degrees do not yield anticipated returns. This has led to increasing fragmentation in higher education offerings; mini degrees and specialized short-term certificate programs satisfy some employment requirements without the larger investment of time and money. Investing four years (or more) and significant cash, and perhaps carrying large debt, begins to make less sense if certificates suffice and if a new certification may be necessary every few years in order to keep up with a changing job marketplace. New School prepares versatile, agile, resilient students for the new reality. Their learning cuts across many topics and categories. They envision more than one career.

New School shifts the responsibility for learning from teacher to student. School provides the facilities, structure, and access to resources and teachers. Parents and peers provide the encouragement. The community provides the best available resource for learning—for every student.

School has become a community service center in communities where necessary services are otherwise unavailable. This is understandable: Parents are busy, many work more than one job, people work on different schedules, transportation is often a problem, connectivity is better at school than at home, and so on. Outsourcing parental and community responsibility to school adds to the list of things it must now do. School has its own work to do. It has fallen behind, so it's time to return to the basics: educating children and teenagers. The other problems are important, but school probably isn't the answer. Instead, parents and communities may cultivate alternative solutions. What's needed is a venue that makes it possible for children and teenagers to grow and pursue a much wider range of interests and activities than even the most robust version of school could possibly provide.

In other words, students, families, and communities require a high-functioning Not School sector to share the burden that currently falls on school.

CHAPTER 5

Not School

When school is in session, it occupies about forty hours a week. Most students sleep about sixty hours. That leaves about seventy hours to do everything else, including learning in Not School, which is where most of life's learning takes place.

If you hunt from the trees, you need a stand to sit on. You need the bait to get the deer. You also need camouflage. You [need] an orange vest when you go hunting so you don't get hurt. You also need some kind of gun. Or you could use a bow and arrow. I think killing animals is okay because you can eat them. You can make them into a jerky. In our area, I think it's okay to kill animals because we can use the fur, sell it, make it into a little rug.

—Kristian, 12, Kentucky, US

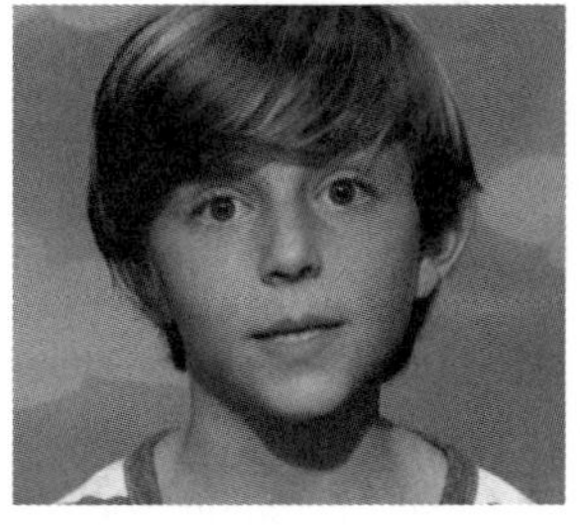

When I grow up, I'd like to be an actor, a singer, or a coder. So, I'd make computer games. Right now, I'm doing quite well down the acting path. I've just got a job with *Priscilla the Queen of the Desert.* It's a big hit! It is about three drag queens who go through the desert in a bus called Priscilla. I heard about it from a friend. I thought that would be quite fun! I went to the audition. I actually made it to the second round. After the first round, they kicked most of the [forty] others out. They kept twelve for the second round. They let you know later the four who got in. [I got in!] At the beginning, I thought, "this is not something I think I can make," but my mom thought I was perfect for the role. That was my motivation to keep going. Now, there are so many posters up [all over the city].

—Thilo, 11, Hong Kong

My hobbies? I love to read books and go outside and cycle. Every weekend, me and my dad go to the park. We cycle, we sit in the grass. And in the winter, we'll have snowball fights, make snowmen. There's always a different hobby for each season. I've been to London, Birmingham, Manchester. I do travel quite a lot. Every year, we try to make a trip to a foreign country. Some of the countries we go to, my dad and my mum's friends stay there, and I make friends with their children. We have relatives in Ireland who I talk to and chat with quite a lot. We just talk about the recent things that go on, the votes, magazines, all the way to Charlie Chaplin and Laurel and Hardy—they are probably my favorite films. I love fantasy books. I've read all the *Harry Potte*r books by J. K. Rowling. I've just started to read *The Three Musketeers*. Another book I adore is Gerald Durrell's *My Family and Other Animals*. You never know what's going to happen next when he puts a snake in the bathtub, a gecko in the ceiling, bumblebees in your father's cigarettes. . . . You just don't know!

—Debanik, Altrincham (near Manchester), England

In the Middle East there are a lot of continuing wars, in Pakistan, Syria, Gaza. And I really feel bad when I watch the news and I see young kids going through that because I'm a kid myself, and if that would happen to my country . . . when I see the pictures, all over the internet when something happens, I really cry. This is something that happened to Kosovo. [In countries with an ongoing war] kids need to be careful where they go, stay with their family. It's not in our hands. How does it stop?

—Mirela, 16, Damanec, Kosovo

I used to try to ignore them, try and push them away. To show them that what they do, it doesn't affect you. Now, I'm going to a different lane. Now, I'm saying, you tell them how you feel. You explain your anger and your frustration. You have to show that you're the superior over them because bullies try and pick the weaker ones. You have to show them that you have the courage to stand up. If you're hurt . . . that's how I found my strength. While I was being hurt, while I was so sad, I showed my sense of frustration in front of them. If you just write it down on a piece of paper, then crumple it up and throw it in the bin, that's good in one way, letting your stress go, but it doesn't stop the bullying in any way. Instead, why don't you speak to the bully and tell them how you feel? . . . You tell them you'd had enough. I don't think the bully will cope. There is a possibility it will make it worse, but you just have to stay strong.

—Nik, 11, Weston-super-Mare, England
(Diana Legacy Award holder for
good work on behalf of others)

Some of the problems are crime and drugs, chemicals and pollution, it goes on and on. The rivers are dirtier, there's trash everywhere, drug addiction, schools are closing because they don't have enough funding. This is really bad! Nobody's fixing it, either. Nobody does nothing about it. I won't be here when I'm eighteen. I am moving to the West Coast and Seattle. I really like Seattle because they have everything that West Virginia wants. They have a good economy. They have good jobs. Good houses. Smart people. Happy people. The only thing they have as bad is the homeless rate. But their unemployment rate is really low. I know all of this because I Google it. I teach myself. The education system here is so bad, I actually learn more from YouTube. . . . I'm just hoping to live in Seattle and be happy.

—Markel, 13, South Charleston, West Virginia, US

I've been in Boy Scouts since, probably, third grade. I know there's troops in other parts of the world. There's this pretty big summer camp that we all go to. There's been troops from Egypt, all over. We each research a Scout troop in a different part of the world. We camped out at this Coast Guard base in New Jersey, the next state over. We got to see some of the people training, and we got to go on the boats. That was really cool. I'm thinking I want to go into the Coast Guard Academy. Once you go there, you've got to go into the military afterwards, for five years. They'll give you, like, four years of college for free. They pay for everything. Then, you have to serve five years. But then, when you get out, you can do whatever. So I was thinking I could be an engineer afterwards. I want to be an engineer because I really like making models, and building.

—Kevin, 14, Richboro, Pennsylvania, US

WHY NOT SCHOOL?

If the question is "Why Not . . . School?," well, even the most ambitious version of New School cannot teach every student everything they want or need to know. School will always be constrained by physical space, number of teachers, site location, community norms, and other factors.

If the question is "Why . . . Not School?," the answer is access beyond school's reach. Not School exists in people's homes, neighborhoods, and in the great outdoors. It is connected to family, friends, the professional world, travel, evenings, weekends, summertime, tromping through deep snow and taking long walks far from home, visiting museums, watching TV, and listening to podcasts. In a lifetime, school fills about 10,000 hours, but Not School occupies more than 150,000 hours. There is more time to learn in Not School, and more flexibility, too.

Admittedly, Not School is not an ideal descriptive term. The best alternative, "learning outside of school" is problematic because it suggests an outdoor area adjacent to a school building. Worse, it positions Not School as secondary. "A growing body of research supports adopting an asset model of education in which curricula and instructional techniques support all learners in connecting academic goals to the learning they do outside of the classroom and through learner experiences and opportunities from various settings that are leveraged for each [individual] learner."[1]

In 2006, Andy, a teenager in suburban Philadelphia, Pennsylvania, collected musical instruments for Hurricane Katrina victims. His project was called Mississippi Music March. It began when his mother noticed an article in a local newspaper. Through the Bux-Mont Katrina Relief Project (combining efforts of Bucks and Montgomery Counties), Andy connected with a high school marching band in Bay St. Louis, Mississippi. The goal: Replace instruments lost to the floods. Andy decided this would be his Eagle Scout project, due for completion before his eighteenth birthday (which was not far off). He began with his local church, then involved his high school marching band. Local newspapers picked up the story; that led to coverage on a local TV station. He collected 110 instruments, including eighty that needed repair. A hoagie (sandwich) sale in space provided by his church raised over $4,000 to pay for those repairs (340 hoagies). Two local businesses provided the sandwiches at cost. Funds raised by Boy Scout Troop 99 families, Andy's church, and the marching band provided $1,000 to buy replacement sheet music. Bux-Mont Katrina Relief sent three trucks filled with instruments to Bay St. Louis—enough to share with a nearby local high school that had lost its instruments in the flood. Andy's long list of thank you notes included his church pastor and board, two professionals who cleaned, evaluated, and repaired instruments, two office workers who managed instrument drop-offs, dozens of local families for their instrument donations, and the band director.

(With his mom's help and encouragement,) Andy took charge and met his goal. He learned by engaging in personally meaningful public service to help people he never met. He learned a lot about communication (often with adults), soliciting help, assembling and managing a team, acquiring resources, tracking a complex project's progress, and keeping volunteers and helpers engaged and productive. In countless reports and documents, employers, educators, and policymakers describe these as twenty-first-century skills, wondering how they could be taught in school. Maybe school is not the best venue. With fewer rules, more flexibility, greater access to resources, and adults who are not focused on curriculum and test results, Not School offers powerful learning opportunities.

In a growing Paraguayan neighborhood in Remansito, just up the Paraguay River from Asunción, Yanina opened a small store. There is constant bicycle traffic, and some motorcycles, too. Mostly, people walk, so they pass her store often and buy because there is no other store nearby. Yanina's store is open all day—when Yanina is not there, her mother tends to customers.

This is my store, as you can see. If you want to buy something, you are welcome. The vegetables, the lettuce, are my own production from my vegetable garden. You can make juice from the bananas, right here. There's also Paraguayan tea if you want that. What I want to do, what I want to be in the future is accounting or a business manager.

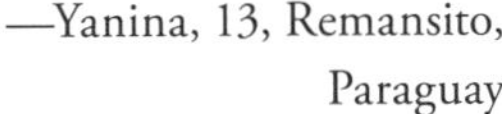

—Yanina, 13, Remansito, Paraguay

A BRIEF HISTORY OF NOT SCHOOL

Before humans invented writing, before school became a common idea, children and teenagers learned about the world through observation, mentorship, and direct experience. They figured out social hierarchies, how to make and care for babies, how to fight, how to participate in groups. They learned to hunt, farm, and prepare food. They endured rough circumstances (many died young), cared for people in need, did chores, shared stories, made up games, and apprenticed to develop useful skills.

Widespread development of public education started over three hundred years ago, but in some places, less than one hundred years ago. France was an early proponent of organized schooling: "By the middle of the 18th century, nearly every parish in Paris had a free school for boys, though only half as many provided for girls. Most children stayed in school long enough to read and write."[2] In the US, a newer country, about half of children attended public elementary school in 1830, which increased to about three-fourths of children by 1870.[3] In many countries, most children did not attend public elementary school until after World War II, and in many cases, not until the 1970s. Instead, most of the world's children and teenagers learned in Not School.

In the US, after the Civil War ended in 1865, more people moved to cities, which became vibrant places to shop, eat, drink, enjoy entertainment, and meet new people. Public venues became popular: lecture halls, theaters, opera houses. Railroads made it easier to travel. Lecturers and entertainers began to travel from one venue to another, sometimes sharing the gospel, performing circus acts, selling goods, telling inspiring stories, and more. Sometimes, parents brought their children so they could learn a thing or two. Sports clubs began to compete and form leagues; drawing a crowd, they constructed local facilities. Public libraries opened their doors to many (not always all) people, and encouraged them to borrow books. In the US, even minorities became welcome (if they followed the rules)—and there were a lot of immigrants who traveled to the US for economic opportunity. Everywhere, children and teenagers took it all in, participating with or without adult permission. Social movements emerged, some to keep children and teenagers occupied: Scouting, church youth groups, Little League and other organized sports, 4-H clubs (learning agriculture), and more. Mostly, though, kids figured out what to do on their own. As public school was just finding its footing, Not School was well established. That was a century ago—before recorded music, radio, telephones, television, the internet, and pickleball courts.

NOT SCHOOL IS UNDERVALUED

It is the lack of formal attention, structure, and perhaps, investment, that makes Not School so valuable as a learning environment. In Not School, all learning is personal, relational, and active. There's no grand design to it; that's just the way learning works.

Over the past century, school has, mostly, become a unified, well-organized, adequately funded, consistent operation with features that would be familiar almost anywhere: students, teachers, full-time staff, curriculum, school buildings, graduation, grades, tests, homework, and so on. Not School has been around much longer, but never as a unified concept, never held in the same regard as school.

This limited view of Not School is counterproductive. It devalues huge swaths of learning, engagement, and human development. It suggests that ideas and capabilities developed outside of school are unimportant, except, perhaps, to list on a college application.

And yet, before, during, and after school, most children and teenagers learn essential skills and build a useful knowledge base under the leaky Not School umbrella. Not School is not perceived as a coherent, proscribed, or significant collection of activities. Lashing long logs to build a twenty-foot-high signal tower matters less than learning about iambic pentameter.

This unfortunate, but pervasive, view discourages scholarly study of Not School and disrespects almost everything not learned in school. Despite its robust, resilient approach to learning, despite its orientation toward community service, despite its role in developing curiosity that often leads to careers, Not School remains a modest, mostly nonscalable candidate for community, government, and philanthropic investment—even though most of the work is carried forward by kids, parents, and volunteers. All over the world, examples abound.

In and around Pittsburgh, Pennsylvania, US, Kidsburgh brings together museums, local television, universities, caregivers, and other community resources, including schools.

Ara Taiohi is "a network aimed at providing 'one voice' for the youth sector" of Aotearoa (New Zealand). Originating in Maori culture, it "organises an annual Youth Week campaign, biennial national *wananga* and regional workshops. Ara Taiohi supports lesbian, gay, queer, trans, and bisexual youth through advising mainstream youth organisations on how they can provide safe and positive activities for all young people."[4] Related activities and organizations include Girls' Brigade New Zealand: "'Empowering girls to succeed in tomorrow's world.' The aim is to combine confidence in outdoor activities, friendship, learning new skills and faith. Like Boys' Brigade, it's associated with ICONZ, whose girls' programmes are aimed at 5–17 year olds and offer 'values based activities in a safe environment.'"[5] Zeal's mission is to make transformative spaces and experiences accessible to all young people, supporting *rangatahi* to connect to their mana, innate self-worth and sense of belonging. Its vision is for "all young people in Aotearoa [to live] full lives of meaning and purpose" and for "all *rangatahi* (young people) [to] feel seen, valued, safe, empowered and have an equitable shot to thrive."[6]

> I think Not School is a chance for people to expand on their interpersonal skills and also to learn more about themselves. The opportunities we get in school are . . . for learning in academics. Learning who you are as a person, about other people—what we learn in Not School is just as valuable, if not a little bit more, because those are the skills we will be building on later in life, day-to-day skills that are not learned in the classroom. They can only be learned by experience. . . . I believe that I have a responsibility I choose to educate myself. . . . After the whole Black Lives Matter movement in 2020, and the rest of the political movements that occurred after that. Even though it's not a lot, I still have [Jamaican] Black heritage, and I take pride in that. Especially speaking with my parents, I believe there was a responsibility, I wanted to search different sources from different perspectives and learn more Black history in America, and about my own history.
>
> —Jaime, 16, Kobe, Japan

STRUCTURE OF NOT SCHOOL LEARNING

In school, learning takes place within a curriculum, a schedule, mandatory attendance, government laws, paid staff, and physical facilities built for school's purpose.

In Not School, form follows function. Learning takes place anywhere, anytime. It makes use of every available resource. Taking a walk in the forest, students of any age (including adults) find plenty to learn about the growth of trees, regeneration, water flows, temperature, humidity, canopies, and more. A branch is more than a dirty piece of wood; it becomes a walking stick, a sword, an art object, a dog's fetch toy. Nearer the shore, sand, rocks, sticks, and mud become castles; wet sand becomes a sculpted mermaid. The mermaid becomes part of a story.

Not School is spending unstructured time at home and in the neighborhood, reading a book, making media, following stories about the wildfires. There is no plan for every six-year-old in the state of Connecticut. In Not School, the structure of learning often materializes at the moment the learning takes place. With exceptions: Learning the catechism, for example, requires structure. So does baking a cake.

If you're hoping to discover the inner structure of Not School here, you will find it only in pieces and parts. Some Not School experiences are almost entirely without structure or rules—daydreaming, taking a walk, falling in love, following links on the web, gazing at the night sky. It's been a long day, and you've collected a lot of shells on the beach. Now, it's time to figure out what you've got, who or what lived in those shells before you found them. Doing that research adds some structure. So does organizing the shells with the prettiest ones first. Some Not School activities are structured from the start—starting a new 4-H club and following procedure to set it up properly. Others begin simply—a group of people getting together to read books, as in the example below—and take on a structure because expansion would be impossible without it.

WE LOVE READING

Around 2010, Rana Dajani, a molecular biology professor, returned to her home country of Jordan. Raising her children, hoping to instill a love of reading, she realized that Jordan had no public libraries, Dajani approached her imam, and asked to use the local mosque as a public place for a small read along. Local mothers thought it was a good idea, so they took their children to read religious books in the mosque. They were surprised to find that the read along was secular, intended to encourage children to love books. The read along just happened to take place in a mosque. This small effort grew into a big idea. The read-along program became popular. Dajani trained other mothers to conduct read alongs in more than seven thousand other places! Today, We Love Reading operates in more than sixty countries, and also in many refugee camps. It publishes children's books, runs libraries, participates in scholarly research, and much more. Its theory—that children who read for pleasure develop strong language skills, achieve better academic results, and have more powerful emotional intelligence—has been proven time and again. The effort is managed by Taghyeer, a nonprofit organization. Its "philosophy is based on the butterfly effect—the concept that small actions can have far-reaching consequences. We believe that just one person can make a difference and that the contribution of each individual matters. Through collective effort, transformation unfolds."[7]

SCOUTING

Despite serious problems in the US, the World Organization of the Scout Movement (WOSM) and the World Association of Girl Guides and Girl Scouts (WAGGGS), which together comprise World Scouting, were "nominated for the Nobel Peace Prize for their work in 'giving young people the tools they need to solve the challenges of the future, while building strong civil society.'"[8] WAGGGS is the global organization for Girl Scouts and Girl Guides; it focuses on ten million girls and young women in 152 countries. Collectively, WOSM, which welcomes boys and girls, has been associated with sixteen million community service projects and nearly three billion community service hours (WAGGGS adds even more).[9] Both are actively involved with "a wide network of partners, including UN agencies and non-governmental organizations, to support local projects led by Scouts."[10] Most work is conducted by children and teenagers with some help and guidance from adult volunteers. Every Scouting organization is similar, but most have adapted to serve local needs.

> The national Scouting organization of Burundi was founded in 1940. . . . The coeducational Association des Scouts du Burundi has 32,340 members, [ages seven to nineteen]. [It] is oriented towards rural needs of the population [including] farming, reforestation, erosion control, and village health.[11]

Scouting was founded in 1914 in East Bengal, now Bangladesh. The organization changed its name to Bangladesh Scouts in 1978. There are about 1.5 million members.

> Scouts are involved in community service, major areas being agriculture, health and sanitation, child welfare, community development, construction and repair of low cost housing and sports. During national disasters, Scouts . . . help with flood control, relocation of citizens and organizing shelters. Membership is open to youth between 6 and 25 years of age, regardless of caste, creed or color. Bangladesh Scouts receive strong support from the government, which recognized Scouting's value in citizenship training.[12]

Girl Scout Daisies (kindergarten and first grade) are encouraged to express their individuality: learning that there isn't just one way to look, feel, act or think, for example. And, girls are trusted to plan and make key decisions, try new things, and make mistakes.

Scouting is based on individual achievement by children and teenagers with minimal adult intervention. Mostly, Scouts learn from one another—older ones teaching young ones, learning in groups, learning from other Scouts. There is a formal rank structure—rank is always earned by satisfying specific, but often flexible, criteria. Merit badges are earned by demonstrating early-stage mastery of topics that are personally interesting to each Scout. Most are connected to useful skills and ideas, such as citizenship, cooking, first aid, or in the case of Filipino Scouts, coconut growing. By learning the fundamentals about coconuts as food, seedlings and soil, plantations and harvesting, pest control, and the importance of coconuts in the world market, they earn a badge.[13] Some merit badges are required for rank advancement, but mostly, the choice of what to learn is an individual decision based on curiosity and personal interest.

NOT SCHOOL AT HOME

Before they're old enough to go to school, kids learn at home from family, friends, play, observation, experimentation, and experience. All of this fits under the Not School umbrella, too. Remember: Learning is relational. Everyone and everything in a child or teenager's life is a teacher, and that includes pets, friends who visit, and what children see and hear and read on TV and on the internet. Kids watch their mother or father put on a uniform, perhaps save a life. We all learn by asking questions: What's it like to serve in a peacekeeping force in the Middle East? To shop in Mexico City? To study in a university where nobody looks or talks like you do? To fall in love with someone who doesn't speak Farsi?

Many children and teenagers are attracted to the jobs that their parents do. Based on whatever information presents itself, children and teenagers learn.

> I don't live in . . . a close-knit community [the way] my parents did or my grandparents did. Talking to grandparents, I learn so much. I remember once I went to one of my friend's grandparents—she's also a South African Indian, like me. My friends came and we all watched her grandma knitting. And we learned how to knit in those three hours. We knit our own squares, and we knit all those squares together to make a blanket. I think that was a big part of our grandparents' culture—actually making their own clothes when you couldn't go out and buy the clothes.
>
> —Almaaz, 15, Johannesburg, South Africa

Almaaz told us she thought a lot about the world in which her grandmother grew up. Families spend much more time together, raising children, cooking and cleaning, relying on others who lived across the road. Today, there is less multigenerational street life, less vibrancy, less informal interaction. Technology and the conveniences of modern life have reduced direct, physical interaction, but they have increased our ability to communicate anywhere, anytime, over great distances. Each has its pros and cons, but all of it fits within Not School learning.

Public Spaces

In Sevilla, Spain, there are many public squares. They're busy all the time: kids, families, businesses. Kids have a place to play that's safe, within eyeshot of adults. The squares are lively, filled with activity. This is common throughout much of Europe and South America, and in many other parts of the world. So, kids need a place to play, somewhere that's safe, easy to reach, well lit, with restrooms, water and food nearby, and caring adults within shouting distance.

In some places, Not School is a busy market parking lot, but it's a place where kids at play compete with drivers and vehicles who seem to think they own the place. Safety is a concern, kids may be disruptive, and it's not an ideal situation. Instead, communities, regardless of their available resources, regardless of available funds, need to provide places where kids can safely gather and play.

It is even better if the facilities are designed for multigenerational use. As John Ratey, author of *Spark: The Revolutionary New Science of Exercise and the Brain,* points out: "Exercise encourages optimum brain function, decreases stress, reduces the tendency to gain weight, improves outlook, mitigates the severity of illness and disease, extends healthy life, and reduces reliance on pharmaceutical solutions. In fact, the single most important job of 21st century school is to prepare students to keep their bodies, and minds, operating in optimum condition for a lifetime."[14]

According to Ratey, alertness, attention, and motivation are improved through exercise. "Nerve cells are prepared and encouraged to bind together"—and this is the cellular basis for cataloging new information. And, exercise "spurs the development of new nerve cells in the hippocampus," which "receives new input from working memory, cross-references that information with existing memories for the sake of comparison and to form new associations." [15]

We tend not to think that way about Not School, but we can learn to do so.

MANY PLACES TO LEARN

Learning happens everywhere. It does not require a school, museum, or protection from the weather. It may not even require other people. What it does require is a degree of freedom, and, at least, a lack of discouragement. If there is a bedrock principle at the heart of Not School, it's the idea that learning happens wherever and whenever a child or teenager finds the time to imagine. It shows up in so many different ways, in so many different places—and most of those places would not merit inclusion in a reasonable adult's plan for community or human development.

Still, there are some very good things that adults can do, with the help of children and teenagers, to help a community to support learning.

Every place on Earth is part of nature. Therefore, every community could build, operate, and benefit from a nature center, with marked trails and signs that tell a story. Updated annually. Who does the work? Students, seniors, local businesses, Scouts, 4-H, and anybody else who wants to help.

Every place can build and maintain a garden—even if it's located indoors using containers instead of outside in open fields. Building community projects around food promotes intergenerational relationships. Growing a community garden invokes emotional nourishment. The magic of starting from seed and serving homegrown food at a community picnic is a positive, loving experience. In fact, more than a half-million volunteers work with more than seven million people in 4-H clubs in more than fifty countries. Many Not School structures are well established, so this is something adults know (or can find out) how to do.

Every place on Earth can trace its history. Therefore, every community can tell its own story on the walls of buildings, on signs and pathways. People learn as they walk their own history. And remember: Stories don't begin when humans show up; lots of interesting stuff happened before "civilization."

However, it is unwise to limit available pathways to nature paths and historical signage. Animals, children, and teenagers all cut their own pathways—and it's always lovely to find that some caring person placed a bench, or access to clean water, or a small bridge across just the right spot on what would otherwise be a soggy mud patch. That is: If adults and others pay attention, it is possible to exert some positive influence on Not School without transforming it into a different kind of experience

A maker space requires a physical location, machinery and supplies, and key people to make it all work. It's wonderful for people of all ages to learn from one another as they create, build, repair, and learn through the use of physical tools and materials. The lab becomes the factory where new benches are made for community street corners, where those in need can get their furniture repaired, where trail markers are designed and constructed, where communities come together to breathe new life into downtrodden properties.

A visual arts space may be devoted to drawing, painting, and more. It should include easy access, volunteer and professional support, and ample exhibit space for all ages. If there are adults around, they will suggest free classes for kids and seniors. Happens all the time.

Consider a performance space, too—a place to operate a theater and teach students many different hard (build scenery) and soft (accept criticism) skills. This can be the ultimate Not School experience—but it need not be fancy. Given any reasonably safe space, a creative community may take shape. Developing and producing a show brings people of all ages together—with hard work and laughter, and pleasure when community members show up to see the show. A theater, in whatever physical form it may take, is also a place to rehearse and perform music, watch movies, and attend lectures from visiting luminaries. More interactions between students and the adults who live in the community, more frequent contact, generates more opportunities to learn from one another and have fun. The availability of space for creativity and expression that can flourish outside of school may prove to be much more than it seems. It may become the most important place in a child or teenager's life, a place where, for the very first time, they find themselves and others who think and behave in similar ways.

Public Libraries

A public library can provide a community with a heart and soul—a place for multigenerational learning. A safe, air-conditioned and heated place for seniors to spend time with one another, in comfort, acquiring and sharing ideas, and for books to survive otherwise challenging weather. A place to read at leisure, where the youngest are told stories and begin to accept responsibility as they borrow their first books. A place where children and teenagers of any age can explore, study, read, do other work, make friends, use a computer, connect to the internet, even borrow other stuff they may need, like a camera tripod or an easel. Mostly, libraries are free to users because they are funded by communities, foundations, and governments. This is a model that could be expanded.

Yes, communities can and do build their own public libraries in the twenty-first century. Clarie Odhiambo and John Malamba were the local community members whose hard work brought a public library to Siaya in southwestern Kenya, near Kisumu, Kenya's fifth-largest city.

> Construction of the Siaya Community Library was funded by the World Bank. The project was completed in late 2014. In the meantime, the county government of Siaya offered to provide space for the Library at the Siaya Cultural Centre, Department of the Ministry of Culture for more than two years. The management of the Library and the Integrated Development Africa Programme, the sponsor of the library project, are grateful to the World Bank, the government of Kenya, the county government of Siaya and all other stakeholders.[16]

Libraries are very popular. "Five times more people visit U.S. public libraries each year than attend U.S. professional and college football, basketball, baseball and hockey games combined."[17] We wonder: Why are cities building new stadiums, but not new libraries?

For every paid library worker in Europe, there are nearly five volunteers.[18] *The Library Policy and Advocacy Blog* of the International Federation of Library Associations and Institutions (IFLA) describes a very wide range of community benefits associated with the presence of a public library. Clarie and John are now developing a floating library—a book boat—to travel to other places around nearby Homa Bay. It is akin to the bookmobile used in several boroughs of New York City, Detroit, and back in 1858, in Warrington, England (with a horse-drawn van). In Bangladesh, book mobiles are active in 1,900 communities.[19]

Some countries are heavily invested in public libraries. Others are not. Former Soviet republics are home to a lot of public libraries. Only about 4 percent of the world's people live in the US, but it's home to 14 percent of the world's libraries.[20]

Media and Learning in Not School

For about two hundred years, most countries on Earth have been creating, producing, marketing, and distributing media. Some, and sometimes much, of it survives in the form of printed material, recorded music, pictures, sounds, stories, audio, video, interactive media, social media, and more. To share that media, we've invented books, newspapers, magazines, the telegraph, radio, motion pictures, motion picture theaters, recording equipment, record players, CD players, MP3 players, television sets, video game consoles, mobile phones, VR headsets, podcasts, blackboards and whiteboards, jumbotrons, textbooks, websites, and so much more.

Media is the most prolific, most successful, most ubiquitous educator the world has ever known. The popular 1990s White House drama *The West Wing* introduced tens of millions of viewers to the inner workings of a federal government grappling with terrorism, genocide, a president with multiple sclerosis, AIDS, the War on Drugs, Taiwan's political status, the 1996 Defense of Marriage Act, student loan forgiveness for teachers, and much more.[21] Is this show interesting to, or suitable for, teenagers? Give them the choice of spending one hundred hours watching very good actors perform very well-written, fast-paced scripts, or sitting in an Old School social studies classroom for the same amount of time with a textbook, a teacher, and a bunch of fairly bored students—you know the answer. Especially if the students can watch anytime, anywhere.

In Not School, very few people restrict their learning to curriculum or government frameworks. Nobody gives the idea of tests a second thought. Instead, people learn what they want to learn, and challenge themselves on their own terms. Who knew so many people, including kindergarteners, seniors, and everyone in between, would want to learn about baking?

All over the world, many viewers can now explain lamination, proving, fondant, tray bake, blind bake, and how to make genoise sponge because they watch a television show now seen in more than two hundred countries (just about every country in the world). It's called *El Gran Pastelero* (*The Great Baker*) in Chile, *Den store bagedyst* (*The Great Baking Bout*) in Denmark, *The Great British Baking Show* in the US, and *The Great British Bake-Off* in its home country.

But that's television—left over from the twentieth century with its fussy schedules and its awkward way of requiring viewers to turn to a specific channel to watch a specific show. That's not the direction the world is moving in. Instead, viewers want to watch whatever they want, to learn whatever they want, simply by searching. You want to learn about dark reds to choose the perfect color for your watercolor habit? Try Denise Soden, who paints out swatches of every color. Her "Color Spotlight—Venetian Red, Indian Red & Caput Mortem (PR101)" has been watched over thirty-five thousand times. Those numbers add up to a much bigger story.

Art for Kids, a small family operation, posts a new art lesson daily on YouTube. It offers 2,400 short-form videos on its YouTube channel with more than seven million subscribers, resulting in more than 2.5 billion views since February 2012. "How to Draw Hello Kitty" has been viewed sixty-eight million times, but "How to Draw a Dachshund," with about six million views, is more typical.

Danny LaBrecque used to be a classroom kindergarten teacher. Not anymore. Now, he spends his time (and a lot of his own money) in his basement studio where he and his wife Stefani design, write, produce, build puppets and props, and perform an internet video series that updates the concept of a 1960s children's show—without a studio or a staff. He explains, "*Danny Joe's Tree House* invites kids to slow down and engage with a wide range of topics, providing them with valuable life lessons, strategies for self-regulation, early STEM concepts, and digital media literacy skills, while also sparking their imaginations with arts and crafts projects, sing-along songs, and other DIY activities."[22]

With video games leading the way, today's media is becoming interactive. Technology, including but not limited to portable computers, adds dimensions to media: interactivity, quick access of related information, storage for later use, connectivity, sharing, extended reality, and making your own content.

We are experiencing a power shift. Longtime incumbents are watching disruptors gain ground. Not School is already more powerful than Old School because it can do so many things that Old School cannot. While Old School is banning cell phones in the classroom, Not School's media operations are figuring out how to connect every student in the world to most of its media assets. With Clayton Christensen at the Harvard Business School, Michael Horn helped to develop theories about disruptive and incremental innovation. He explains,[23] "Our schools, as they were built, were not built to optimize learning . . . our society has fundamentally changed. We're no longer living in an industrial economy. We're living in a knowledge economy where every single student needs to be able to find their passion, and fulfill their potential. . . . We need a system that can customize or personalize for every single individual learner."[24] Even young students understand how core assumptions about learning have radically changed. What they may not realize is that the change has just begun.

> I learn from family, I learn from friends, anybody! I learn from teachers, my principal . . . and even in books, I learn stuff, like reading, math, science, stuff like that. I watch YouTube, but I don't watch YouTube all the time. There's not that many videos on there that teach you about stuff. Whenever I have free time, I do watch stuff that isn't about learning. Sometimes, our teacher lets us watch a little bit of YouTube, like at recess. I want to be a teacher when I get older.
>
> —Jamesyn, 9,
> South Charleston, West Virginia, US

Thought Experiment: Starfish

Unlike most animals, starfish are found all over the world—"from warm, tropical zones to frigid, polar regions."[25] Starfish date back at least 450 million years (not many animals are older). They have five, six, seven, even ten or more arms. If they lose an arm, they can generate a new one. Some starfish change gender from male to female. Many starfish live in tide pools or near the shore, so it's easy for a young child to take a picture of a starfish or record a short video.[26] And, they look cool and they're easy for a child to draw.

Imagine a global starfish project. Children, teenagers, classes, and teachers gather, collect, generate, and share information about starfish. They organize the information in an international database with built-in language translation, post their insights, and ask one another questions. It's fun, it's a great way to learn from and about one another, it builds human knowledge. It builds self-confidence, too.

If they have questions, they can reach out to an expert, someone like Dr. David Pawson, a senior research scientist and curator of echinoderms (emeritus) at the US's Smithsonian Institution. With less than five minutes of work, we found Dr. Pawson's email address on the Smithsonian website: *pawsond@si.edu*.[27] Many experts are easy to find and already field questions from students.

Today, about one billion students enjoy internet access. If one in ten of them, or one hundred million students, generated one media asset per year—a photograph, a brief essay, a picture, a video, a list of starfish facts—and if educators, science museums, aquariums, park rangers, government agencies, and ordinary people did the same, we might generate a quarter-billion media assets about starfish alone.

The question is not whether they can or would generate one hundred million, five hundred million or a billion assets. The question is how that material would be organized and made available to every student, teacher, classroom, and school in the world.

Global Brain

Wikipedia posted its first edited article on January 15, 2001, two weeks after the twenty-first century began. It is about twenty-five years old, but it remains one the world's largest websites and the largest collection of collective knowledge ever assembled on Earth. Mostly, Wikipedia presents information in text, supported by graphics and photographs and some sound files, so each page loads quickly and does not require much bandwidth. Operated by the Wikimedia Foundation—a nonprofit—Wikipedia is one of the world's most visited websites, attracting about fifty million unique device visits per day, and delivering its information in more than three hundred languages.[28] In 2023, the Wikimedia Foundation's expense budget was about $170 million.[29] By comparison, Portland, Maine's city council approved $143.8 million for 2024[30] to serve about 6,500 primary and secondary school students.[31]

Wikipedia is not written or produced for children or teenagers. Many kids use the service, but the articles tend to be long, complicated, and not easily adapted for their existing knowledge or facility with the material. For example, "In physics, gravity (from Latin *gravitas* 'weight') is a fundamental interaction which causes mutual attraction between all things that have mass. Gravity is, by far, the weakest of the four fundamental interactions, approximately 10^{38} times weaker than the strong interaction, 10^{36} times weaker than the electromagnetic force and 10^{29} times weaker than the weak interaction."[32]

That's material written for a high school senior or a college student, not for a fourth grader, so we asked ChatGPT to "rewrite for a ten-year-old." It responded immediately, did a good job, but failed to explain strong and weak forces clearly: "In physics, gravity is a force that pulls things toward each other. It's like a special magnet that makes objects with mass (or weight) stick together. Gravity is the weakest force compared to other forces in the universe. It's much, much weaker than the strong force, the electromagnetic force, and the weak force. Actually, it's so weak that it's about a trillion times weaker than the strong force! But even though it's weak, gravity is still really important because it's what keeps everything on Earth and in space from floating away."[33]

As technology tools learn what students want and need to know, and follow their pathways, they become smarter and more useful. This is the way many large internet sites operate in the commercial sector.

Imagine a Global Brain The need is clear and immediate. Every child and teenager in the world requires reliable, low-cost internet service, and they require access to vast numbers of free internet media assets for learning. They also require a modern, interactive workspace that allows them to gather, create, share, fact-check, revise, and store their learning and the knowledge they acquire through school and Not School. With this essential tool—we call it Global Brain—they will learn individually, in small groups, and through local and international collaborations, and make use of every available asset that adults can provide. Existing and new media assets, Wikipedia, AI, real-time translation—each of these provides a piece of the puzzle. What is needed, however, is a comprehensive plan, rapid implementation, and secure tools that allow students to learn effectively and assess their progress, regardless of where they happen to live or what kind of school they attend.

Global Brain becomes a tool that adapts to every student's curiosity, interests, pace, depth, and breadth. It presents reading material based on a comprehensive evaluation of each student's history. Most important, it collects and collates the work of a great many students who are otherwise unaware of their similar or complementary interests. In this way, Global Brain lives up to its name: It takes Wikipedia's place as the largest collection of human knowledge ever assembled. And the work is being done by students as they learn.

Is Global Brain a tool for school? Maybe, but it's best if the system is neither built nor managed by school. In part, that's because school isn't a single entity—it's a million local buildings that do not, as a rule, collaborate with one another, and do not possess the time, expertise, resources, freedom, or focus to devote to such an enterprise. And schools do not operate with independence—they are subject to local governance and existing laws and regulations that would impede and probably prevent progress. Also, if Global Brain was a massive school project, it would probably be tied to curriculum, and homework, and formal assessment, all ideas whose useful time has passed.

Instead, Wikipedia's got the right idea. Global Brain needs to be constructed independently, coordinated by a nonprofit or NGO without agenda, managed by volunteers and students, and open to all competent contributors. Global Brain becomes a workspace, a repository, a means to share learning about any and every topic generated by the curiosity of young people. Given the contributors and the audience, it's likely to rely more on sounds and images, with far less reliance on text that Wikipedia. Growing up alongside AI, it would make good use of new technologies, constantly adapting to each student's status quo—which may be a flip phone, a radio, or a more versatile device.

From the start, Global Brain is intended to be a contributory system. Here, a science or art museum or a university professor could show and tell students what they might want to know. A diabetes association could help students understand how to manage their blood sugar before they're diagnosed with diabetes. A river guide could take students on an unforgettable journey. Every panda at every zoo could be recorded by a local student. A great deal of useful information is already available, and much more could be made—and Global Brain solves the problem of how to put it all in a place where children, teenagers, parents, and teachers can find it and make use of it with suitable confidentiality and security.

By design, Global Brain complements the New School structure (but it could be organized in other ways, customized by each individual user). Perhaps it makes sense to organize material under headings such as My Body, My Mind, Our Countries & Cultures, and so on. This would help contributors know where to place their assets—video, podcasts, charts, animations, interactive games, articles, book excerpts, and the like—and would also help teachers and communities construct Fundamentals. As young people develop their own ideas, Global Brain can be a very useful platform for nearly all Personal Education activities. This becomes a place for everyone to share their knowledge, on a safe and vetted platform, for the good of all humankind.

As Global Brain develops, it will face questions about the use of intellectual property. Does Danny LaBrecque decide to post *Danny Jo's Tree House*? Is usage tracked? Is he paid some sort of royalty? Or does a random user post episodes of the series—as they might on YouTube? If that happens, what happens? Where does fair use and copyright protection begin and end? What if the material is, say, a song composed and performed by a twelve-year-old? Whose permission is required? What if the song becomes a hit? Does the twelve-year-old receive royalties, or do incoming revenues flow to the parents, or the school, with a promise of future fiscal responsibility? These questions are not new, but the potential scale of Global Brain raises their profile.

Every student follows their own learning journey. If school participates in Global Brain, then teachers (and parents) can see students' work in progress. Each student's learning history—and their approach to learning—can be plugged into various measures of competence and potential, which may link to possible community service, employment, higher education, and other opportunities. The result is a kind of portfolio, a permanent record of each student's curiosity, collaborations, and progress.

Global Brain's Interactive Engines Learning about the human heart is not easy to do. Mostly, that's because the heart is inside the body nestled amid bones, muscles, and organs. To get a good look, you need to go inside and push the other stuff out of the way. It would be dark and yucky. And if you didn't know what you were doing, the patient could die. Instead, what you want is something that operates just like a real body but without the mess and without the risk of serious consequences. What you need is Global Brain's Human Body Engine, a simulation that allows you to play—yes, play—with the body and see what happens.

You might begin with something resembling your own body. Feed it ridiculous amounts of pizza for a simulated year and see how it reacts. Have it run ten miles in summer heat, let it nearly collapse, give it some water, and see the improvement. Turn it from a girl into a boy. Make it older.

Start again. This time, the body is not human at all. It's your dog.

Here's another Global Brain interactive engine. History can be difficult to learn because, once again, we can achieve only a limited view with current technology. And yet, there are all sorts of photographs, stories, paintings, wardrobe items, museum collections, biographies, movies, video games, and family trees that could be put together to tell a more complete story. Global Brain's History Engine scans the internet for useful materials—an AI trick we already know how to do—and constructs contextualized stories to more fully explain what happened, where it happened, and why. It delivers a sense of time and place akin to time travel, with ample opportunity to communicate with people who appear on screen. Think in terms of riding in a carriage down Broadway in NYC's Manhattan before cars, when department stores were a new idea, and people dressed up before they left home. Then take the same ride down Broadway, but now it's 1945, and World War II just ended so people are celebrating. Now, it's 1976 and parts of Broadway are in sad shape. You could explore the 1939–1940 New York World's Fair and find out about the new invention called television. As more people contribute materials from their homes, their families, and their experiences, historical storytelling becomes richer, more detailed. This is a collective project of the highest order, one that's likely to attract considerable interest from museums and their funders.

To understand the impact of numbers and money, to understand possible futures, what you want is a Data Analysis Engine. By feeding local climate data into a DAE, every student contributes to global knowledge on a massive scale. Map that onto medical data or atmospheric data over time and over space, and new discussions take shape.

More brainstorming about more Global Brain interactive engines begins. Students and teachers pivot from memorization of stale information to the generation of new knowledge.

Adults Want to Help (Proceed with Caution!)

Not School is a kid-centric world. Adults always want to make it better. Maybe that's not such a good idea.

It's getting dark outside. And it might rain tomorrow. Playing with that cardboard box is fun, but it'll get destroyed unless it spends the night in a dry place. Some kids kick around a ball and forget about the box.

Two big brown dogs run by. The kids run after the dogs. Then they go home.

Next morning, no rain, but also no box and no ball. The box has been torn apart. The kids find the ball, but it's in use by eight other kids they don't know.

They play football (soccer, to US kids). Teams coalesce. Out-of-bounds is the pile of decrepit tires and those big rusted-out cans.

It starts to rain really hard, with lightning and thunder. Everyone is soaked. Some kids slide around in the mud. Some kids go home. The dogs are back, and they've taken the ball.

Weeks later, some of the kids come back to see what's up. There's a fence around the vacant lot. Kids complain. Parents get involved, schedule meetings, and come up with a plan. They negotiate. They raise money. They get results. There will be a new facility that includes restrooms and a food stand. It will be open to kids from 8:00 A.M. until 2:00 P.M. on weekends, and used by senior citizens in the afternoons and early evenings. Garbage will be picked up daily. No dogs allowed.

The kids lost control of the ball. Some wander off to look for another box.

CHAPTER 6

Adults

Solomon Schwartz was an art teacher in a public school in Brooklyn, New York. Norman was a young teenager from a poor family who drew pictures for fun. Mr. Schwartz arranged for Norman's admission to the prestigious High School for Music and Art. Norman was grateful. He enrolled, and he quickly realized the school was not the place to learn to earn the money his family needed to survive. Norman returned to his neighborhood school, but he struggled. One day, Mrs. Cozzens, his French teacher, asked him to stay after class. He was failing French, and worried about being expelled. Mrs. Cozzens smiled when she told him that "it was a crime to waste his talent at a school like this." Mrs. Cozzens did some research. With her help, Norman became a student in Manhattan's School of Industrial Art. The school lived up to its promise: "To Train Artists and Designers for Industry."

By his own admission, Norman was a competent artist, not a shining star. In fact, he spent most of his time writing, producing, directing, and emceeing stage shows. Later, he did the same thing in the US Navy, entertaining several thousand men on the USS *Oklahoma City*. After military service, Norman worked briefly as a commercial artist, then switched to a more promising young industry—television—initially as an art director, then as a producer of popular long-running network series.

Luvelle, who later became a school superintendent, tells a somewhat similar story about boyhood in rural Virginia: "An English teacher broke policies, broke rules in the school district to allow me to take Honors English at our high school. Now, people didn't like it. They were upset! They were mean!! I saw how educators and my peers, people treated me differently. I had access to vocabulary, ways of writing stories I couldn't have imagined [before]. I think the key to me achieving in school was 'Yeah, go ahead man.'"[1]

Norman in New York City and Luvelle in rural Virginia got lucky. A teacher (in Norman's case, two teachers) paid attention to a student and changed a life. As adults, our job is to increase the odds of young people getting lucky.

TWENTY-FIRST-CENTURY ADULTS

Only about one in four adults live with schoolchildren. Half of adults never marry. Many adults know almost nothing about the lives of twenty-first-century children or teenagers, but they fund public primary and secondary school by paying taxes. When school funding issues arise, many adults favor road and bridge repair, or new sports stadiums.

In theory, government would focus on education as essential to development. In practice, development is a long-term issue, but government is organized, mostly, to deal within elected officials' terms of service. Senior government officials rarely deal with primary and secondary school issues. Legislators deal with immediate problems, but long-term education policy is not their concern. The ministry or department of education is focused on short- to medium-term issues. Although they are aware of trends, taking action is difficult because governance of education is usually distributed among national, provincial (state), and local entities. In the US, more than thirteen thousand local school boards deal with logistics, compliance, budgets, community relations, facilities management, transportation, technology, public health regulations, and food services.[2] They are not experts; they are citizens with an interest in schooling and local politics, not, as a rule, professional educators. They hire a superintendent to employ and manage staff and handle operations. Sometimes, at the school board level, members discuss what teachers teach and what students learn, but those decisions are made higher up the chain. Local boards sometimes face cultural issues that may include, in the US, book banning or other culture wars issues.

Parents

To varying degrees, more than two billion parents are involved in their children and teenagers' schoolwork. Many work long hours to earn a living, care for young and old and otherwise who require assistance, or deal with other issues. Not only is their time limited, many lack the knowledge, skill, confidence, competence, understanding of curriculum, or relationship with their child that is needed to be helpful. And, as so many teachers have learned, every student's family situation is special in its own way.

> I have three foster siblings and three of my sisters and brothers, so there's seven kids. There's so many! My foster siblings . . . their mom couldn't take care of them anymore, so my mom decided to take them in as her own, and do the best she can to provide them the family they weren't able to have. It just happens kind of unexpectedly. In the end, it's the thought of giving them a roof over their heads. There's a lot of love. It has taught me a lot as a person about how to care for myself. Actually, when I grow up, I want to be in the medical field to help other people. I want to be either a doctor or a nurse. I want to give back to other people. Any way that I can help. In low-income neighborhoods, locally. Maybe a fund for Christmas gifts for children. Maybe Fridays, we do dinner, and we come together and we become a community. And then, after all that, we can make the project go bigger and do worldwide things. I don't know, maybe people in villages that don't have much and try to give them water and food and school supplies. It's going to be a long time until we get to that, but I know it's possible to accomplish that.
>
> —Sianni, 14, Richboro, Pennsylvania, US

Most parents do not involve themselves in school issues. If they speak out, they fear there may be consequences for their child. If the parent or student has a problem with a teacher, it's not worth fighting because there will be a different teacher for the next school year. And it's rarely clear whether the cause of the problem is actually related to the teacher and not to other events in the student's life. Parents try to be supportive and helpful, but they're often reluctant to initiate a battle.

If a situation is intolerable, the parent can decide to move their offspring to another school, perhaps a private school, a religious school, a military school, or a boarding school, or they may decide that homeschooling is best. Flight is often preferable to fighting.

School Principals

A principal can make a big difference in the life of a student. "Next to teachers, principals are the most important factor in improving student achievement. By one estimate, about 25 percent of a student's academic gain can be attributed to an effective chief administrator."[3] In the US, "public K–12 school principals spent an average of 58.3 hours per week on all school-related activities." On average, more than half of that time is spent solving problems and working out short-term plans with teachers, students, and parents.[4]

Ideally, a principal provides a stabilizing influence, but "nearly 30 percent of principals who lead troubled schools quit every year. By Year 3, more than half of all principals leave their jobs."[5] The demographics of US school principals have changed. Females now slightly outnumber males.[6] Racial diversity is taking longer, but progress has been steady.[7] Students see themselves in school leaders.

Teachers

Teachers are professionals who know more about how students learn, succeed, fail, get distracted, forget, remember, and behave than any other adults, but there is too much material and not enough student interest in learning or remembering the curriculum. Teachers are caught in a difficult reality. Much of their time is spent planning, meeting, dealing with paperwork, preparing and grading tests, and doing other things that school requires but feels a step or two away from helping students learn.

Attempts at transformative change are usually futile. And yet, few careers offer the joy and the sense of personal and professional accomplishment that teaching provides.

Teaching Workforce Worldwide, seventy-plus million people work as schoolteachers. If the world's teachers gathered in one country, its population would be larger than France, the world's twentieth most populous country.[8] By 2030, UNESCO estimates a need of forty-four million more teachers worldwide.[9] Given the growth of Africa's population, and Asia's large numbers, we will probably need more than one hundred million teachers on Earth by 2050.

For a very long time, men were in charge and women did their bidding—usually with low salaries. This has begun to change, but in most places, most schoolteachers are female. In 2020, 87 percent of primary school teachers in Europe and Northern America were female, and 78 percent were in Latin America and the Caribbean. In Asia, the numbers average about 70 percent. In secondary school, about 60 percent of teachers in these areas were female.[10] To be fair, in sub-Saharan Africa—where more than a third of today's children are being born—47 percent of primary teachers are female, as are 32 percent of secondary teachers. The distinction is significant: Africa is moving away from the US and UK gender model adopted by much of the world.

Appeal Rosa Nabulonde teaches in Kawempe High School in Kampala, Uganda.

> My mother was a teacher. She used to teach primary. I used to go with her to school and watch her teach. She taught for thirty-eight years, and [even after retiring] she has never really stopped teaching! I want to be like my mother. All of our neighbors were teachers, so I used to see teachers every day, teaching and interacting with students. I also admired an old man who used to teach history. When I teach, I have ideas in my head. And there's a bunch of students who want to go play or do something else. The first thing you have to do—identify each student according to their ability. You get to know that this one is quicker and this one needs extra time. There might be a student who hasn't understood. When you know something, and a student knows a different thing, you have to give them time to express their views. The student brings their own research, so you share. Every kid, in every country, thinks they know better than the teacher. Every kid can be naughty. Every kid thinks their point is always correct, that they are smarter than the teacher. Oh . . . I do love teaching!

Teaching can be a very appealing profession, a long-term commitment to make the world a better place one child at a time. While acknowledging the low salaries, stress, lack of respect, and other tiresome issues, spending days in a classroom with students and helping them learn and find their way ranks teaching among the world's most satisfying work—if the conditions are right. Unfortunately, too often, teachers are not afforded the respect they require to do their jobs. It is a system in need of repair, but most teachers lack the available time to deal with the big picture. Unions may be helpful, but often their concerns go beyond the local school or district and they attempt to hold ground or manage larger issues.

Power

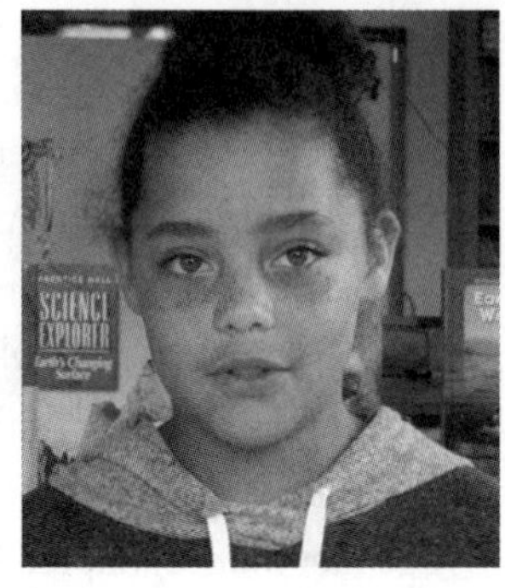

I want to be a teacher. When I was younger, I wanted to be a veterinarian, but I'm not so good with blood, so I don't think I could do surgery or anything. I want to be a teacher because I was right in the middle of the teacher's strike a month ago, and that just made me want to be a teacher even more. I really love kids. When I was in sixth grade, West Virginia didn't really spend that much money on education, and I guess the teachers, they didn't feel like they got paid enough, so they all got together and there was this big strike. Since we didn't have school, I stayed with a friend whose mom was really close with a lot of teachers. We went to the capitol every day of the strike. We met up with the teachers. We were socializing—me, my sister, a couple of other kids. When West Virginia went on strike, it caused people in other states to go on strike. I actually liked it. I liked how the teachers took a stand and actually caused other people to stand up, too. They fought for better wages. They fought for better health benefits, like insurance. They also fought for better things, like some schools in West Virginia, they didn't have iPads or laptops. It was pretty hard to learn. They were taking a stand so other kids would have a chance to learn.

—Kaia, 12, South Charleston, West Virginia, US

Teachers on strike! Kaia is clearly benefiting from lessons about taking a stand and fighting for a better life, but teachers should never be put into this position. Instead, the system should be respectful of their professional role. When the system is unresponsive, is it wise for teachers to coordinate their efforts and brandish power to bring about meaningful change?

Nathan McAlister teaches history at Seaman High School in Kansas in the US. In fact, he was Kansas's Outstanding Teacher of the Year, well-regarded by his peers. He works on the front lines and sees the need for change every day, and says, "Instead of trying to cover every single thing, how do we give . . . students skills with which they can . . . understand how . . . topics are interconnected? This *Trivial Pursuit* model of [social studies and] history just doesn't work. Maybe if we're getting ready for *Jeopardy!*, great, but we're getting ready for life, and we need the skills necessary to navigate, and to vote!"[11]

Quality, Impact, and Effectiveness As in any profession, there is great variability in the teaching workforce. Some teachers are naturally talented, fully prepared, and focused on the success of every child or teenager in their classroom, and their work is consistently excellent over decades of instruction. Some are less talented, less likely to prepare, and more focused on their own lives than the lives of the students in their classroom. And there's everything in between.

In the beginning, kindergarteners and first graders learn so much from their teachers, not only about basic skills like reading and arithmetic, but also about how to get along and how the world works. There's lots of affection between teachers and their students, lots of trust, lots of room for imagination and discussion (and naps!). Apart from an occasional (and inevitable) upset and crying fit, students and teachers are happy most of the time. Learning is fun, rich, and abundant.

Later in primary school, some problems emerge, but may not be a big deal. Students begin to express disinterest in certain topics, then certain subjects, and begin to find better things to do and other things to learn. It's not that they don't want to learn . . . they just don't want to learn what's in front of them. It's a bit mind-numbing—learning something that doesn't hold much interest—but in the years before adolescence, children tend to comply.

However, adults are telling them what to do. Students are not learning to think and act for themselves. To please their adults, students comply. Teachers watch as initiative, creativity, and curiosity melt away. Students want to concentrate on interesting, relevant, useful topics and skills. At a time when their brains and bodies are orienting toward independence and self-actualization, their freedom in school is restricted. If they misbehave, they are threatened with disciplinary action. The result: lots of unhappy students, unhappy parents, unhappy teachers. For many middle school students, it's a mess; schools blame raging hormones, but that's a misdiagnosis. Aggressive government-mandated curriculum conflicts with what these emerging teenagers want and need to learn. School's structure conflicts with their developmental needs.

For much of secondary school, teachers do their best in a system rooted in the belief that every student equally benefits from the mandatory curriculum. It's a lousy design because students are not allowed to pursue their own interests and teachers are not free to guide them to more relevant or useful work. And again, some teachers are better suited to the job than others.

Project-based learning (PBL) can cleverly mask the core problems. Students and teachers follow a curriculum, but PBL provides a gentle workaround. Teachers hand students some responsibility for learning. Students develop and implement projects of their own choosing. It's a step in the right direction, but students who try to make more decisions about their own learning often find themselves within a system not designed for that purpose.

Teachers, principals, and school districts frequently experiment with new approaches. Although some and perhaps many have merit, most in-system solutions are difficult to scale and sustain within the Old School philosophy.

Respect Given a chronic shortage of fifteen-plus million teachers in sub-Saharan Africa, and more around the world, the obvious solution is to spend more money, and perhaps address some of the working conditions.[12] Unfortunately, this is insufficient motivation for a difficult job that requires great dedication. In Thailand, for example, "Teaching is not an interesting job like doctors or engineer, so a mindset shift is the solution."[13] Still, more money would help.

In the US, public school teachers spend their own money to make their classroom an inviting place to learn. Many US teachers now work second jobs because their salary is insufficient to fund a decent place to live, food, clothing, and transportation. They work long hours to teach a curriculum many know to be excessive, largely irrelevant, and dull, but they teach what they are told to teach. Teachers are professionals, but they are not allowed to make the big decisions about teaching or learning.

As explained by former teacher Charles Fournier in his popular podcast series, *Those Who Can't Teach Anymore*, reasons for ending a teaching career include low pay, insufficient support, long hours, overcommitment, inadequate resources, mental health issues, and, in lower-income districts, insufficient funding. Violence, poverty, crime, family challenges, and drug abuse are among the toxins that make their way into schools and impact teachers.

When the pandemic hit in the US, teachers were required to convert in-person teaching to virtual lessons for students via videoconferences. No matter that students lived with other people, and quiet places to participate in group conversations were hard to find. No matter that students found it difficult to focus with sixteen or twenty-five other tiny faces on the screen. No matter the problems with technology, attention, distraction, boredom, or suitable material for this type of learning.

Teachers learned a lesson. Without in-person, one-on-one interaction with students, the new learning model was a nonstarter. Teacher and student needed to be in the same physical space. Human presence mattered.

Just before Norman, who started this chapter, died at age ninety-seven, he wrote a thank you essay to Mr. Solomon and Mrs. Cozzens. His respect for them, and what they did for him, stayed with him all his life. (Norman's son, Howard, is happy to deliver the heavenly message.) Were those teachers the rule, or were they the exception? Statistics cannot answer that question, but perhaps you can ask yourself, given the wide range of people you know in your own life, did a teacher change a life? And given what we now know, have the odds of that happening improved? And might the New School approach increase the probability to any meaningful extent?

Student Engagement "We guide. Your work is only to guide this student, depending on what he or she wants. We are not supposed to be a dictator," explains biology teacher Abdullah Turinawe, also in Kawempe High School, Kampala, Uganda.[14]

Student engagement requires a teacher's keen understanding of, and deep experience in, human development, relationships, and cognition. The teacher provides expertise and guidance rooted in scholarship and academic excellence, careful and effective research, and many practical skills and benefits. Teachers mentor and guide. Students improve project planning, relationship building, project management, flexibility, resourcefulness, mitigation of obstacles, resilience, work-arounds, reshaping, navigation of shady information, managing frustration, dealing with changes in direction, and insufficient context. A teacher's toolkit is huge, and teachers willingly pass on everything they know to their students.

Teachers help students exploit New School's flexibility. A project begun in one Learning Category can be pursued in others. Ideas are connected and frequently lead to more ideas.

Learning Categories and Fundamentals Within each Learning Category, the first step is to motivate student engagement with a Fundamental. In this example, students in every grade face the same question in Our Countries & Cultures: "What is a country?"

Typically, a Fundamental lesson takes about twenty minutes—about ten minutes to present key ideas and another ten minutes for discussion leading to Personal Education projects. The teacher decides whether to use maps, lists, information about the country where the school is located, whatever makes sense based on grade level, student interest, and power to ignite each student's imagination.

To begin with, a teacher might consider facts and nuances—there are about two hundred countries in the world, but they are difficult to count. The oldest country in the world is probably Algeria, and the newest is South Sudan (look on the map—they're not far from each another). Another approach, perhaps for older students: Many of today's countries were part of much larger empires, so today's borders do not make sense. People from one culture may live in several countries, and people from one country may come from many different cultures.

After about ten minutes, student questions begin to percolate. As the teacher finishes the Fundamentals presentation, students are encouraged to share ideas, ask questions, offer examples, look at maps and timelines, be curious, wonder. This is precisely what the teacher wants—the actual information is secondary. It doesn't matter how much each student remembers. What matters is their desire to explore.

During those first critical minutes, the teacher is constantly aware of attentiveness and saliency. After the Fundamental lesson, the teacher immediately goes to the students who don't seem to get it, don't seem to care, seem confused or unmotivated. All the students understand what's happening. One-on-one and in small groups, students work together to discuss possible Personal Education projects, vetting their own ideas, offering to partner or work in small groups, debate what is and is not worth pursuing. They do this to refine their own projects, to get them started, and to make sure the teacher can spend as much time as possible with the students who require direct, sustained attention.

By the end of this first hour, every student is engaged and working on their Personal Education project. And everyone knows there will be ample time in the afternoon to work on their projects, with their own or another teacher available to help. Afternoon meetings are not long because they are intended for guidance, feedback, and access to resources, not dissemination. Students also organize time to help one another. They reach out to members of the local and online community for help and to collaborate. Students know how to reserve time on teachers' schedules.

Students are confident that the teacher knows them as individuals and has their interests in mind. They also know how to post their project-in-development, objectives, deliverables, and anticipated completion dates in Global Brain. When they need help, other students are the first place they look for assistance. Teachers are always available if and when they are needed—and some students will require more time with teachers than others. This, too, maximizes teacher time for every student.

In short, teachers are the key to personalizing Personal Education.

Learning Categories and Personal Education Along with several other students, Abraham is especially interested in the history of his own country, India. They are familiar with the earlier history, a time when what became India was "a powerhouse, called The Golden Bird because we were so rich in agriculture," as Abraham (below) explained. They know parts of their history thanks to the epics—the *Mahabharata*, for example—but recording their complicated regional history was not common practice.

> We were economically great. The British came about 250 years ago. They conquered us. . . . They took advantage of how we were always divided and always at war . . . we were divided into many kingdoms. They hit us right where we were weak. They took advantage of one kingdom, and made that kingdom attack another kingdom, and that whole chain spread. They took over the royal castles. They got to a safer and higher position. That was the work of the East India Company: divide and rule, basically.
>
> —Abraham, 12, Gurugram, Haryana, India

Abraham struggles to understand their strategy. "I still think there were problems that they could have rectified. They should have been kinder to us. . . . They put us under slavery instead of actually having fair trade with us. Instead of being equal to us, they let their greed take over."

Clearly, learning is personal, but interaction with a clear-headed adult is needed. As Abraham and several other students struggle with the idea of a kind conquest and their resentment about being enslaved, with the help of both parents and teachers, and students with some contrary opinions, the relational aspect of learning takes shape.

"But in the end, they did unite us [as one country]. They introduced a lot of technology to us. And I don't think we'd be here without the conquering that they did."

Abraham and his friends are not the only formerly colonized people who understand both the negatives and positives of British control. By connecting with students in Uganda, sometimes called "the Pearl of Africa," they find similar responses to the benefits of British control, including, for example, clean water. In the future, this may ignite a joint Personal Education project by students in both countries, looking at the British Empire from a modern, local perspective, again demonstrating that learning is active.

Meanwhile, what are other students doing? Several second-grade students are asking their parents and grandparents what country their whole family is from. They're finding those places on a map, looking at photographs. Several sixth-grade students are in the library finding historical maps of Brazil, Argentina, Paraguay, and Chile to figure out how war changed those countries' borders—which transformed their size and shape. Mostly, the librarian is getting the kids to focus on the story that caused those maps to change.

In the new paradigm, on any given subject, teachers will always know less than their students. Since the teacher's job is student engagement, not information dissemination, the core skills are related to paying attention, listening, clear thinking, project definition, project management, resource access, resource management, critical and creative thinking, building relationships, dealing with errors, recuperating from failure, and helping partners resolve differences. Not every question requires an answer. Not every project includes a clearly defined endpoint. Sometimes, the teacher's most valuable contribution is to ask students when they feel they have learned enough.

Student Management Angie Mikula was an art teacher in a K–8 school in Sergeantsville, New Jersey, US. Her large classroom was organized by workstation (Drawing, Painting, Collage, more). Beginning in first grade, as Angie's students entered the art room, each one selected their workstation. Each student placed their personal marker on a planning board, then went to that workstation. The board allowed each student to choose among available seats (Relaxation Station was full, but Fiber and Print/Stamp offered open space). This eliminated disruptive arguments, removing Angie from the mediator role. Angie would remind students to keep every workstation clean, but rarely inspected or cleaned. Shifting responsibility from teacher to students—remember, these children are six years old—Angie spent her time with individual students and their projects.

Day In and Day Out There is no excuse for teaching to be stress filled and emotionally exhausting. It can no longer require a fifty-plus hour work week. In New School, any task that draws a teacher away from the engagement of individual students is secondary—minimization through administrative reshuffling, technology solutions, reshaping the work so students can self-manage or help others is a good idea. For example, students enter details, software prepares progress reports. If two dozen teachers are presenting a Fundamental about Bukhara, the Silk Roads, and Uzbekistan, it's helpful if they know what one another are doing, work together, and share—it's senseless for each teacher to prepare the same material. Forget about test prep, testing, proctoring, and grading tests—students do not learn the same things, so this idea mostly disappears.

A new school day begins. Students are ready with their questions, which do not include "Can I have one more day to finish my report?" Instead, they ask, "What's the best way to start on . . ." or "Do you know someone who can help me with . . ." Forget "The dog ate my homework." (Dogs have better things to do with their time.)

Not Everything Works Out as Planned Hitting the target on the first try is darned lucky. With teaching, it's always a game of where to go next and how to correct course and get back on track, figuring out what kinds of supports and challenges are appropriate for the specific student and the specific situation. Although less obvious in a New School setting, much of the teacher's job is calibrating each student's engagement with each specific goal and activity. What's more obvious is allowing space for errors and corrections, dealing with the emotional response, then finding a way forward.

Some mistakes are just mistakes. Some flops are just flops. Learn what you can, fix them, or just move on.

Teachers are trained to identify, and help, a student who is prone to errors, doesn't pay attention, plans poorly, does sloppy work. They can also identify the ones who fail quickly by intention.

Other School Specialists

The school nurse makes sure the condition of a student's body is not an impediment to learning. The job of a school psychologist is to do the same thing for each student's mind. Both know a lot about the health of children and teenagers. As it happens, so does the physical education teacher, and if New School takes shape as we suggest, so do the teachers responsible for at least three Learning Categories: Your Body, Your Mind, and Movement. They work together to support every student's Personalized Education interests.

Guidance counselors perform some similar roles—particularly related to emotional well-being—but their world also includes Your Life, and Our Future(s), and sometimes, Our Country & Cultures. Guidance counselors already work one-on-one with students, but the connection to Personal Education in a formal structure would be new.

Librarians have always been associated with Personal Education—helping a student who is interested in caterpillars find books about caterpillars. In its most basic form, that's what Personal Education is all about. Another good thing about librarians: They know the resources available in the school building, in other schools, in the district, and from other sources. If a student needs video footage of Italy in the 1920s, the librarian will probably know where to find it. The job of a librarian is to provide every available resource for learning in response to every student's need. In public schools, there may be one or two people working in a school library, but often there is no school library at all (something adults can fix if they make libraries a priority).

Other school specialists include people who work in logistics, facilities, food services, and special education. Their knowledge and experience is useful to students, too, but Old School is not organized with every available resource in mind. New School makes use of everything in school, near school, at home, in the community, and more.

Should Adults Decide What Children and Teenagers Learn? Times have changed, but deep down, many adults continue to subscribe to a very old English saying, "*A mayde schuld be seen, but not herd.*"[15] That is, roughly, girls or children, should be seen but not heard. In the twenty-first century, not many kids think this way because they are human beings, not wallpaper. Their ideas may not be completely reasonable or fully formed, but that doesn't mean adults should dismiss them. Students practice active listening in school, but adults sometimes forget how to do that.

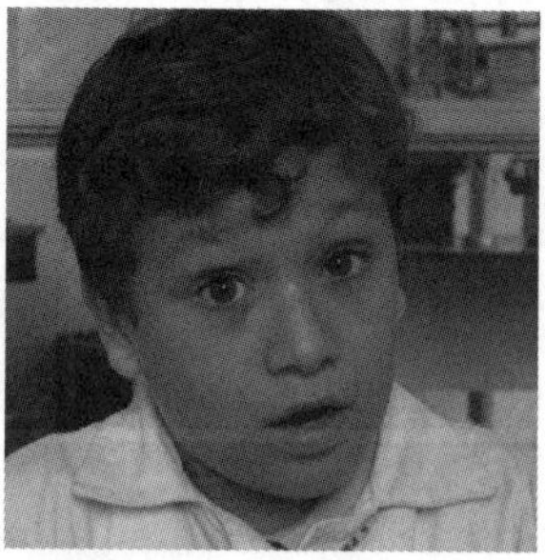

> [We could design a robot that's similar to a person.] It's possible. It's possible! But it's difficult!! There is a big difference between a human and a robot. We could develop something similar, but two will not be identical. Human beings think differently. But robots can save lives.
>
> —Lucas, 10, Montevideo, Uruguay

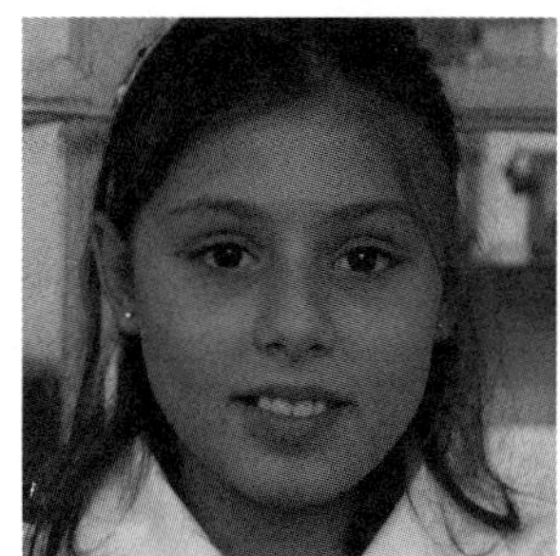

> When I grow up, I would like to be an inventor. One of my dreams is to fly. I would like something that you could put into your hands and fly away. Above the clouds. Something like a motorbike and a skate, but the skate has an engine, and the skateboard can fly.
>
> —Guillermina, 8, Montevideo, Uruguay

Kids are interested in lots of different things. When a student decides to learn about the connection between apartheid and Jim Crow, or the sexual behavior of bonobos, do they require anybody's permission?

Who is responsible for keeping parents informed? Parents are legally responsible for the actions of their minor children and teenagers, so parents would, as a rule, face no barriers with regard to their access to their children and teenagers' schoolwork. If students use Global Brain for research, notes, reports, and finished projects, their parents may freely review their work.

In a free society, it is difficult to prohibit learning. If a student wants to learn about the sex lives of bonobos, that's what he, she, or they do. The role of the adult is to channel that inquisitive energy. Acknowledge that kids do become interested in the sex lives of animals, and perhaps promote the fact that bonobos share 99 percent of their DNA with humans.

"Partnership with Families" is a claim many schools make. In New School, that claim becomes meaningful through an ongoing dialogue between student, teacher, and parent about what is being learned, why and how it is being learned, obvious and less obvious concerns, personal relevance of the learning experience to the student, and more. Those conversations are unusual in Old School, but everyone benefits if they are front and center in New School.

Trust A trusting relationship between each student and a teacher is the foundation of learning.

Based on contemporary measurement of educational activity, it would be reasonable to assume relationships have nothing to do with school or student success. Survey data tells school and community leaders about the importance of belonging and supportive relationships in the school environment, but Old School just goes on. Widespread change is so difficult, there is little confidence things will ever change.

Trust is not a given. It's easily damaged, difficult to repair. When a teacher insists a student do something that the student doesn't want to do, trust hangs in the balance.

Trust cannot be constructed or mandated from the top down—the education system is too big, and the top is too distant from individual students' lives. Instead, trust is cultivated by individual teachers, one student (and parent) at a time. Teachers build trust by engaging with each student on that student's terms. Trust becomes the license for a teacher to guide each student in new directions, away from unproductive projects and bad behaviors. Students share their feelings of trust (or distrust). As relationships grow, trust becomes stronger.

For meaningful learning to take place, the teacher trusts each student to take responsibility for learning, and to be honest. Each student trusts the teacher to do everything possible to help listen with an open mind and heart, open the door to additional resources, and not buy into the student's bs.

Parents, communities, and government trust the teachers they've hired and trained to function as autonomous, expert professionals. Each student is aware that somebody is actually paying attention.

> Myself, I want to be a software engineer, but my parents want me to be a doctor. I guess I will win because I really believe in myself. I want to take the option myself, not by my parents' choices.
>
> —Rahil, 13, Gurugram, Haryana, India

Robin Gregory, a senior researcher in decision sciences in British Columbia, Canada, emphasizes the importance of a *decision mentor*—"a parent or teacher or coach, elder sibling, aunt or uncle, counsellor or neighbor who can be there to help support a 10–25 year old in learning who they are (their values, what matters to them), gaining access to accurate information (e.g., concerning consequences), and framing the decision in ways that incorporate curiosity, compassion, and flexibility in light of what is learned over time."[16]

A student is not an unsolved puzzle or a powder keg about to explode. A properly selected, well-trained, unencumbered teacher is able to cultivate potential and help overcome negative feelings—if not for every student, then for most of them. When there's conflict, neither student nor teacher (nor parent) has reason to call trust into question. There should be no doubt that the parties are listening to one another, being taken seriously, and will find a reasonable solution. Without wall-to-wall scheduling, every teacher has time to work with every one of their students. This is a massive cultural shift. We all have a lot to learn.

Change Change does not happen by magic. It requires planning, leadership, management, cooperation, collaboration, incentives, evaluation, in-course improvements, and more.

The locus of change is adults, and that comes with certain responsibilities—including paying close attention to what children and teenagers are learning, and why.

Everything begins with people in high places. They learn to see Old School clearly, and endorse New School and Not School, or their kin. Structural changes are required. Facilities, budgets, compensation plans, union contracts, community expectations, and state and national laws and practices are aligned with new ways of thinking and doing.

Parents will speak out. The media will pay attention. Some teachers will embrace a new way of working, but some will resist (for all sorts of reasons). Some students will realize just how much responsibility falls on their shoulders, and they may resist, too. The system's inability to hide behind state frameworks, curriculum, testing, and test scores will generate insecurity for governance, administrators, and teachers as students assert their right to learn on their own terms.

How does any of this actually happen in the real world? It begins by bringing students, parents, teachers, principals, superintendents, governance, foundations, and the media together with a profound commitment to figure out how to make it happen. Bear in mind that change is iterative, so nothing happens in just one meeting or one series of meetings. Instead, change takes shape through experimentation, coordinated efforts, discontinuities, and a persistent drumbeat over a reasonable period of time, in lots of places, with clear objectives related to R&D, pilot testing, software development, weekend tryouts, week-long and month-long tryouts, the first and second and third rounds of full-years in multiple schools, coordinated efforts, sharing of best practices, constant reassessment, and seemingly endless attention to cultural change. And, change requires different sets of metrics because, for example, it may be engagement or support from teachers that benefits from measurement to unearth paths for potential reshaping or improvement.

Retraining a million or more teachers begins with a commitment to pivot from Old School to New School at scale. Whether this decision, or this set of decisions, is made at a national, regional, state/provincial, or local level, it requires a lot of teacher and student involvement in the planning process, a clear operating plan, updated governance and support, and general agreement on new forms of assessment. Clearly, these activities involve more than just the teachers, but it is the teachers who manage the process because they are the ones who interact with students every day.

The importance of local governance cannot be overstated because, locally, they are the people who employ the superintendent and the teachers. With their engagement and support, progress becomes possible; but remember, these people are not, by and large, trained educators. And they are already putting a lot of time into their school board work, usually without compensation. And this approach involves a lot of discussion about change management, which tends to result in political dustups bound to generate stress for many of these people. One way to solve this problem is to concentrate on state and provincial governance, and to mandate change.

Perhaps a better way is to involve not only the school board members, but the students, parents, teachers, and higher-level governance so that (a) many people understand the current situation, (b) the situation and its alternatives are discussed with the benefit of knowledge and clear thinking, (c) hypotheses and experimentation begin, and (d) results are shared and discussed, and used as raw material for further exploration.

And, as with any large-scale (think: corporate) exercise in significant cultural change, there will be "me issues"—resistance, a sense of displacement, sadness, disbelief, fear, astonishment, aggression, denial. Some teachers will threaten, or at least, consider, leaving the profession. Some teachers will resist and organize greater resistance by joining with other unhappy teachers, attempting to explain why the new concepts will never work and will harm students over time. Most adults will stay because no other job offers so much joy and fulfillment and, usually, convenience (near home, summers off, etc.). Although schools are unique, there is a great deal of change management knowledge and training in the marketplace.

Preparing Teachers for Success From Fedrick C. Ingram, secretary-treasurer, AFT (American Federation of Teachers): "Teachers understand what responsibility is. We're in the 21st century. Maybe it's time for us to relook, reimagine, rethink, refocus. But we simply won't do it by simply hoisting more responsibility on teachers without thinking about the professionalism and the respect that we deserve."[17]

Although parents and governance may be involved, it's the students and teachers who do the hard work. Change in the workplace is not a new idea, but it is a new idea in school. And it is more complicated because change affects not only teachers and other adults, but also children, teenagers, and parents whose lifetime success may rely on the effectiveness of this transformation. Training runs wide and deep. It includes many conversations with students, parents, governance, and teachers in other schools and districts, all over the world. There are in-person and online support groups.

For teachers accustomed to teaching students about a growth mindset, it may feel strange to look in the mirror and see the work of noted American psychologist Carol Dweck affecting their own lives and careers. Staying with a system of education that offers frustration and lackluster results has resulted in a *fixed mindset* (Dweck's term) of global proportions. Envisioning a future that embraces a more productive and satisfying role for each teacher leads to a growth mindset for both students and teachers. A teacher developing a growth mindset becomes a role model. As Dweck explains, "The passion for stretching yourself and sticking to it, even (or especially) when it's not going well, is the hallmark of the growth mindset. This is the mindset that allows people to thrive during some of the most challenging times in their lives."[18]

Worldwide, colleges and universities prepare undergraduate students to become new teachers with courses that may include, for example, "Diagnosis and Assessment in Reading and Literacy," "Educational Technology for Teaching and Learning," and "Managing Engaging Learning Experiences." New School will require such training to be updated with students, not school, at the center of the solar system. With that Copernican shift, students begin to see teachers as real people, not the embodiment of fixed curriculum. In New School, students and teachers have more to talk about. A teacher who volunteers at a local animal shelter may be planning a trip to Japan to study Buddhism, spends winter mornings snowshoeing, and bakes French pastries (currently, mille-feuille) often with terrible results (and keeps trying).

Quickly, this becomes an exercise in teachers training teachers at a never-before-seen scale. There is an immediate need for information, access, and tools for collaboration—universal internet service, devices, and something like Global Brain. Teachers will not have time to design such as system. Instead, it is more likely to be developed and operated in Not School, where there is greater freedom and access to resources. As with the internet, students will learn how to use it in Not School, but put it to use for all sorts of learning activities in school and out.

Teaching becomes a much more satisfying profession. Teachers serve as a conduit to a world of relationships, opportunities to learn, exploration and discovery, and people who share interests. In New School, teachers are exposed to many ideas and requests for resources from students, so they communicate with other teachers in other countries almost daily. Teachers connect with scientific, medical, museum, archaeological, anthropological, arts, theater, and music professionals. Teachers are trained to pay attention and encourage students to learn from one another. This is not something students easily do on their own.

To-Do List for Adults

Before we even consider making a list, there are two items that require immediate global attention.

Poverty hits children and teenagers very hard and makes their education especially challenging. Poverty is often multidimensional—associated with abbreviated schooling, inconsistent attendance, inadequate nutrition, questionable drinking water and food supply, unreliable electricity, lack of family assets, housing issues, and more.[19] Eradication, or near-eradication, of poverty is not an impossible dream. Generally, the percentage of people living in poverty in many parts of the world is about half what it was in the second half of the twentieth century.[20] Adults possess ample evidence of what works to substantially reduce poverty. According to the Borgen Project, the list includes access to basic social services, removal of barriers to resources, rapid and sustained economic programs, social protection systems for health and safety, and, of course, access to technology and innovation.[21]

Reliable internet access is now essential for every primary and secondary student. A third of the world's students cannot reliably access the internet. Service requires (a) reliable electricity, (b) reliable hardware and software, and (c) reliable connections. In some places, the combination remains a struggle. Often, the problem is not technology—it is political will. Provision, maintenance, repair, and replacement are practical and logistical problems to solve. No excuses! Adults, please work together and get this done! A student growing up without connectivity places that student at a significant disadvantage in the workplace, and as a global citizen. A region or a nation in which many students, and many other people, cannot access the internet assures economic strife and political unrest (which is dangerous for the whole world).

That said, here's the list of items that adults need to address, preferably immediately, certainly before 2030.

1. *Respect every child and teenager.* Engage and appreciate young people on their own terms. Adolescent development allows them to be especially passionate and vital—they are well suited to change the world. Once activated, and comfortable with their role, subsequent increases in experience and wisdom invigorate the next generation. Adult interaction with teenagers is vital to their self-confidence and power—and teaches adults a lot about how to live their own lives.

> We now know that adolescence is a similarly remarkable period of brain reorganization and plasticity. This discovery is enormously important, with far-reaching implications for how we parent, educate, and treat young people. If the brain is especially sensitive to experience during adolescence, we must be exceptionally thoughtful and careful about the experiences we give people as they develop from childhood into adulthood.[22]
>
> —Lawrence Steinberg, *Age of Opportunity*

> I think the world has to stop eating meat. We have a lot of (what is the word in English?) . . . deforestation! The Amazonia is at risk. They have a lot of wildfires. A lot of animals are dying. It is something that we have to preserve. It's our home! We have to preserve it. No pollution! We use a lot of plastic that causes a lot of ocean deaths. The future affects us!!
>
> —Brenda, 17, Rio de Janeiro, Brazil

2. *Remove every significant obstacle to learning for every child and teenager.* Every student needs a safe place to live and study, nourishing food to eat, and clean water to drink. They require reliable transportation to and from school, medical care, and places to exercise. Growing bodies require lots of sleep. Often, these local issues require collaborative assistance—without harming the local culture—from people who may not live nearby. This is not easy, but adults can figure it out.

3. *Build, fund, and support a twenty-first-century framework and practical operation for learning.* Please stop replicating your own twentieth-century education on behalf of your children and teenagers. Stop insisting that every student

learn the same things in the same way. Stop incessant testing. Stop homework. Stop pretending that standards are essential for modern public schooling. Instead, involve the entire community—especially the students and the teachers—in a collaborative global framework. New School provides such a model. Use it! Encourage others to use it, too!

4. *Stop telling teachers what to do.* Trust teachers to do their jobs as education professionals. Hire the best available teachers, pay a fair wage, make sure working conditions are safe and appealing. Support teachers and students with trust and the resources they need to succeed. Do not second-guess. Get in there and help students by expanding available resources and sharing your experience—without a political or social agenda. Eliminate government frameworks, mandatory curriculum, and standards-based testing because their time has passed.

5. *Guide young people toward ideas that matter to them.* Although New School students are responsible for their own learning, they are influenced by adults. Get the community involved!

Maybe start in New York City—How is it possible that one in four kids there are poor? Who are these children? Do they live in troubled neighborhoods? Why are their neighborhoods troubled? Why are their families suffering? Is this true in other cities in the US? How do we get lots of students, lots of teachers, lots of schools to talk about this, do the research, get media attention? Is this happening everywhere in the world?

Most people can't name many African countries or cities and can't distinguish between Nairobi and Namibia. Adults can change this—they can promote the idea of learning about Africa, build relationships, produce learning materials, write and perform songs, and set up conversations with real kids and real grown-ups in Kenya (where Nairobi is a city) and Windhoek (the biggest city in the country of Namibia).

Figure out how your community can learn about the local impact of climate change, why it is happening, what is being done today to mitigate the problem, and what needs to be done in the future. Get it started, get other communities on board, build a movement. What are we waiting for?

6. *Focus on resources and collaboration.* Left to their own devices, adults will continue to ignore problems or chase short-term solutions. We need adults to do a lot more than that.

Students require safe and secure outdoor spaces to run, walk, play, and exercise from early morning through the evening, with restrooms, with proper lighting and security, and available food and water. They need small, medium, and large places to gather, and probably, fewer traditional classrooms. They want maker labs, with people to teach them to use equipment and materials safely and responsibly. Some want to grow their own food, tend to animals (if practical), and cook for themselves—with appropriate instruction. They can access an in-school medical facility, with staff, because learning about the human body is essential for everyone, and because, from time to time, everybody needs care. (First aid is a core skill for every student, teacher, and staff member.) They benefit from more and better public and school libraries. More community interaction—local and global—is necessary, too. There are enough adults in every community to check this item off the list—and have fun doing it.

7. *Engage government and philanthropy.* Although they operate in very different ways, government and foundations spend a great deal of money on primary and secondary education. Although there are many examples of impressive results on a local level, large-scale collaboration and sustainable transformation has been elusive. As a result, progress moves slowly, and many of the grant makers find themselves associated with routine projects, but little that will make a profound difference for very large numbers of students. This chronic problem is difficult to solve within the bounds of Old School, but there is considerable opportunity for advancement in both Not School and New School. Of course, neither government nor philanthropy are single entities: There are federal, provincial/state, and local governments, and there are corporate and family foundations that operate internationally, nationally, regionally, and locally.

8. *Keep the ball rolling, even if the direction is uphill.* Change is difficult. And yet, as this book has insisted, Old School offers an unreasonable solution because it disregards the wants and needs of many and perhaps most students, relies on misbegotten ideas about learning, disrespects and disengages teachers, does not produce a desirable return on investment, and fails to provide most students with the necessary training to earn a good living. Pivoting to New School requires adults—many adults—to understand that Old School is a poor solution, and to support a new solution. Models that describe change are useful here. New ideas are fragile. They are easily criticized, wounded, and destroyed. People are easily

discouraged. Take action, keep making progress, build relationships, and demonstrate what can be done so others will do even more.

If adults listen to children, pay attention to the enormous changes taking place everywhere, and commit to a coherent twenty-first-century philosophy, everyone makes progress. This is not a given. It requires adults, everywhere, to work together for the common good of their children, their children's children, and everyone on Earth.

CHAPTER 7

Progress

If you want to pursue your passion, you've got to take things into your own hands. Go out and find that information for yourself. Learning about chickens is my responsibility because I'm the one who is "that chicken person." I don't think that's the school's responsibility to do that for me. [At school,] there are other "chicken people" and it's really nice to hang out with them. There's definitely some stuff we need to teach most people, if not everyone, about the egg and meat industry . . . there are actually more chickens on Earth than there are people, and most of them are in cages. That meat is not going to be as easy or as healthy for you. I reckon everyone should know more about raising chickens.

—Annika, 14, Lismore, Australia

All over the world, every day, kids make progress on their own terms. They make use of school, Not School, and every available resource to learn what they want and need to know. They cannot rely on school because, at best, school deals with such a small portion of their evolving lives. They are in motion, growing up, changing, forging new relationships, wondering about their future. They know they're growing up in the midst of a whirlwind.

THE IMPORTANCE OF SCHOOL

Many of today's children and teenagers will be alive to see the turn of the next century. They will live more than eighty years, but they will attend school for only a fraction of their time on Earth. They require more from school than learning to read, learning to count, and learning some science and social studies. They require discipline, structure, and a means to continue learning after the years of formal schooling end. It's not so much what they learn that matters. Instead, it's their ability to learn on their own for a lifetime. They need to learn in order to make progress on their own despite formidable obstacles and misinformation, and to collaborate to solve present-day problems and build a viable future for an increasingly diverse and complicated planet.

Annika is learning about chickens. She knows it sounds silly; we laughed about it during our *Kids on Earth* interview. But she also knows it's important because she's genuinely concerned about Earth's food supply. There is a micro picture—raising some chickens in a small city in New South Wales (population: 44,334)—and a macro picture—feeding the world.[1]

> I take school as my primary source of knowledge, and books, and if I go to websites online, I take that as secondary which would build upon my knowledge at school. Of course, school doesn't teach you everything, but I'd like to think about school as my primary source of knowledge.
>
> —JD (Jongwon), 14, Kobe, Japan

GLOBAL PROGRESS

As evidenced by hundreds of *Kids on Earth* interviews, the current batch of children and teenagers are the first generation of truly global citizens. They regularly see and hear stories from all over the world, listen to and watch music from many countries and cultures, make friends with peers who live far away, plan to study abroad and travel, and live in places their parents wouldn't have given a second thought. In all but a few regions, they can talk to one another—and use emerging technology to clear language hurdles.

The word *foreign* is becoming objectionable because no place is "the other." Attitudes are changing, have changed. Unfair treatment based on the color of a person's skin is no longer acceptable public behavior. Girls must be afforded the same opportunities as boys. Food must be safe to eat and produced with sustainable practices. Everybody is entitled to personal safety, good health, clean water, decent work, economic stability, safe energy, peace, justice, and a long list of other emerging rights detailed in the UN's SDGs. Everybody is entitled to quality education, too. Collectively, this is now the way kids on Earth define progress.

PROGRESS REQUIRES TRUSTWORTHY INFORMATION

For decades, secondary school students in the southern US state of Mississippi were taught history curriculum that "omitted the horrors of slavery, lynching, the Ku Klux Klan and Jim Crow and largely skipped over the civil rights movement." Charles Sallis, a history professor, "had long realized that what he had been taught was wrong: Slave owners were not benevolent, Reconstruction was not a tale of Black corruption, and white supremacy was not inevitable." For four years, Dr. Sallis and sociology professor James W. Loewen worked with faculty and students on what became "a ninth-grade history textbook so vigorous, frank and unsparing in its review of the state's grim history that the Mississippi State Textbook Purchasing Board barred its use in schools almost as soon as it appeared."[2] Sallis and Loewen, and their associates, fought for the right for students to think clearly about the authentic history of a US state and its people.

Information's supply side has always been murky. In the past, we valued gatekeepers. Some remain. Gatekeepers gather information in accordance with industry standard practices, prepare their information with careful fact-checking and copyediting, and submit their work to well-trained and experienced superiors for comment and approval. Changes are made, facts are rechecked, and the material is released. The multistep process, the interaction of professionals who held one another accountable, the public profile of television networks, textbook publishers, book publishers, magazines, and schools all suggested a unified view that the information was reasonably correct. Some or most of it probably was, but not all of it because of errors and sometimes, because of intent. Bias has always been part of media. For many years, people in New York City chose their daily and weekly newspapers based on the paper's bias (*Daily News*—conservative; *Village Voice*, exceedingly liberal). Often acknowledging their bias, each paper adhered to professional standards.

With social media, information flows from many to many—and without the steps in between. Much of it is opinion, or belief, or misguided information, not facts or traditional journalism, but there is a larger problem, a sin of omission.

Nigeria may soon overtake the US as the world's third most populated nation. That's not something most people know because there's not a lot of media coverage about Africa, certainly not in the US. It's a story that doesn't get told, so most people don't know that Nigeria, Pakistan, and Indonesia are on track to become the third-, fourth-, and fifth-largest nations by population, making the US number six if it does not aggressively liberalize its immigration policy. The populations of Tanzania, Uganda, Kenya, and Sudan will almost certainly overtake the UK, France, Germany, or South Korea by 2050. Meanwhile, Russia continues to lose ground—after World War II, it was the world's fourth-largest nation in terms of population, but by 2075, it will probably be around number fifteen on the list, much diminished, which may help to explain its aggressive stance on international relations.

It's not just a matter of mis- or disinformation. It's our Old School philosophy that teaches us to see a very narrow view of the world. If everybody must learn the same things, and there are lots and lots of things they must learn, then the future of Tanzanian and Russian demographics won't get much attention. Better that some people focus on those things, and share. And that at least a few people focused on, well, chickens.

PROGRESS REQUIRES NEW WAYS OF THINKING

Given the diversity of problems to be solved over the next twenty-five years, and the need to move forward on so many fronts, generating new ideas and bringing new ideas to life must become priorities for teachers, students, and schools. Right now, we don't have a way to do that, but we do see glimmers of hope.

Among many examples . . . "Vertical farming can use up to 99% less water to grow crops and can produce up to 20 times more crops per acre compared to traditional farming. . . . It condenses the space required for agriculture by stacking plots vertically, optimizing the units of horizontal land used. . . . Because the vertical farms are in a controlled environment, virtually no pesticides or herbicides are necessary. Most plants are also certified organic."[3] That's why Dylan Chung of Portola High School wrote about vertical farming in a *Los Angeles Times* opinion piece. It's why Mountain Vista High School in Colorado, US, has been farming inside railroad freight cars since 2017. In fact, Freight Farms is an international for-profit enterprise, and Mountain Vista High School is just one of more than six hundred outposts associated with high schools, colleges, community organizations, and commercial operators.[4]

> Well, I think it's more like I feel safe enough to go outside by myself at night and not have the need to look behind my back or think something happens to me. I just feel like I can go out, walk along the park, the street, and nothing bad will occur to me. Younger kids, too. In elementary, students taking the train by themselves in the morning to get to school. It's the mindset, the culture in Japan. In our society, we don't like to break the harmony that we live in which includes disturbing other people. It's really rooted into our culture.
>
> —Conrad, 17, Kobe, Japan

PROGRESS REQUIRES SAFETY AND SECURITY

In many places, children and teenagers are not safe, but they do the best they can under the circumstances. Climate change is becoming more disruptive. In many places, coping with difficult local weather has become part of life.

> What worries us here is giant storms, because they bring so much water. There are very hard rains, and there is the river. So water goes up to half a meter, more or less, and enters into the houses. Then, I have to wait for the water to leave, for everything to start to dry. You get a lot of snakes and spiders. Everything in your room gets destroyed. Some of the dogs [protect themselves] by living on the roofs.
>
> —Analiz, 13, Remansito, Paraguay

Conflict, irrational leadership, corruption, power plays, incompetent governance, war—these issues are interwoven with prejudice, refugee crises, climate migration, social injustice, inability to provide food and water, and much more. When information is quickly and efficiently enflamed and engorged with misinformation, as is now common in the world's media, the pace and intensity increases the likelihood of misguided action, and dangerous behavior. The need for investment, reliable infrastructure, productive employment, and social services is becoming essential—on a scale never before contemplated. The inability to provide these services in a timely, responsive manner, over the short and long run, to students and teachers and everyone else, combine with advanced weaponry and intensify potential threats. It is time that primary and secondary students learn about these aspects of twenty-first-century life—in a manner appropriate to their emotional development.

Security threats are often invisible. A technology weapon may be deployed to destroy communication or transportation, food or water supply, or trust and confidence in government or the military. In the past, attackers were easily identified—they wore recognizable uniforms, they could be seen at a distance. In the twenty-first century, weapons are used by individual agents (school shooters, for example), and technologists who can wreak havoc from the comfort of their parent's basement. Media makes them celebrities. To be critical thinkers and smart consumers of information, students must understand twenty-first-century technology. They must also be familiar with investigation, law enforcement and defense, economic unrest, social instability, and other core concepts. Some students will learn more and build careers in this growing industry.

This is a lot for children to absorb. It's scary. As frequency and complexity continue to increase, attacks will become more aggressive. The biggest impacts are likely to occur in fast-growing regions where employment and personal income are still evolving.

It turns out that systems theory, urban planning, decision sciences, and other college-level studies have a place in primary and secondary school learning. Set a high bar. Do not underestimate the capacity of children and teenagers—but do provide the necessary emotional support so we don't terrify them.

MAGICAL THINKING AND PROGRESS

Climate change is not going to take care of itself. If humans do not change the way we live, the result will be more and more extreme heat, unmanageable water conditions, severe storms, more unmanageable wildfires, destruction of local habitat, dramatic issues with food supply, and lengthy periods of discomfort and misery.

Belief that the Old School curriculum (mathematics, science, social studies, language arts) and mandatory government frameworks will change any of that is magical thinking.

> Stepping on a crack cannot, given what we know about the principles of causal relations, have any direct effect on the probability of your mother breaking her back.[5]
>
> —*Scientific American*

Electing a demonstrably unethical national leader with a criminal record, poor judgment, and irrational ethics who claims to be the only person who can solve the biggest problems is the result of magical thinking. This is a global problem.

Learning how to read in English without decoding letters, words, sentences, or paragraphs is magical thinking.

Between now and 2050, Africa's population will triple. Most people in Africa will be young. Essential systems for social services, employment, economic growth, and political stability are not in place. The media pays almost no attention. Old School ignores the situation. Unreasonable optimism can be indistinguishable from magical thinking.

According to the Organization for Economic Cooperation and Development (OECD), millennials in the US workforce tied for last on tests of mathematics and problem-solving among workforces of industrial countries analyzed. "We now have the worst-educated workforce in the industrialized world. Because our workers are among the most highly paid in the world, that makes a lot of Americans uncompetitive in the global economy. And uncompetitive against increasingly smart machines. It is a formula for a grim future."[6]

Is it possible to distinguish between magical thinking and new knowledge? Just over a century ago, Alfred Wegener's theory of continental drift—continents moving over time—was thought to be magical thinking, because "scientists held fast to the traditional theories they'd spent careers developing."[7]

Is it possible that forest bathing—immersing yourself in the forest's atmosphere—provides significant health benefits? Initial scientific research suggests reductions in a stress hormone, higher levels of cancer-killing proteins and immune cells, and regulation of blood sugar. "Forest therapy can have a positive impact on the oxygen levels in your brain," Dr. Susan Albers explains. "That's because you're surrounded by trees and vegetation that engage in photosynthesis. The result: Plants absorb carbon dioxide and release oxygen into the air."[8]

To teach that Columbus discovered America when we know that's nonsense, to celebrate this historical nonevent with a national holiday—that's what we've been doing since 1934—this does not promote progress. Christopher Columbus never stepped foot in what became the United States.

To explore continental draft or forest bathing with the rigor of competent research, well, that's how we build knowledge. Sure, a lot of ideas turn to dust. As adults, our job is to make sure that the dust doesn't define what people learn in school or in any other part of their lives.

LEARNING AND SELF-PRESERVATION

> I think it is confusing living in our world. I don't know what I should do. . . . I am spending most of my days wondering what I, what life I want to lead and how I should live. It is really hard to answer. School is helping, but I think the important part is to learn about me and my desires. To know about me, more deeply. And maybe that's what school needs to do to help. To help me.
>
> —Bo-seop, 16, Seoul, South Korea

Among students, and teachers, the intensity and pervasiveness of stress, anxiety, unhappiness, and mental health problems keeps growing, but social-emotional learning, mindfulness, resilience, and other positive interventions are still treated as curriculum supplements. Here's why. In Old School, individual freedom is restricted: Students cannot leave the classroom without permission, cannot learn what they want to learn, must pay attention to the teacher, whether the material is interesting, useful, or relevant.

In many countries, when interviewing children and teenagers, it was not unusual to hear a student say: "School feels like a prison." They were describing a day-to-day existence that limits intellectual freedom.

"A lot has happened. I grew up in the '80s. I went through a lot of struggles to figure out who I was as a person—not the messages I was receiving from society." For years, Jule lived in prison. As an adult, along with other prisoners, Jule chose to become a student. Intense academic learning provided his way out. His cell was filled with books that even the most serious students would rate as challenging. He read them all. He graduated. Now, he proudly describes himself as the first formerly incarcerated person to be hired full-time by the Ford Foundation. His job: To analyze data and develop strategies for grants to advance gender, racial, and social justice.

> Now . . . people are so passionate about self-determination, about social justice, about equity. It's really beautiful. I don't know what brought us here, but I think we're in a good space to move forward. I am so honored. While I was in prison

> and taking classes, I knew we were doing something special. I believe you need to meet people where they are and provide them with tools to learn what they are more comfortable with. For some, it may be watching a documentary. For others, it's maybe reading a book. Nonetheless, we are in a society that prides itself in being diverse, but we have only one way of teaching. I think it's really important that we understand that with diversity comes diverse ways of learning.[9]

LEARNING AND PROGRESS IN THE MODERN WORLD

COVID-19 demonstrated the inadequacy of public health systems and illuminated the likelihood of future viral outbreaks. Climate change is ravaging communities with dangerous storms, floods, extreme heat, wildfires, and threats to water and food supply. Years of inadequate attention to infrastructure are resulting in road and bridge failures and revealing other structural deficiencies. Being outdoors becomes dangerous when the Air Quality Index exceeds 150 (for some people) or 200 (for most of us).

It's not that we're doing nothing. Many people are battling issues related to climate change, but they're not winning the war. Similarly, schools are not entirely resistant to change or modernization. All over the world, teachers work long hours and develop new ideas to keep students engaged. Districts do their best to provide modern technology. States update their frameworks. It's just not enough.

Similarly, higher education continues to evolve, improve, and embrace contributions from people all over the world. It is no longer unusual to meet someone like Rana Dajani, who we met in chapter 5—a Palestinian-Jordanian microbiologist who earned her PhD at the US's University of Iowa. Modern universities thrive on their peoples' diversity and difference. This is real progress, but universities still struggle with their inability to engage half the world's population, and with connecting their academic programs with their graduates' need to earn a living.

Our institutions are doing their best, but keeping pace with modern life, and the future, is exceedingly difficult.

Fortunately, students—and adults, through tax dollars—invest in primary and secondary school education because they believe the return-on-investment will be high. And yet, students sense a diminishing need for humans in the workplace. From customer service to manufacturing, routine jobs requiring only primary and secondary education are becoming replaced by technology. Steady income from employment demands versatility and learning for a lifetime—and protecting a career from robots and other technologies that could do the job faster, cheaper, and better. It is difficult to convince Old School-skeptical students that they will be well prepared to compete effectively in a rapidly evolving marketplace. This is true in Europe and the Americas, and is a very harsh reality in much of Africa and Asia (where, you will recall, most of the world's children grow up).

> Bulgaria is a small country. There's no danger that war will break out. I love living here. I have many choices. I like dinosaurs and when I grow up, I want to be a paleontologist. Or a lawyer—I like to speak! On the news, they say that in Florida, that one child, he has a gun, and he shot some people and killed them! I was really sad because when I grow up, I want to go the United States. I think Russia has many problems with guns [too]. So, I may stay here in Stara Zagora, but I could live in many places. When it happens, I will think about that. The future will show me.
>
> —Vicky, 12, Stara Zagora, Bulgaria

Assuming Vicky continues to live in Bulgaria, paleontology might be a good choice. There are not many paleontologists in Bulgaria, but the profession is being enhanced, not destroyed, by technology. There is a strong international community of paleontologists working in museums and universities in Europe and throughout the world. She can easily connect with them digitally or in person. What about law? Maybe, maybe not. There are certainly more lawyers than paleontologists in Europe, but AI and other technologies are handling more and more routine legal work. If Vicky starts learning about paleontology in secondary school, she gains marketplace advantage and a better sense of whether this career might be one she loves. She can easily connect school and her potential future, so it makes sense to invest time (and, later, money) in a paleontology career.

Study, get good grades, do your homework, keep the teacher happy and everything will work out fine! Many parents support the Old School strategy—it worked well enough for them! Children and teenagers are wise to be skeptical.

There are holes in the safety net. Wages and housing costs are out of sync. In the US, companies avoid hiring full-time employees to shirk responsibility for health benefits. To make up the difference, teachers and other undercompensated workers develop side hustles in the gig economy or work a second job. They lack the funds to cover emergencies. Saving for rainy days and for old age may be an impossible dream.

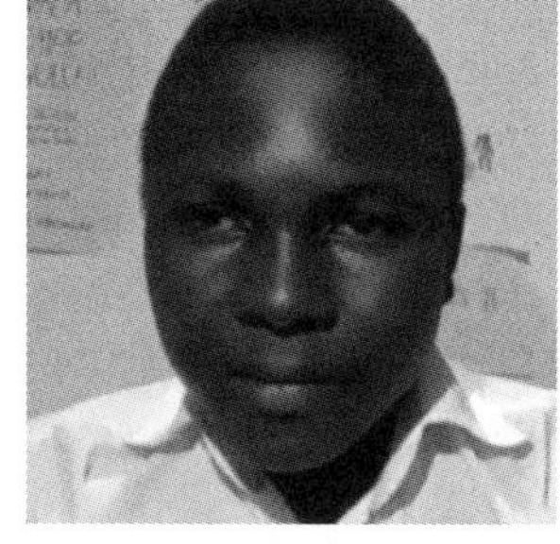

> In East Africa, there are many wars. If I become a soldier, I can help people. I am not afraid. You are protecting people with your life. If I fight, I fight for purpose. I am brave. I am not yet strong enough. I will become stronger by exercising every day. I watch YouTube videos to learn. I work with my friends. Some of them want to become engineers. I want to be a soldier for my whole career. I want to achieve a top rank. I begin at a military college, then add on.
>
> —Rhodin, 18, Kampala, Uganda

PROGRESS THROUGH STRATEGIC ACTION

> You don't make progress by standing on the sidelines, whimpering and complaining. You make progress by implementing ideas.
>
> —Shirley Chisholm, US congresswoman, 1977–1981, secretary of the Democratic House Caucus

For centuries, the region that became western New York State in the US was controlled by the Haudenosaunee (Iroquois) and Seneca nations—indigenous tribes. That changed on May 31, 1779, with this directive from General George Washington to General John Sullivan: "The immediate objects are the total destruction and devastation of their settlements and the capture of as many prisoners of every age and sex as possible. It will be essential to ruin their crops now in the ground and prevent their planting more."[10]

Eighteen years later, the US government finished "clearing" the land. The first peoples were basically gone—the region was in the hands of land speculators—and this was progress (through domination). Jeremiah Wadsworth, a sea captain who made his first fortune in the West India trade, and later became a US congressman, bought large amounts of rich agricultural land in the area. As Wadsworth's sons increased their own holdings, they benefited from the 1825 completion of the Erie Canal (connecting New York City to the Great Lakes) and the 1850s coming of the railroads (connecting the Genesee River Valley to prosperous Baltimore, Pittsburgh, Rochester, and Buffalo). As they settled the area, they needed schools and teachers for their children.

In 1867, the Wadsworth Normal and Training School was born—to train teachers. In time, the school became part of New York's new state university system but remained limited to teacher training—slowly expanding to teacher-librarians, teachers of teachers of speech and hearing and the "mentally handicapped," teachers of foreign languages, and early childhood specialists. Other than education degrees, the State University of New York College at Geneseo did not offer a four-year bachelor's degree until 1964.[11]

Slowly, the small rural college began to diversify. In 1980, a school of business was added, with programs in accounting, management, and economics. By 1983, there were degrees in computer science and biochemistry, followed by biophysics in 1993.[12] "In 2003, the college began the largest capital improvement project in the history of the SUNY system. The Integrated Science Facility [is] . . . a 105,000-square-foot $32 million building equipped with a nuclear accelerator." It opened in 2007.[13] New curriculum and new facilities attracted new students with new interests, and their version of progress.

Today, SUNY Geneseo is New York State's public honors college named "a 'best and most interesting' college by *Fiske Guide 2023* "for the quality of academics and students' social and quality-of-life ratings." There are eighteen academic departments including theater and dance, anthropology, music and musical theater, philosophy, geography and sustainability studies, political science and international relations, and more, serving fewer than four thousand undergraduate and graduate students. It is now partnered with Rochester Institute of Technology (RIT) for a joint program in sustainability.

People recognized potential opportunity, took action, and a small-town teacher's school grew into an honors college. SUNY Geneseo was able to develop the necessary relationships, muster the resources, cultivate necessary influence, and maintain its bearing. There are challenges ahead—enrollment, questions about the value of higher education, competitive institutions, and more—but they continue to make progress. Every student and every adult should know about what was done to Indigenous people, everywhere, for other peoples' progress. A chief diversity officer is now a standard role on every SUNY campus—there are sixty-four campuses, serving more than 350,000 students—and we cannot reverse the horrors of the past, but we can help everyone to think differently about the present and the future.[14]

LEARNING FOR A LIFETIME

Geneseo's story unfolds over nearly 250 years. If you're a student today, your story will unfold over seventy, eighty, perhaps ninety years or so. You might spend ten or twenty of those years in school. As an individual, how do you keep learning what you need to know for a half century or more? And how do you figure out what you need to know?

If you attended New School, and you participated in Not School, you've got a structure, you know how to learn on your own, and you're probably resourceful, too. If you attended Old School, your structure might feel creaky, you may struggle to learn on your own, and resourcefulness may not come naturally. If you attempt to learn without any particular structure, your natural curiosity may be all you need, but that's asking a lot because a half century is a long time. Most likely, you'll learn about whatever happens to capture your imagination, and maybe follow the crowd by watching, reading, and listening to whatever marketers are pushing at the time, or whatever algorithms determine you would enjoy.

Instead, if consider the structure of New School, you could choose to learn about Your Body, Your Mind, Our Country & Cultures—let's just stop there for a moment. If you made a list, right now, today, of things you'd like to know about your heart, your lungs, your legs, your brain, your emotions, and your memory, you would be approaching your life's learning with intention and by your own design. How would you do that? Well, you could start with some of the more reputable websites and their YouTube videos. For more depth from credible sources, visit a public library. Following our own advice, one of this book's authors read a library book called *Healthy Heart, Healthy Brain* which helped him understand his circulatory system with a focus on memory, reducing the risk associated with heart attack and stroke, and chronic illness. There is always a lot to learn, but once you finish school, it's up to you to manage the what, where, how, and why of your learning.

Serious issues are easier to explore if they're presented in compelling ways. John Oliver's television series, *Last Week Tonight*, has covered organ and body donations, cryptocurrency, critical race theory, voting rights, elections in India, televangelists, the British monarchy, patents, debt, wrongful convictions, the ethics of Supreme Court justices, sex work, ransomware, school lunch programs, and UFOs. He's a smart, well-informed class clown who performs for grown-ups.

Of course, you can explore on your own and see whether the road takes you. Type “President of Bolivia” into Wikipedia’s search bar. Suddenly, you’re captivated by Gustavo Petro, who started his career at age seventeen with a guerrilla group called the 19th of April Movement. The movement evolved into the M19 Democratic Alliance, a political party.[15] He became Bolivia’s president. You can watch him speak in Spanish (with English translation) on several dozen YouTube videos and in a fifty-four-minute-long interview on the September 22, 2023, episode of the public media series, *Democracy Now!*[16]

Now, if you’re like most people in the US, you may have some trouble finding Bolivia on a map. In fact, you may not know much about Bolivia at all. Or, you might know only what the media has deemed important. As of January 2025, the most recent BBC news stories about Bolivia were about smuggling cocaine and the homes of poor people nearly falling off the side of a cliff. Surely there’s more to Bolivia than that!

You could stop there—if you’re learning on your own, you can stop anytime, anywhere—but it would be nice to know more. The best way to do that: Book a flight and spend a week or a month down in Bolivia. The second best: Learn from people who live there. And if that’s not easy, learn from people who have traveled there. They may tell you about “stargazing at the space-like Uyuni salt flats,” enjoying a parade with folk dancing that lasts for days and enjoys UNESCO Heritage status, seeing the ancient textiles at the museum of Indigenous art in Chuquisaca (also known as Sucre), and watching capybaras and macaws in their native habitats at the Madidi National Park in Bolivia’s Amazon region.[17]

If you gather information this way, you may have fun, but the lack of structure makes coherent knowledge, understanding, and wisdom difficult to attain. There are better ways. One is experience. Go play, make music, travel, read, hike, kayak, make art, listen to music, go to the theater, dance, cook and bake and try all sorts of foods. The other is relationships. Make friends, cultivate acquaintances, talk to people you don’t know, get out of your comfort zone, travel to spend time with family members you don’t see very often, approach anyone who seems interesting and request a conversation, keep in touch, reach out via email and social media and set a time to talk, then another. Do things you might not otherwise do. Have fun. Surprise yourself. Can you do this for the next fifty years? Absolutely! Will you learn a lot? That’s completely up to you.

> I am planning to be the mother of six children. I am presently at the University of Nairobi, Kenya. The reason why I chose this university is it is the best in Kenya. I was actually looking forward to getting my undergraduate in another country, but then, I also wanted to get the experience of studying in Kenya first. I am studying nutrition and dietetics . . . this will be my start to save a lot of lives not only in my community and in Kenya, but in other countries as well. I would like to volunteer with the United Nations when I am done with my undergraduate, and other organizations in nutrition and diets and food, so I can get myself out there, and gain more experience. When I am around thirty-five or forty years old, I will be an ambassador of Kenya to another country . . . to learn from leaders in other countries. And I will have my own organization in the field I am working in, providing more employment for youth in my country.
>
> —Binti, 21, Nairobi, Kenya

NOTHING LIKE SCHOOL

Wherever people live in communities, there is at least one functioning school nearby. School is a place where young people learn with guidance from trained adults, get to know peers who live nearby, and make friends. It provides a structure and set of standards for meaningful learning that can last a lifetime. Its presence is visible. It is always there, and for at least half the days each year, is bustling with activity. It touches every parent and every school-age child or teenager. With notable exceptions, school is a safe place with clean water, reliable electricity, connectivity, at least one nutritious and free (or low-cost) meal a day, plus some mental and physical health care, and regular adult supervision. Although the ride is bumpy right now, school remains the world's best, most trusted source of public education—with staff, facilities, structure, and resources in more than a million communities all over the world.

Adults are accustomed to paying for school with their tax dollars, not only for their own children and teenagers but for all students. Local government is trusted and experienced in administering funds. Management is solidly in place. Parents and communities instruct their children and teenagers to attend school whenever it is in session, pay attention, and work hard. Everyone holds school, teachers, and students to a high standard. In many countries and communities, schools are now educating children under age five, and outside the US, college enrollment continues to increase.[18] All good news—school is a functional system.

But it needs to change. Andreas Schleicher is in charge of education for the OECD in Paris. He knows more about school trends and economics than perhaps almost any other person on Earth. He says,

> Our schools today are going to be our economies and our society tomorrow. When countries and societies . . . make trade-offs between the present and the future, smart countries always prioritize the future. . . . We have good [OECD] data that you spend one dollar, and you get many, many dollars back over the lifetime. There's no better bet that society can make, financially, economically, and also socially than in the education of children. If you come from a disadvantaged background, you have only one chance, and that's a good teacher and a good school.[19]

In the US, more than three million public school teachers work about 180 days a year with nearly fifty million students in nearly one hundred thousand school buildings.[20] In the first fifty years of the twenty-first century, about half of the US population will have been educated in US public schools. Nothing in the world comes close to school in terms of service, number of people involved, or economic impact. There is nothing else like school, not at this scale, not with its value to individuals and society, longevity, and potential. Nothing!

Health care is administered locally through hospitals, clinics, and doctor's offices, but most visits are occasional and rarely last more than a half hour. With the exception of patients who regularly schedule repeat visits and those in chronic need, most people do not interact daily or weekly with health care.

Similarly, most people do not interact with law enforcement. In some countries, under some conditions, police may be more or less visible, but daily contact between law enforcement and large numbers of children and teenagers would be exceptional. The same is true for local fire departments.

Military presence is unusual in most local communities, except during strife. Most people see or interact with uniformed personnel, weapons, or conflict only on occasion. In India, about one in one thousand people serve in the military—but personnel are not usually seen in the daily lives of most citizens.[21]

In the US, over ten million people work full time for local and state governments and the federal government (some education workers are government employees). About 6 percent work in hospitals and 5 percent work in the military. The remaining 42 percent work in many other roles, typically with less direct regular daily interaction with specific members of the public.[22]

Besides school, no institution employs very large numbers of adults to supervise a nation's children and teenagers day in and day out. Only school does that. Given the sheer size, scale, and presence of school, and its potential future impact, it makes sense to help school through this difficult period so it can be strong and resilient. School is the answer to the question, "How do humans assure progress and social good for everyone?," but not in its Old School form.

WHAT SCHOOL MUST DO

Given the extraordinary position and value of school, and the lack of reasonable alternatives, school should be held to the highest standard within its core purpose. It can also lean on Not School to do the things that it cannot, need not, should not, or will not do on its own.

There are many good reasons to support the idea and operation of school as the preeminent public provider of useful, relevant, meaningful learning for children and teenagers. There are, however, some things school could do to reestablish its diminished glory. Mostly—in the words of some kids consulted for this project—school needs to "get over itself!" That is, school ought to stop demanding everybody salute its woefully outdated model. The model was never that great, even if it did serve a purpose for a time. That time has expired.

Throughout the world, there are small-bore examples of students engaged in future-facing programs in all sorts of schools. Many suggest what New School (and Not School) could be, but they rarely prove a concept at scale. Now is the time for Old School to make the shift for the good of the five billion people who are or will soon be in school—for the good of half of the people on Earth.

Here's a note to school everywhere. Please excuse the direct language and candor; it's offered with the greatest love and respect . . .

1. Think in terms of what students will learn and remember, not what you think they ought to know. With the best intentions, *you are teaching far too much information*. Students are massively overwhelmed. They forget most of what you tell them, and they cannot extract the big ideas. Teach less! Instead of presenting twenty-five thousand or thirty thousand items of interest in twelve-plus years, think closer to five thousand. That's about 350 Fundamental items in each school year—roughly two or three ideas

per day, not ten or twenty. If you choose those ideas carefully, students will learn, remember, focus, and care about what's important.

2. Stop organizing learning with twentieth-century school subjects. When most students hear the word "mathematics," many (perhaps most) of them run in the other direction. Old School subjects were never perfect, but they've served their purpose. They are bloated, irrelevant, disconnected, and unhelpful to students who making sense of the modern world. *Your subjects are no longer effective organizing structures.* They should be replaced. Fairly big changes are necessary because school schedules and staff assignments are based on this Old School structure. Transformation is within reach; please do not underestimate the resilience of teachers.
3. Fill school days with ideas and activities devised by students. Allocate school's instructional hours for each student's Personal Education, based on Fundamentals devised by the community (including students) and learned by everyone. Instead of disseminating information and managing classroom activities, support one-on-one and small groups of students who pursue a wide, diverse range of ideas.
4. Design a new structure based on the modern world. One new structure: a reasonable, interlocking set of new Learning Categories, such as: (1) Your Body, (2) Your Mind, (3) Your Life, (4) Our Country & Cultures, (5) Our Planet & Beyond, (6) Our Future(s), (7) Words & Stories, (8) Numbers & Money, (9) Sounds & Images, and (10) Movement.
5. Do not assign homework. Students have plenty to do outside of school, and they learn a great deal from Not School. Your allocated time is roughly 9:00 A.M. to 3:00 P.M., half the weekdays of the year. Don't expand the school day or the number of school days per year. *Get your work done within the allotted time*—a good lesson for students and teachers to learn.
6. Stop mandatory testing. This is a major cause of stress for students, teachers, and parents. It requires a lot of time that could be spent in more productive ways. These tests do not respect teachers and do not respect students. Standardized results do not measure learning when it is happening, so they are not very useful. Students welcome assessment if it helps them learn what they want to learn.

7. Stop trying to do the job alone. It is difficult to manage learning for more than a billion children and teenagers. Keeping every individual student engaged and productive for more than eight thousand hours of their lives is really hard! You are part of a local community where there are lots of useful resources—and there are many more outside your community. There are people who want to help. Ask for help! Even better, present a design for collaboration (borrow the design from the million other schools in the world, or make up your own). Rethink your structure so students and teachers can build safe and secure relationships, not only with people nearby, but with people they meet on the internet. Connect people all over the world. Diversity helps everyone. Be sure to work with your community to make sure school is safe and secure—no student should be afraid to go to school because they might get shot!
8. Recruit, hire, train, support, and value the best teachers you can find—and pay them a living wage. Hold them to high standards for professionalism, contemporary knowledge, best practices, and skills in engaging and relating to students. Respect their professional achievement, their stature in the community, and their leadership. Support them with time, attention, and resources so they can learn from each other and from their students. Make teachers' relationships with students a top priority. Pay teachers enough money so they can live without secondary employment; do not allow them to pay for classroom supplies; guarantee great benefits, too. If progress is sluggish, work with your community to pressure government to change these unreasonable, arbitrary decisions. Accept nothing less than the best solution. This investment yields a very high return.
9. Mental health and mindfulness are essential to learning. "Mental awareness builds cognitive and emotional skills that cultivate inner strength, a sense of purpose, and the capacity for continuous learning and flexible adaptation," explains University of Virginia professor of education Patricia (Tish) Jennings, whose expertise in this field and ideas about learning have been instrumental in devising New School, understanding Not School, and developing this book.[23]

   A culture of mindfulness provides every student and every teacher with a personal toolkit filled with practical strategies to regain focus, manage stress and negative emotions, and deal with the flow of daily life. In a New School environment, mindfulness becomes even more powerful, elevating hope and purpose to propel student curiosity into accomplishments never before contemplated by the human race. As Tish explains, "Positive emotions are self-reinforcing. Once you [the teacher] have mindfully and intentionally established a positive emotional climate in your classroom . . . your students will help reinforce it."[24] Without this philosophy, New School feels like Old School.

10. Stop pretending school possesses magical powers. School is a place where adults help children and teenagers learn skills, gain confidence, and acquire knowledge. Initially, students acquire capacity in order to feel good about themselves and to please adults, but after a few years in primary school, students begin to connect their life at school with their potential future life as a productive global citizen. Work with community and media to expose every student to the world, its issues, its opportunities, and the wide range of possibilities offered by life in the twenty-first century. Think very carefully before restricting access, basing your decisions on clear guidance from teachers and university researchers as well as contemporary scientific understanding of human growth and maturity. And remember: Every student is unique, so every student's path is unique, too.
11. Get to work on preschool. There is now sufficient evidence to support preschool education for every young child on Earth. That's more than two hundred million preschoolers. They require teachers, classrooms, and their own smaller-sized facilities, mostly in Africa and Asia, but in many other places, too. Get serious about the value of learning for people who are under five years old—and the teachers who provide them with the foundation for a lifetime of learning. Pay preschool teachers a reasonable salary with benefits. Provide appropriate facilities—by design, not as an afterthought in a church basement. And it's not too early to start on New School's Learning Categories, even if the children are three or four years old—they have bodies, they have minds, they have lives, they think about the future, and they love words and stories and sounds and images.
12. Get to work on lifelong learning. People older than eighteen or twenty or twenty-five continue to learn for their entire lives. Media will not satisfy

that need. The first ten items on this list will keep you plenty busy, but this one is every bit as important because the solutions set up a half century of learning for almost every person on Earth.

13. Connect ideas. Do not segregate ideas in subject areas. Every idea should immediately generate a mind map that weaves in and out of every Learning Category. Think in terms of networks of related ideas and relationships, not single ideas to be memorized. Center your thinking on real people with whom you have engaged in one-on-one conversation in order to understand their needs, what they do every day, their plans for the future, their connections to the outside world, their reliance on community. Nothing is simple. Everything opens a door to a world of ideas.
14. The best way to learn is to talk to other people. There are forty-four schools in Nunavut, and several thousand students. Most of those children and teenagers, and teachers, know as little about your life as your students and teachers know about their lives. Where to start? For general background, contact the *Nunavut News*. Their phone number is (867) 873–4031. Their website—www.nunavutnews.com—is helpful—but some of it is written in visual characters you may not understand: ᓄᓇᕘᒻᒥ ᐱᕚᓪᓕᐊᔪᑦ means "Nunavut News." If you're a student or a teacher, ask an editor or reporter to connect you with the office at Inuksuk High School. Or contact the school directly—they have a Facebook page. The school's phone number and office email address are (867) 979-5281; IHS@gov.nu.ca. It took us less than ten minutes to learn all of this. If you get in touch, say hello for us.
15. Do everything possible so that every student learns based on their own interests. If you do that, students will share what they learn, and a tree of knowledge will grow. Like magic.

I like listening to music, mostly rock, heavy metal, Guns N' Roses, Metallica. I really like Queen. In my free time, I mostly play guitar and sometimes, I study. I like being on my computer, so I watch YouTube. And I watch television. I play electric guitar, but he didn't play guitar, and Einstein played violin (here he is on my T-shirt playing electric guitar, thanks to Photoshop). Einstein was dyslexic. I know he created the theory of relativity. I want to be a physicist. When I was young, I wanted to know how nature works. From what parts is

this made? Now, I know that it's made from atoms, but there are still some things we don't know about the world. I want to discover it. I want to be a doctor of physics. I want to invent new stuff like rocket ships, and . . . do research on quantum theories. I learned about quantum theory on TV [watching] Nat Geo, Discovery Science, and other scientific programs. None of my relatives are physicists or scientists. Quantum physics is hard to explain. It's a theory [about] how particles move through space. So: Quantum duality . . . there is this experiment in which an electron generates a wave of probability of where it will land. This theory started in Einstein's time. We still don't know the answer. It's very hard to test, to measure. These are geniuses working on this . . . is it real, is it fake? Or (laughing) is it *magic*?

—Teo, 14, Piran, Slovenia

OUR NEXT STEPS

Mostly, we have learned what we have conveyed in this book by connecting and collaborating with children, teenagers, teachers, and experts—perhaps a thousand people in all. You've met some of them in this book. We want to build on the work we've done so far. We hope you do, too.

We will interview more children and more teenagers and share those interviews on the *Kids on Earth* platform. In fact, most countries and most cultures are not yet represented, so there's lots of work ahead. We want to interview many more kids. If you want to help, let us know via www.kidsonearth.org. These conversations keep us grounded and provide fuel that allows us to continue to learn.

We've begun a parallel service, *Teachers on Earth.* We want to understand how teachers deal with student engagement. We want to connect teachers so they develop a global network of their own. We promise to stay close, but this is work others do for themselves.

Everything starts at the top, so we plan to use this book, and the plan we have envisioned for learning, as the North Star for an iterative process with governance, including people who work in government, policy, planning, and implementation. And we continue to work with decision-makers and their teams so they fully understand the objectives, actions, and consequences of this important work. This is work to be done worldwide and at the community level. With relentless collaboration. And without fear of consequences.

Engage a very wide range of stakeholders—that's students, parents, teachers, principals, superintendents, school board members, elected officials, government staff, technologists, and journalists who do not, as a rule, talk to one another. Convenings and media coverage are essential—local, national, and international—with a growing list of partners.

Experiment with Learning Categories, Fundamentals, and Personal Learning; try with a few students, then more, then lots more. Share ideas, gather feedback, learn from mistakes, increase scale and intensity. More multigenerational, multidisciplinary convenings, more partners, more media coverage.

Prototype Global Brain to learn how it works. Solicit participation by teachers, students, technologists, funders. Help it grow.

Resist the temptation to analyze, discuss, and debate. Use Not School to develop ideas that school cannot digest. Don't wait for an invitation. Don't ask for permission. Get started. Don't let perfect be the enemy of the good.

TRANSFORMATION

Students who begin kindergarten in 2023 will be twenty-seven years old in 2050. As they grow, they find more and better ways to learn. They will not require permission from adults. They embrace already independence, intellectual freedom, and their own curiosity. They make use of every available resource for learning. They find their own way—because, beyond a certain point (which arrives early), being told what to do is not a good way to learn. They set high expectations for themselves and their teachers—and have fun doing it. If Old School is unwilling or unable to solve its own problems, they move on.

They won't pay much attention to the material taught if it's not worth learning. If someone demands that they learn material lacking purpose or utility or that is just plain boring, they will find something more interesting to learn. Beyond Fundamentals, most students need not learn what other people learn. To remain relevant and useful, school must adapt to each student's individual interests and their natural inclination to learn in their own ways. Learning in school diverges from uniformity and adopts diversity as the common standard.

Students and teachers connect, communicate, and collaborate with peers nearby, in person, and throughout the world, via digital technology. Students and teachers schedule around time zones; they wake up early or go to bed late, but that's no reason for students in Kingston, Jamaica not to talk to peers in Singapore, which is a dozen time zones away.

Students become very aware of their use of instructional time. A student deeply engaged in quadratic equations may not wish to be distracted by African literature. It is their learning, their life, their freedom that is at stake.

However, if their particular school or classroom is poorly managed or stuck in Old School culture, there will be chaos.

Please stop complaining about school or trying to reform it. Please don't blame the students or punish them with meaningless testing and by wasting their time.

Collectively, we can make the necessary decisions and take the necessary action to change the rules, put Old School to rest, bring New School to life, and animate Not School so it becomes an equal partner in learning. Adults can do this, but so far, we have chosen not to, with every good excuse to explain why not.

Together, we—students, teachers, parents, governance—can think clearly. We must work together to make life on Earth better not only for ourselves, but for the children who will grow up during our lifetimes, and not only the ones in countries whose names we know. For the good of families, communities, nations, and more than ten billion people who happen to live nearby, it is time to transform learning and school for the twenty-first century.

Notes

Introduction

1. Data based on United Nations, Department of Economic and Social Affairs, Population Division, "Births per Year," Our World in Data, last updated July 12, 2024, https://ourworldindata.org/grapher/number-of-births-per-year, and average 80 percent enrollment (95% primary, 80% early secondary, 60% late secondary, with 134 million births per year and no assumption for increased enrollment beyond the current estimates).
2. "World Population Prospects 2024," United Nations, DESA, Population Division, https://population.un.org/wpp/graphs?loc=900&type=Probabilistic%20Projections&category=Population&subcategory=1_Total%20Population.
3. Life expectancy graph from Esteban Ortiz-Ospina and Max Roser, "Global Health," Our World in Data, last revised February 2024, https://ourworldindata.org/health-meta.
4. Homi Kharas, "The Unprecedented Expansion of the Global Middle Class," Working Paper No. 100 (Brookings Institution, Washington, DC, February 2017), 2, https://www.brookings.edu/wp-content/uploads/2017/02/global_20170228_global-middle-class.pdf.
5. World Bank Group, "Decline of Global Extreme Poverty Continues but Has Slowed," press release, September 19, 2018, https://www.worldbank.org/en/news/press-release/2018/09/19/decline-of-global-extreme-poverty-continues-but-has-slowed-world-bank.
6. Moira Herbst, *The Changing Childhood Project: A Multigenerational, International Survey on 21st Century Childhood* (UNICEF, 2021), 52, https://www.unicef.org/innocenti/media/566/file/UNICEF-Global-Insight-Gallup-Changing-Childhood-Survey-Report-English-2021.pdf.
7. Herbst, *Changing Childhood Project*, 52.
8. Herbst, 38.
9. Herbst, 73.
10. Herbst, 19.
11. Herbst, 73.
12. "HIV," The Global Health Observatory, World Health Organization, https://www.who.int/data/gho/data/themes/hiv-aids.
13. "K–12 ALICE School Safety Training," ALICE, Navigate 360, https://www.alicetraining.com/our-program/alice-training/k12-education/.
14. "Historical Estimates of World Population," United States Census Bureau, last revised December 5, 2022, https://www.census.gov/data/tables/time-series/demo/international-programs/historical-est-worldpop.html.
15. Data based on UNESCO Institute for Statistics, "Net Attendance Rate of Primary School," Our World in Data, last updated June 16, 2024, https://ourworldindata.org/grapher/primary-school-attendance-selected-countries?tab=chart.
16. Max Roser and Esteban Ortiz-Ospina, "Literacy," Our World in Data, last revised March 2024, https://ourworldindata.org/literacy.

17. R. C. Pianta, "The Case for Radical Redesign: A Working Paper" (Charlottesville, VA: Center of Advanced Study of Teaching and Learning, University of Virginia, 2024).
18. Interview with Jonathan, *Kids on Earth*, https://vimeo.com/kidsonearth.
19. *Reinventing School*, web video series, https://www.youtube.com/@ReinventingSchool/videos.
20. Matt Rosenberg, "The World's Newest Countries Since 1990," *ThoughtCo.*, updated July 10, 2019, https://www.thoughtco.com/new-countries-of-the-world-1433444.
21. "Population Pyramids of the World from 1950 to 2100," World 1980, PopulationPyramid .net, 2024, https://www.populationpyramid.net/world/1980/.

Chapter 1

1. "Population Pyramids of the World from 1950 to 2100," World 2050, PopulationPyramid .net, 2024, https://www.populationpyramid.net/world/2050/.
2. "Height-for-Age Boys," WHO Child Growth Standards, World Health Organization, https://cdn.who.int/media/docs/default-source/child-growth/child-growth-standards /indicators/length-height-for-age/cht-hfa-boys-p-2-5.pdf?sfvrsn=b6ff59f8_10.
3. "Normal Growth," Children's Wisconsin Hospital and Health System, https://childrenswi .org/medical-care/adolescent-health-and-medicine/issues-and-concerns/adolescent-growth -and-development/normal-growth.
4. UNICEF, "New Year's Babies: Over 370,000 Children Will Be Born Worldwide on New Year's Day," press release, December 31, 2020, https://www.unicef.org/press-releases/new -years-babies-over-370000-children-will-be-born-worldwide-new-years-day-unicef; Saloni Dattani et al., "Child and Infant Mortality," Our World in Data, 2023, https:// ourworldindata.org/child-mortality#child-mortality-by-cause-of-death.
5. Lydia R. Anderson et al., *Living Arrangements of Children: 2019* (US Census Bureau, 2022), 3, https://www.census.gov/content/dam/Census/library/publications/2022/demo/p70-174.pdf.
6. Jessica Bahr, "Census 2021: Almost Half of Australians Had a Parent Born Overseas," SBSNews, updated June 28, 2022, https://www.sbs.com.au/news/article/census-2021 -almost-half-of-australians-had-a-parent-born-overseas/5r9mi7esi.
7. Susan Engel, *The Hungry Mind: The Origins of Curiosity in Childhood* (Harvard University Press, 2015), 38.
8. Engel, *Hungry Mind*.
9. Engel, 24.
10. Engel, 29.
11. "Recent Inductees," Inducted Toys, Strong National Museum of Play, https://www .museumofplay.org/exhibits/toy-hall-of-fame/inducted-toys/.
12. "The Science Behind the Spin: The Physics of Spinning Tops Explained," (blog), Bruce Charles Designs, January 26, 2022, https://www.brucecharlesdesigns.com/blogs/news/the -science-behind-the-spin-the-physics-of-spinning-tops-explained.
13. "Spinning Tops."
14. Amanda Morin, "Skills Kids Need Going into High School," Understood, https://www .understood.org/en/articles/skills-kids-need-going-into-high-school.
15. William Shakespeare, *Julius Caesar*, ed. Barbara Mowat, Paul Werstine, Michael Poston, and Rebecca Niles (Folger Shakespeare Library, n.d.), https://www.folger.edu/explore /shakespeares-works/julius-caesar/read/.
16. "List of Census Metropolitan Areas and Agglomerations in Canada," Wikimedia Foundation, updated August 16, 2024, 13:56 (UTC), https://en.wikipedia.org/wiki/List_of_census _metropolitan_areas_and_agglomerations_in_Canada.

17. "Census Profile, 2016 Census, Moose Jaw [Population Centre], Saskatchewan and Saskatchewan [Province]," Statistics Canada, November 29, 2017, https://www12.statcan.gc.ca/census-recensement/2016/dp-pd/prof/details/page.cfm?Lang=E&Geo1=POPC&Code1=0549&Geo2=PR&Code2=47&SearchType=Begins&SearchPR=01&B1=All&type=0.
18. "2SLGBTQI+ Terminology—Glossary and Common Acronyms," Women and Gender Equality Canada, Government of Canada, last modified September 17, 2024, https://women-gender-equality.canada.ca/en/free-to-be-me/2slgbtqi-plus-glossary.html.
19. Jason G. Antonio, "Moose Jaw's Crime Rate Ranked 37th Nationally in 2021, Data Shows," *Moose Jaw Today*, August 2, 2022, https://www.moosejawtoday.com/local-news/moose-jaws-crime-rate-ranked-37th-nationally-in-2021-data-shows-5654825.
20. Government of Saskatchewan, "SaskTel Investing an Additional $100 Million in Rural Fibre Initiative to Help Bridge the Digital Divide for Dozens of Rural Communities," news release, November 15, 2022, https://www.saskatchewan.ca/government/news-and-media/2022/november/15/sasktel-investing-an-additional-$100-million-in-rural-fibre-initiative.
21. "Neighborhoods Matter: Children's Lives Are Shaped by the Neighborhoods They Grow Up In," Neighborhoods, Opportunity Insights, https://opportunityinsights.org/neighborhoods/.
22. "Neighborhoods Matter."
23. Total HIV/AIDS deaths in Africa in 2022 were 630,000, compared with about 200,000 deaths in the rest of the world. *HIV Statistics, Globally and by WHO Region, 2023* (World Health Organization, 2023), https://cdn.who.int/media/docs/default-source/hq-hiv-hepatitis-and-stis-library/j0294-who-hiv-epi-factsheet-v7.pdf.
24. In comparison with other parts of the world, the impact of COVID on Africa was relatively small: about 260,000 deaths in Africa vs. one to two million deaths in North America, Europe, and Asia. World Health Organization, "Cumulative Confirmed COVID-19 Deaths by World Region," Our World in Data, last updated March 13, 2025, https://ourworldindata.org/grapher/cumulative-covid-deaths-region.
25. Bloomberg, "How Chennai, One of the World's Wettest Major Cities, Ran Out of Water," *Economic Times*, last updated February 4, 2021, https://economictimes.indiatimes.com/news/politics-and-nation/how-chennai-one-of-the-worlds-wettest-major-cities-ran-out-of-water/articleshow/80680182.cms?utm_source=contentofinterest&utm_medium=text&utm_campaign=cppst.
26. Insights about adult engagement from Andreas Schleicher, PISA 2022 Mathematics Education Presentation for Excel in Education, OECD Education, December 8, 2023.
27. "Infographic: Women's Rights and the Law," UN Women, July 1, 2021, https://www.unwomen.org/en/digital-library/multimedia/2021/7/infographic-womens-rights-and-the-law.
28. "The 17 Goals," United Nations Department of Economic and Social Affairs, https://sdgs.un.org/goals.
29. Julia Haines, "Places the U. S. Government Warns Not to Travel Right Now," *U.S. News & World Report*, March 6, 2024, https://www.usnews.com/news/best-countries/articles/places-the-us-government-warns-not-to-travel-right-now.
30. Jeanne Batalova, "Top Statistics on Global Migration and Migrants," Migration Policy Institute, July 21, 2022, https://www.migrationpolicy.org/article/top-statistics-global-migration-migrants.
31. Caitlin Davis and Jeanne Batalova, "Filipino Immigrants in the United States," Migration Policy Institute, August 8, 2023, https://www.migrationpolicy.org/article/filipino-immigrants-united-states.

32. "President McKinley Asks for Declaration of War Against Spain," History.com, last updated April 19, 2024, https://www.history.com/this-day-in-history/mckinley-asks-for-declaration-of-war-with-spain.

Chapter 2

1. *Britannica*, "Plant Cell," last updated February 15, 2025, https://www.britannica.com/science/plant-cell.
2. Stephen T. Jackson, "Climate Change Throughout History," Global Warming, Saving Earth, Encyclopedia Britannica, https://www.britannica.com/explore/savingearth/climate-change-throughout-history.
3. Stanislas Dehaene, *How We Learn* (Penguin, 2020), 145–146.
4. Alison Gopnik et al., *The Scientist in the Crib: What Early Learning Tells Us About the Mind* (Harper Perennial, 1999), 87–88.
5. Susan Engel, *The Intellectual Lives of Children* (Harvard University Press, 2021), 8, 12.
6. Johanna Calderon, PhD., Assistant Professor of Psychology in the Department of Psychiatry at Harvard Medical School; Johanna Calderon, "Executive Function in Children: Why It Matters and How to Help," Child and Teen Health, Harvard Health Publishing, Harvard Medical School, December 16, 2020, https://www.health.harvard.edu/blog/executive-function-in-children-why-it-matters-and-how-to-help-2020121621583.
7. Committee on Developments in the Science of Learning, *How People Learn: Brain, Mind, Experience and School*, rev. ed, ed. John D. Bransford, Ann L. Brown, and Rodney R. Cocking (National Academy Press, 1999), 31.
8. Committee on Developments, *How People Learn*, 9.
9. National Academies of Science, Engineering, and Medicine, *How People Learn II: Learners, Contexts, and Cultures* (National Academies Press, 2018), 2, https://doi.org/10.17226/24783.
10. Celeste Kidd and Benjamin Y. Hayden, "The Psychology and Neuroscience of Curiosity," *Science Direct* 88, no. 3–4 (2015): 449–460.
11. Susan Engel, *The Hungry Mind: The Originals of Curiosity in Childhood* (Harvard University Press, 2015), 7–9.
12. Engel, *The Hungry Mind*, 10.
13. Dehaene, *How We Learn*, 188.
14. Dehaene, 189.
15. Engel, *The Hungry Mind*, 17.
16. Dehaene, *How We Learn*, 194.
17. Dehaene.
18. Engel, *The Hungry Mind*, 75.
19. Engel, 77.
20. Engel, 193.
21. *APA Dictionary of Psychology*, "Cognition," last updated April 19, 2018, https://dictionary.apa.org/cognition.
22. "Hearing Range," Wikimedia Foundation, last edited February 25, 2025, 13:28 (UTC), https://en.wikipedia.org/wiki/Hearing_range#/.
23. Anne Marie Helmenstine, "The Visible Spectrum: Wavelengths and Colors," *ThoughtCo*, updated June 7, 2024, https://www.thoughtco.com/understand-the-visible-spectrum-608329.
24. Mindy Joyner, "How Do Dogs See the World?," PetMD, October 29, 2021, https://www.petmd.com/dog/general-health/how-do-dogs-see-world.

25. "MRI," Tests and Procedures, Mayo Clinic, September 9, 2023, https://www.mayoclinic.org/tests-procedures/mri/about/pac-20384768.
26. Daniel Simmons, "But Did You See the Gorilla? The Problem with Inattentional Blindness," *Smithsonian Magazine*, September 2012, https://www.smithsonianmag.com/science-nature/but-did-you-see-the-gorilla-the-problem-with-inattentional-blindness-17339778/.
27. Susan Magsamen and Ivy Ross, *Your Brain on Art: How the Arts Transform Us* (Random House, 2023), 137.
28. Mihaly Csikszentmihalyi, *Flow: The Psychology of Optimal Experience* (Harper Perennial, 1991), 3.
29. Nancy Costello et al., "Algorithms, Addiction, and Adolescent Mental Health: An Interdisciplinary Study to Inform State-Level Policy Action to Protect Youth from the Dangers of Social Media," *American Journal of Law & Medicine* 49, no. 2–3 (2023): 135–172, https://doi.org/10.1017/amj.2023.25.
30. Magsamen and Ross, *Your Brain on Art*, 12.
31. Matt Johnson, "The Power of Intrinsic Motivation," *Psychology Today*, January 5, 2021, https://www.psychologytoday.com/us/blog/mind-brain-and-value/202101/the-power-intrinsic-motivation.
32. Johnson, "The Power of Intrinsic Motivation."
33. Johnson.
34. Johnson.
35. National Academies of Sciences, Engineering, and Medicine, *How People Learn II*, 109.
36. Dehaene, *How We Learn*, 89–90.
37. Anne Trafton, "In the Blink of an Eye," MIT News, January 16, 2014, https://news.mit.edu/2014/in-the-blink-of-an-eye-0116.
38. Dehaene, *How We Learn*, 89–90.
39. National Academies of Sciences, Engineering, and Medicine, *How People Learn II*, 4.
40. National Academies of Sciences, Engineering, and Medicine, 75–76.
41. Dehaene, *How We Learn*, 70–71.
42. Magsamen and Ross, *Your Brain on Art*, 146–147.
43. "Xun Kuang," Quotable Quotes, Quotes, Goodreads, https://www.goodreads.com/quotes/7565817-tell-me-and-i-forget-teach-me-and-i-may; The misattributed quote, "Tell me and I forget, teach me and I may remember, involve me and I learn" is often attributed to Benjamin Franklin, but the source has not emerged.
44. Melissa Jenco, "AAP Endorses New Recommendations on Sleep Times," *AAP News*, June 13, 2016, https://publications.aap.org/aapnews/news/6630/AAP-endorses-new-recommendations-on-sleep-times.
45. "Sleep and Health," Physical Education and Physical Activity, US Centers for Disease Control and Prevention, July 2, 2024, https://www.cdc.gov/physical-activity-education/staying-healthy/sleep.html?CDC_AAref_Val=https://www.cdc.gov/healthyschools/sleep.htm.
46. Hermann Ebbinghaus, *Memory; A Contribution to Experimental Psychology*, trans. Henry A. Ruger and Clara E. Bussenius (Columbia University Teachers College, 1913), https://archive.org/details/memorycontributi00ebbiuoft/page/n5/mode/2up. A 1913 historical research text, in original form, by Ebbinghaus. It includes his calculations, explanations, and research.
47. Jonathan Hancock, "Ebbinghaus's Forgetting Curve," Mindtools, https://www.mindtools.com/a9wjrjw/ebbinghauss-forgetting-curve.

48. Anne-Laure Le Cunff, "The Forgetting Curve: The Science of How Fast We Forget," Ness Labs, accessed April 3, 2025, https://nesslabs.com/ebbinghaus-forgetting-curve.
49. Le Cunff, "The Forgetting Curve."
50. Dehaene, *How We Learn*, 222–224.
51. Rita Carter, *The Human Brain Book: An Illustrated Guide to Its Structure, Function and Disorders*, 2nd ed. (Dorling Kindersley, 2014), 158.
52. Carter, *Human Brain Book.*
53. Committee on Developments, *How People Learn*, 9.
54. Mike Shatzkin, "How Book Publishing Has Changed in Recent Decades and the Puzzling Question of What Comes Next," *The Shatzkin Files* (blog), June 19, 2022, https://www.idealog.com/blog/how-book-publishing-has-changed-in-recent-decades-and-the-puzzling-question-of-what-comes-next/.
55. Mike Shatzkin, "The Problem with Bookstores Is the Problem for Bookstores," *The Shatzkin Files* (blog), June 5, 2023, https://www.idealog.com/blog/the-problem-with-bookstores-is-the-problem-for-bookstores/.
56. Brad Adgate, "The Rise and Fall of Cable Television," *Forbes*, November 2, 2020, https://www.forbes.com/sites/bradadgate/2020/11/02/the-rise-and-fall-of-cable-television/?sh=361f8b1c6b31.
57. Tony Maglio, "All 124 Cable Channels Ranked by Average Viewership in 2021," The Wrap, Yahoo Entertainment, December 17, 2021, https://www.yahoo.com/entertainment/124-cable-channels-ranked-average-193000903.html.
58. Jason Wise, "How Many Videos Are on YouTube in 2025? New Stats, EarthWeb, last updated February 5, 2024, https://earthweb.com/how-many-videos-are-on-youtube/.
59. "Internet Users by Country 2025," *World Population Review*, accessed April 3, 2025, https://worldpopulationreview.com/country-rankings/internet-users-by-country.
60. Karen White, *Publications Output: U. S. Trends and International Comparisons* (National Center for Science and Engineering Statistics, NSF, 2021), https://ncses.nsf.gov/pubs/nsb20214/publication-output-by-country-region-or-economy-and-scientific-field.
61. Dehaene, *How We Learn.*
62. L. S. Vygotsky, *Mind in Society: The Development of Higher Psychological Processes* (Harvard University Press, 1978), 88.
63. "Firefighter," Signing Savvy, https://www.signingsavvy.com/sign/firefighter/6898/1.
64. *Seen, Counted, Included: Using Data to Shed Light on the Well-Being of Children with Disabilities* (UNICEF, 2021), 18.
65. "General Prevalence of ADHD," CHADD, https://chadd.org/about-adhd/general-prevalence/.
66. *Seen, Counted, Included: Using Data to Shed Light on the Well-Being of Children with Disabilities* (UNICEF, 2021), 18, https://data.unicef.org/resources/children-with-disabilities-report-2021/.
67. "Children in Poverty in United States," Kids Count Data Center, The Annie E. Casey Foundation, last updated September 2024, https://datacenter.aecf.org/data/tables/43-children-in-poverty#detailed/1/any/false/2048,1729,37,871,870,573,869,36,868,867/any/321,322.
68. "Goals 4: Ensure Inclusive and Equitable Quality Education and Promote Lifelong Learning Opportunities for All," Department of Economic and Social Affairs, United Nations, https://sdgs.un.org/goals/goal4.
69. "Education," World Bank Group, last updated March 25, 2024, https://www.worldbank.org/en/topic/education/overview.

70. *Connecticut Elementary and Secondary Social Studies Frameworks* (Connecticut State Department of Education, 2015), 60, 70, 120, https://portal.ct.gov/-/media/SDE/Social-Studies/ssframeworks.pdf.
71. *Connecticut Elementary*, 1.

Chapter 3

1. Pasi Sahlberg, *Finnish Lessons: What Can the World Learn from Educational Change in Finland?* (Teachers College Press, 2011), 1.
2. https://designintech.report/2019/03/09/design-in-tech-report-2019/
3. *Quick Reference Guide for the North Carolina Standard Course of Study: Grade K* (North Carolina State Board of Education, 2024), https://www.dpi.nc.gov/documents/publications/catalog/is183-quick-reference-guide-k/open.
4. Home, Australian Curriculum, https://www.australiancurriculum.edu.au/.
5. "Mathematics (Version 8.4)," Australian Curriculum, https://australiancurriculum.edu.au/f-10-curriculum/mathematics/?strand=Number+and+Algebra&strand=Measurement+and+Geometry&strand=Statistics+and+Probability&capability=ignore&priority=ignore&elaborations=true.
6. "Accountant and Auditors," Occupational Outlook Handbook, US Bureau of Labor Statistics, last modified August 29, 2024, https://www.bls.gov/ooh/business-and-financial/accountants-and-auditors.htm.
7. Simon Barker, "Skills Required to Be a Full Stack Developer: A Checklist," (blog), DEV Community, edited September 7, 2021, https://dev.to/allthecode/skills-required-to-be-a-full-stack-developer-a-checklist-2805.
8. *2023 Indiana Academic Standards–Mathematics: Geometry* (Indiana Department of Education, 2023), https://media.doe.in.gov/standards/indiana-academic-standards-geometry.pdf.
9. "Nitrogen," Wikimedia Foundation, last updated January 23, 2025, 1:30 (UTC), https://en.wikipedia.org/wiki/Nitrogen.
10. "Great Barrier Reef," *National Geographic*, last updated, January 22, 2025, https://education.nationalgeographic.org/resource/great-barrier-reef/.
11. Michael Hansen and Diana Quintero, "The State of the Nation's Social Studies Educators," Brookings, July 3, 2017, https://www.brookings.edu/articles/the-state-of-the-nations-social-studies-educators/.
12. Tennessee Social Studies Standards, p. 2, accessed April 3, 2025, https://www.tn.gov/content/dam/tn/education/standards/ss/Social_Studies_Standards.pdf?utm_source=chatgpt.com.
13. *Britannica*, "Ukraine Summary," last updated February 20, 2025, https://www.britannica.com/summary/Ukraine.
14. "Russian Invasion of Ukraine," Wikimedia Foundation, last updated March 25, 2025, 11:02 (UTC), https://en.wikipedia.org/wiki/Russian_invasion_of_Ukraine.
15. "Vechornytsi," Wikimedia Foundation, last updated October 14, 2024, 19:48 (UTC), https://en.wikipedia.org/wiki/Vechornytsi.
16. "Culture of Ukraine," Wikimedia Foundation, last updated January 9, 2025, 21:39 (UTC), https://en.wikipedia.org/wiki/Culture_of_Ukraine.
17. "Paraguayan War," Wikimedia Foundation, last updated March 23, 2025, 22:18 (UTC), https://en.wikipedia.org/wiki/Paraguayan_War; and John Charles Chasteen, *Born in Blood and Fire: A Concise History of Latin America*. (W. W. Norton, 2006).

18. Justine Harrington, "25 Best Soups from Around the World," Far & Wide, updated December 9, 2024, https://www.farandwide.com/s/worlds-best-soups-a922c02329244086.
19. Markus Kampl, "33 International Soups: Unlock the World's Favorites," *The Roaming Fork*, May 21, 2023, https://theroamingfork.com/international-soups/#2-egusi-soup-west-africa-.
20. Alexandria Ocasio-Cortez, "Ocasio-Cortez Reflects on Her Evolution, Politically and Personally," *New York Times*, September 5, 2023.
21. "About UN Women," UN Women, https://www.unwomen.org/en/about-us/about-un-women.
22. This is difficult to calculate. One useful source is the *National Teacher and Principal Survey* (US Department of Education, National Center for Education Statistics, 2017–2018), https://nces.ed.gov/surveys/ntps/tables/ntps1718_21022407_t12n.asp, but the categories blend and segregate social studies and language arts, so 150,000 is a reasonable estimate for US social studies teachers (in secondary school).
23. Jane Oakhill et al., *Understanding and Teaching Reading Comprehension: A Handbook* (Routledge, 2015).
24. *The Reading Framework* (UK Department for Education, 2023), 21, https://assets.publishing.service.gov.uk/government/uploads/system/uploads/attachment_data/file/1178136/The_Reading_Framework_2023.pdf.
25. "Speech and Language Developmental Milestones," Health Information, National Institute on Deafness and Other Communication Disorders, NIH, last updated October 13, 2022, https://www.nidcd.nih.gov/health/speech-and-language.
26. "Speech and Language."
27. John McPhee, *Draft No. 4* (Farrar, Straus and Giroux, 2017), 138–9.
28. Emily Sohn, "It's Time to Stop Debating How to Teach Kids to Read and Follow the Evidence," *ScienceNews*, April 26, 2020, https://www.sciencenews.org/article/balanced-literacy-phonics-teaching-reading-evidence.
29. *Reading Framework*, 88.
30. *Reading Framework*, 12. Sources cited in the original text quoted here include S. E. Mol and A. G. Bus, "To Read or Not to Read: A Meta-Analysis of Print Exposure from Infancy to Early Adulthood," *Psychological Bulletin* 137, no. 2 (2011): 267–296; Federico Batini et al., "The Association Between Reading and Emotional Development: A Systematic Review" *Journal of Education and Training Studies* 9, no. 1 (2021): 12–48, https://doi.org/10.11114/jets.v9i1.5053; Christina Clark and Anne Teravainen-Goff, "Mental Wellbeing, Reading and Writing: How Children and Young People's Mental Wellbeing Is Related to Their Reading and Writing Experiences," *National Literacy Trust Research Report* (National Literacy Trust, 2018), https://files.eric.ed.gov/fulltext/ED593894.pdf; and Eliza Kennewell et al., "The Relationships Between School Children's Wellbeing, Socio-Economic Disadvantage, and After-School Activities: A Cross-Sectional Study," *BMC Pediatrics* 22, no. 297 (2022), https://doi.org/10.1186/s12887-022-03322-1; David Kidd and Emanuele Castano, "Reading Literary Fiction and Theory of Mind: Three Preregistered Replications and Extensions of Kidd and Castano (2013)," *Social Psychology and Personality Science* 10, no. 4 (2019): 522–531, https://doi.org/10.1177/1948550618775410; and Raymond A. Mar et al., "Exploring the Link Between Reading Fiction and Empathy: Ruling Out Individual Differences and Examining Outcomes," *Communications* 34, no. 4 (2009): 407–428, https://doi.org/10.1515/COMM.2009.025.
31. Thomas G. White et al., "What Does 'Below Basic' Mean on NAEP Reading?," *Educational Researcher* 50, no. 8 (2021): 570–573, https://www.readingrockets.org/sites/default/files/2023-09/What-Does-Below-Basic-Mean-on-NAEP-Reading.pdf.

32. Rebecca Rolland, "Why Kids Aren't Learning to Read, and How to Help," *Psychology Today*, February 12, 2022, https://www.psychologytoday.com/us/blog/the-art-talking-children/202202/why-kids-arent-learning-read-and-how-help.
33. *The Economic & Social Cost of Illiteracy* (World Literacy Foundation, 2018).
34. Gemma Cherry and Anna Vignoles, "What Is the Economic Value of Literacy and Numeracy?," *IZA World of Labor* no. 229 (2020), https://doi.org/10.15185/izawol.229.v2.
35. "Common Credits Ralph Ellison for Pointing Him Toward Music," *New York Times*, Sunday Book Review, January 14, 2024, https://www.nytimes.com/2024/01/11/books/review/common-interview-and-then-we-rise.html?.
36. "Children's Picture Books," *New York Times*, https://www.nytimes.com/books/best-sellers/picture-books/.
37. Lindsay Ann, "31 Student-Approved Books to Read for High School," *Lindsay Ann Learning* (blog), September 21, 2020, https://lindsayannlearning.com/books-to-read-for-high-school/.
38. "Get Schooled on 'School'," Word History, Merriam-Webster.com, https://www.merriam-webster.com/wordplay/get-schooled-on-the-origins-of-school-twice.
39. "Hispanic Population to Reach 111 Million by 2060," United States Census Bureau, last revised October 8, 2021, https://www.census.gov/library/visualizations/2018/comm/hispanic-projected-pop.html.
40. Howard Blumenthal, *Our Whole World in Their Hands: 21st Century School & Our Global Future*, unpublished, May 18, 2021), 25.
41. *Reinventing School*, "Episode 43: Language Learning, Part 1," *Reinventing School*, web videwo interview series, posted May 5, 2021. https://www.learningrevolution.com/reinventingschool/episode-43-language-learning-part-1.
42. *The National K–12 Foreign Language Enrollment Survey Report* (American Councils for International Education, 2017), https://www.americancouncils.org/sites/default/files/FLE-report-June17.pdf.
43. *Foreign Language Enrollment Survey*.
44. Blumenthal, "Episode 43: Part 1."
45. Quoted in Blumenthal.
46. Quoted in Blumenthal.
47. Gaston Dorren, *Babel: Around the World in Twenty Languages* (Atlantic Monthly Press, 2018), 325.
48. "Our Story," Yiddish Book Center, https://www.yiddishbookcenter.org/about/saving-literature.
49. "Michelle Obama," National Portrait Gallery, Smithsonian, https://npg.si.edu/learn/classroom-resource/michelle-obama.
50. "Music Teacher Demographics and Statistics in the US," Zippia, updated January 8, 2025, https://www.zippia.com/music-teacher-jobs/demographics/.
51. "Internet Publishing Employment Up 48 Percent, First Quarter 2016 to Second Quarter 2020," *Economics Daily*, US Bureau of Labor Statistics, December 3, 2020, https://www.bls.gov/opub/ted/2020/internet-publishing-employment-up-48-percent-first-quarter-2016-to-second-quarter-2020.htm.
52. Note: Some of these careers were included in the Mathematics summary as well.
53. *Reinventing School*, "Episode 38: Physical Education & Public Fitness," web video series, posted February 17, 2021, 1 hr., 6 min., 53 sec., https://www.learningrevolution.com/reinventingschool/episode-38-physical-education-public-fitness.
54. "Childhood Obesity Facts," US Centers for Disease Control and Prevention, https://www.cdc.gov/obesity/childhood-obesity-facts/childhood-obesity-facts.html.

55. John J Ratey and Eric Hagerman, *SPARK: The Revolutionary New Science of Exercise and the Brain* (Little, Brown & Co., 2008), 53.
56. "Registered Nurses," Occupational Outlook Handbook, US Bureau of Labor Statistics, last modified August 29, 2024, https://www.bls.gov/ooh/healthcare/registered-nurses.htm; "Physicians and Surgeons," Occupational Outlook Handbook, US Bureau of Labor Statistics, last modified August 29, 2024, https://www.bls.gov/ooh/healthcare/physicians-and-surgeons.htm; "Pharmacists," Occupational Outlook Handbook, US Bureau of Labor Statistics, last modified August 29, 2024, https://www.bls.gov/ooh/healthcare/pharmacists.htm; "29–1224 Radiologists," Occupational Employment and Wages, last modified April 3, 2023, https://www.bls.gov/oes/2023/may/oes291224.htm; "Dentists," Occupational Outlook Handbook, US Bureau of Labor Statistics, last modified August 29, 2024, https://www.bls.gov/ooh/healthcare/dentists.htm; and "Veterinarians," Occupational Outlook Handbook, US Bureau of Labor Statistics, last modified August 29, 2024, https://www.bls.gov/ooh/healthcare/veterinarians.htm.
57. *Report on the Condition of Education 2024* (Washington, DC: National Center for Education Statistics), p. 24, accessed April 3, 2025, https://nces.ed.gov/pubs2024/2024144.pdf.
58. "Tertiary Education Attainment by Country 2025," *World Population Review*, accessed April 3, 2025, https://worldpopulationreview.com/country-rankings/tertiary-education-attainment-by-country.
59. "How Many People Hold Bachelor's Degrees Globally?" last updated August 12, 2024, https://cambridgedb.com/how-many-people-hold-bachelor-s-degrees-globally.html#google_vignette.
60. *PISA 2022 Results (Volume I)* (OECD, 2023), 45.
61. Nicholas Ferroni, "The Teacher's Dilemma: Should I Stay or Should I Go?," *NEA Today*, January 2025, 48.
62. Tim Walker, "Survey: Alarming Number of Educators May Soon Leave the Profession," NEA News, *NEA Today*, February 1, 2022, https://www.nea.org/nea-today/all-news-articles/survey-alarming-number-educators-may-soon-leave-profession.
63. Presentation about school in South Korea at Hakuba Forum, Hakuba, Japan by Yerica Park on March 10, 2023, followed by personal interview with Yerica Park on May 23, 2023.
64. Hyojung Kim and Woongbee Lee, "South Korea: The Life-Changing Exam That Won't Stop for a Pandemic," *BBC News*, December 2, 2020, https://www.bbc.com/news/world-asia-55155217.
65. Jin Yu Young, "South Korea to Drop 'Killer Questions' from College Entrance Exam," *The New York Times*, June 21, 2023, https://www.nytimes.com/2023/06/21/world/asia/south-korea-csat-questions.html.
66. Caleb Silver, "The Top 25 Economies in the World," *Investopedia*, updated January 29, 2025, https://www.investopedia.com/insights/worlds-top-economies/.

Chapter 4

1. *Merriam-Webster Dictionary*, "Assimilate," https://www.merriam-webster.com/dictionary/assimilate.
2. Chris Buckley and Isabelle Qian, "How China Is Erasing Tibetan Culture, One Child at a Time," *New York Times*, January 9, 2025, https://www.nytimes.com/interactive/2025/01/09/world/asia/tibet-china-boarding-schools.html.
3. Ken Robinson, "Do Schools Kill Creativity," TED Talk, February 2006, 22 min., 17 sec., https://www.ted.com/talks/sir_ken_robinson_do_schools_kill_creativity?subtitle=en.

4. *Britannica*, “Monoculture,” last updated February 4, 2025, https://www.britannica.com/topic/monoculture.
5. “Invasive Species,” *National Geographic*, last updated October 30, 2024, https://education.nationalgeographic.org/resource/invasive-species/.
6. Seren Morris, “How Many People Died in Hiroshima and Nagasaki?,” *Newsweek*, August 3, 2020, https://www.newsweek.com/how-many-people-died-hiroshima-nagasaki-japan-second-world-war-1522276.
7. “Non-Jewish Victims of Nazism,” Bitesize, BBC.com, https://www.bbc.co.uk/bitesize/topics/zk94jxs/articles/zh9dwnb#zn7sf82.
8. *Britannica*, “Casualties of World War II,” last updated May 15, 2024, https://www.britannica.com/topic/casualties-of-World-War-II-2231003.
9. “The Bill of Rights: A Transcription,” America’s Founding Documents, National Archives, last reviewed July 10, 2024, https://www.archives.gov/founding-docs/bill-of-rights-transcript.
10. “Cloud Paintings—10 Most Famous,” Artst, https://www.artst.org/cloud-paintings/.
11. *Merriam-Webster Dictionary*, “Subject,” https://www.merriam-webster.com/dictionary/subject.
12. Check potentially troublesome “accuse” in “Late Latin *categoria*, from Greek *katēgoria* predication, category, from *katēgorein* to accuse, affirm, predicate, from *kata-* + *agora* public assembly, from *ageirein* to gather.”
13. “Health Workforce,” Data, The Global Health Observatory, World Health Organization, https://www.who.int/data/gho/data/themes/health-workforce.
14. *Britannica*, “Brain,” last updated March 18, 2025, https://www.britannica.com/science/brain.
15. Miho Nagasawa et al., “Oxytocin-Gaze Positive Loop and the Coevolution of Human-Dog Bonds,” *Science* 348, no. 6232 (2015): 333–336, https://doi.org/10.1126/science.1261022.
16. Laurie Santos, “Teaching Happiness with Dr. Laurie Santos,” Teacher Hub, Dr. Laurie Santos, https://www.drlauriesantos.com/teaching-happiness.
17. “Leading Causes of Nonfatal Injury,” WISQARS Leading Causes of Nonfatal Injury Visualization Tool, WISQARS, US Centers for Disease Control and Prevention, Chttps://wisqars.cdc.gov/lcnf/?y1=2021&y2=2021&ct=10&cc=0&s=0&g=00&a=lcd1age&a1=0&a2=199&d=0. These are US statistics for 2021.
18. Malagasy are Indigenous people who live in Madagascar.
19. Gaston Dorren, *Babel: Around the World in Twenty Languages* (Grove Atlantic, 2018), 9.
20. “During the winter (summer in the Northern Hemisphere), Peruvian Time is the same as North American Central Time, while during the summer (winter in the Northern Hemisphere) it is the same as Eastern Time.” “Time in Peru,” Wikimedia Foundation, last updated March 6, 2025, 15:11 (UTC), https://en.wikipedia.org/wiki/Time_in_Peru.
21. Macquarie University Big History Institute, *Big History* (DK Publishing, 2016), 98–99.
22. Seth Godin, ed., *The Carbon Almanac* (Pantheon Books, 2022), 21.
23. “PM2.5 Air Pollution Claimed 54,000 Lives in Delhi Last Year, Says Study,” *Economic Times*, last updated February 18, 2021, https://economictimes.indiatimes.com/news/politics-and-nation/pm2-5-air-pollution-claimed-54000-lives-in-delhi-last-year-says-study/articleshow/81087341.cms?utm_source=chatgpt.com&from=mdr.
24. Darla Deardorff, “UNESCO Story Circles Train-the-Trainer Event,” online event, February 1, 2024, 10:30 A.M. Eastern Time.
25. *Reinventing School*, “Episode 40: A Fresh Look at Micro-Schools,” weekly web tv series, posted on YouTube April 21, 2021, https://www.youtube.com/watch?v=iNn7GxLhpJA&t=619s.

26. US Bureau of Labor Statistics, "College Enrollment and Work Activity of High School Graduates," news release, April 23, 2024, https://www.bls.gov/news.release/archives/hsgec_04232024.htm.
27. Personal interview with Greg Roberts, University of Virginia, May 4, 2022.
28. Brennan Barnard, "A Decade of Change in College Admission," *Forbes*, December 31, 2019, https://www.forbes.com/sites/brennanbarnard/2020/12/31/a-decade-of-change-in-college-admission/?sh=383d4e313ee9.
29. Personal interviews with Michael Mills, SUNY Geneseo, August 5, 2019, and September 11, 2019.

Chapter 5

1. National Research Council, *How People Learn: Consensus HPL 2* (National Academies Press, 2021), 7.
2. James MacGregor Burns, *Fire and Light: How the Enlightenment Transformed Our World* (Thomas Dunne Books, 2013), 96.
3. Nancy Kober and Diane Stark Rentner, *History and Evolution of Public Education in the US* (Center on Education Policy, 2020), 4, https://files.eric.ed.gov/fulltext/ED606970.pdf.
4. Helen Dollery, "Page 3. Youth Groups over Time," Story: Youth Organizations, Te Ara—Encyclopedia of New Zealand, https://teara.govt.nz/en/youth-organisations/page-3.
5. Helen Dollery, "Page 1. Christian Youth Organisations," Story: Youth Organizations, Te Ara—Encyclopedia of New Zealand https://teara.govt.nz/en/youth-organisations/page-1.
6. "Who Is Zeal?," Zeal, https://zeal.nz/whoiszeal/.
7. "About the Organization: Changing Mindsets Through Reading to Create Change-Makers," Taghyeer, accessed April 2, 2025, https://welovereading.org/about/.
8. "WAGGGS and WOSM Welcome Nobel Peace Prize Nomination," News, World Association of Girl Guides and Girl Scouts, February 18, 2021, https://www.wagggs.org/en/news/wagggs-and-wosm-welcome-nobel-peace-prize-nomination/.
9. Home, World Scouting, https://www.scout.org/.
10. "Explore the Sustainable Development Goals," Scouts for SDGs, World Scouting, https://sdgs.scout.org/goals.
11. "Association des Scouts du Burundi," Wikimedia Foundation, last updated February 25, 2025, 11:27 (UTC), https://en.wikipedia.org/wiki/Association_des_Scouts_du_Burundi.
12. "Bangladesh Scouts," Wikimedia Foundation, last updated December 15, 2024, 11:25 (UTC), https://en.wikipedia.org/wiki/Bangladesh_Scouts.
13. "Coconut Growing," Scout Advancement Resource, Merit Badge Center, Philippines, https://www.mbcenter.org/htm/meritbadges.php?mb=coconutgrowing.
14. Howard Blumenthal, Our Whole World in Their Hands: 21st Century School and Our Global Future, unpublished manuscript, May 14, 2021
15. John Ratey, *Spark: The Revolutionary New Science of Exercise and the Brain*, with Eric Hagerman (Little, Brown, 2008), 41–42, 53.
16. "The Siaya Community Library," WISE, Qatar Foundation, last updated January 4, 2021, https://www.wise-qatar.org/project/siaya-community-library/.
17. *Libraries: How They Stack Up* (OCLC, 2003), https://www.oclc.org/content/dam/oclc/reports/librariesstackup.pdf.
18. "Library Stat of the Week #27: On Average There Are 4.7 Volunteers for Every Full-Time Library Worker," *Library Policy and Advocacy Blog*, IFLA, July 16, 2020, https://blogs.ifla.org/lpa/tag/librarystatoftheweek/page/3/.

19. "Bookmobile," Wikimedia Foundation, last updated March 18, 2025, 23:06 (UTC), https://en.wikipedia.org/wiki/Bookmobile.
20. *Libraries: How They Stack.*
21. "*The West Wing*," Wikimedia Foundation, last updated March 15, 2025, 21:04 (UTC), https://en.wikipedia.org/wiki/The_West_Wing.
22. Danny Joe's Treehouse, "Can You Come Out and Play?," online children's show, posted July 10, 2023, YouTube, 1 min., 7 sec., https://www.youtube.com/watch?v=nvhjQQodu08.
23. "The Essential Clayton Christensen Articles," *Harvard Business Review*, January 24, 2020, https://hbr.org/2020/01/the-essential-clayton-christensen-articles.
24. Bob Greenburg, "Michael Horn—Disrupting Class," Brainwaves Video Anthology, posted August 8, 2017, YouTube, 6 min., 47 sec., - https://www.youtube.com/watch?v=qYb7OcJCMTk&t=1s.
25. "Starfish," Wikimedia Foundation, last updated March 8, 2025, 17:53 (UTC), https://en.wikipedia.org/wiki/Starfish.
26. "Starfish."
27. Courtney Fernandez Petty, "All About Starfish," *STEMvisions Blog*, Smithsonian Science Education Center, September 5, 2017, https://ssec.si.edu/stemvisions-blog/all-about-starfish.
28. "History of Wikipedia" Wikimedia Foundation, last updated February 21, 2025, 00:20 (UTC), https://en.wikipedia.org/wiki/History_of_Wikipedia.
29. *Wikimedia, Inc., Consolidated Financial Statements June 30, 2023 and 2022* (KPMG, 2023), 6, https://wikimediafoundation.org/wp-content/uploads/2023/11/Wikimedia_Foundation_FS_FY2022-2023_Audit_Report.pdf#page=6.
30. "Council Approves FY24 School Budget," Portland Public Schools, accessed April 2, 2025, https://www.portlandschools.org/calendars/news/~board/district-school-news/post/council-approves-fy24-school-budget.
31. "About Portland Public Schools, Portland Public Schools, accessed April 2, 2025, https://www.portlandschools.org/about.
32. "Gravity," Wikimedia Foundation, last updated March 7, 2025, 9:57 (UTC), https://en.wikipedia.org/wiki/Gravity.
33. ChatGPT, https://chat.openai.com/. Access and response on July 6, 2023 at 5:57 P.M.

Chapter 6

1. *Reinventing School*, "Episode 48: Running Ithaca's Schools," web video series, posted September 10, 2021, https://www.learningrevolution.com/reinventingschool/episode-48-running-ithaca-s-schools.
2. *Ballotpedia*, "Analysis of School District and Board Member Characteristics, 2022," August 24, 2022, https://ballotpedia.org/Analysis_of_school_district_and_board_member_characteristics,_2022.
3. Peg Tyre, "Why Do More than Half of Principals Quit After Five Years?," Hechinger Report, September 26, 2015, https://hechingerreport.org/why-do-more-than-half-of-principals-quit-after-five-years/.
4. Soheyla Taie and Laurie Lewis, *Characteristics of 2020–2021 Public and Private K–12 School Principals in the United States: Results from the National Teacher and Principal Survey* (US Department of Education, National Center for Education Statistics, 2022), 3, https://nces.ed.gov/pubs2022/2022112.pdf.
5. Taie and Lewis, *Characteristics*, 3.

6. Jason Hill et al., *Trends in Public and Private School Principal Demographics and Qualifications: 1987–88 to 2011–12* (US Department of Education, National Center for Education Statistics, 2016), 6, https://nces.ed.gov/pubs2016/2016189.pdf.
7. Hill, *Trends*, 6.
8. "List of Countries and Dependencies by Population," Wikimedia Foundation, last updated March 21, 2025, 3:12 (UTC), https://en.wikipedia.org/wiki/List_of_countries_and_dependencies_by_population.
9. *Global Report on Teachers: Addressing Teacher Shortages and Transforming the Profession* (UNESCO, 2024), https://unesdoc.unesco.org/ark:/48223/pf0000384714.
10. *Global Report*.
11. *Reinventing School*, "Episode 36: The Vastness of Social Studies," *web video* series, posted February 1, 2021 https://www.learningrevolution.com/reinventingschool/episode-36-social-studies.
12. "The Persistent Teacher Gap in Sub-Saharan Africa is Jeopardizing Education Recovery," News, UNESCO, last updated April 20, 2023, https://www.unesco.org/en/articles/persistent-teacher-gap-sub-saharan-africa-jeopardizing-education-recovery?TSPD_101_R0=080713870fab20003c6a9c7e6919f57646ece2371d8d8e05643603d5459a813e-3716927b0dd5780a08eef273c2143000a9b9ad800f283fa231cb8fc8d835030b4d0c6d10dc-260f68a07d0c439b278ed808dcac57982fb1d132ae7a52ba29316e.
13. Observation by Ploi Sripoom, a University of Virginia student who grew up in Thailand.
14. Howard Blumenthal and Richard Pianta, "Abdullah–Uganda2024–Teachers on Earth–7-25-2024," *Kids on Earth*, video posted July 25, 2024, Vimeo. https://vimeo.com/990240998.
15. Roughly, and a popular source: "This opinion is recorded in the 15th century collection of homilies written by an Augustinian clergyman called John Mirk in *Mirk's Festial*, circa 1450: Hyt ys old Englysch sawe." Gary Martin, "Children Should Be Seen and Not Heard," Phrase Finder, https://www.phrases.org.uk/meanings/children-should-be-seen-and-not-heard.html.
16. Email correspondence with Robin Gregory, January 5, 2025, related to Robin Gregory and Brooke Moore, *Sorting It Out: Supporting Teenage Decision Making* (Cambridge University Press, 2024).
17. *Reinventing School*, "Episode 49: An AFT Perspective," web video series, posted January 6, 2022, https://www.learningrevolution.com/reinventingschool/episode-49-an-aft-perspective .
18. Carol Dweck, "A Summary of Growth and Fixed Mindsets," (blog), Farnam Street, https://fs.blog/carol-dweck-mindset/.
19. *Global Multidimensional Poverty Index 2021: Unmasking Disparities by Ethnicity, Cast, and Gender* (UNDP, 2021), https://hdr.undp.org/content/2021-global-multidimensional-poverty-index-mpi.
20. Joe Hasell, "Data Appendix—The Fight Against Global Poverty: 200 Years of Progress and Still a Very Long Way to Go," Our World in Data, July 7, 2019, https://ourworldindata.org/history-of-poverty-data-appendix.
21. Mary Barringer, "10 Ways to Reduce Poverty in the World," (blog), The Borgen Project, April 29, 2017, https://borgenproject.org/10-ways-to-reduce-poverty-in-the-world/.
22. Lawrence Steinberg, *Age of Opportunity: Lessons from the New Science of Adolescence* (Houghton Mifflin Harcourt, 2014), 22.

Chapter 7

1. "Lismore: 2021 Census All Persons QuickStats," Australian Bureau of Statistics, https://abs.gov.au/census/find-census-data/quickstats/2021/LGA14850.

2. Adam Nossiter, "Charles Sallis, 89, Dies; Upended the Teaching of Mississippi History," *New York Times*, updated February 19, 2024, https://www.nytimes.com/2024/02/16/us/charles-sallis-dead.html.
3. Dylan Chung, "Is Vertical Farming the Future?," High School Insider, *Los Angeles Times*, August 30, 2023, https://highschool.latimes.com/portola-high-school/is-vertical-farming-the-future/.
4. "Case Studies," Freight Farms, https://www.freightfarms.com/case-studies.
5. Piercarlo Valdesolo, "Why 'Magical Thinking' Works for Some People," *Scientific American*, October 19, 2010, https://www.scientificamerican.com/article/superstitions-can-make-you/.
6. Marc Tucker, "Why Other Countries Keep Outperforming Us in Education (and How to Catch Up)," Education Week, May 13, 2021, https://www.edweek.org/policy-politics/opinion-why-other-countries-keep-outperforming-us-in-education-and-how-to-catch-up/2021/05.
7. Igor Juricevic, "Personal Beliefs Versus Scientific Innovation: Getting past a Flat Earth Mentality," The Conversation, June 13, 2016, https://theconversation.com/personal-beliefs-versus-scientific-innovation-getting-past-a-flat-earth-mentality-58842.
8. Juricevic, "Personal Beliefs."
9. *Reinventing School*, "Episode 6: College Behind Bars," *web video* series, posted June 10, 2020, https://www.learningrevolution.com/reinventingschool/episode-6-college-behind-bars.
10. "From George Washington to Major General John Sullivan, 31 May 1779," Founders Online, National Archives, https://founders.archives.gov/documents/Washington/03-20-02-0661.
11. *Fact Book: State University of New York at Geneseo* (Office of Institutional Research, 2009–2010), https://www.geneseo.edu/sites/default/files/sites/ir/Fact_0910.pdf.
12. *Fact Book*.
13. "State University of New York at Geneseo," Wikimedia Foundation, last updated March 17, 2025, 21:14 (UTC), https://en.wikipedia.org/wiki/State_University_of_New_York_at_Geneseo.
14. *SUNY Diversity, Equity, and Inclusion Phase One Action Plan* (SUNY Office of Diversity, Equity, and Inclusion, 2021), introduction, 1, https://www.suny.edu/media/suny/content-assets/documents/diversity/suny-dei-final-action-plan.pdf.
15. "Gustavo Petro," Wikimedia Foundation, last updated March 15, 2025, 21:09 (UTC), https://en.wikipedia.org/wiki/Gustavo_Petro.
16. Gustavo Petro, "Colombian President Gustavo Petro: Full Interview of Democracy Now!," interview by Amy Goodman, *War and Peace Report*, Democracy Now!, September 22, 2023, https://www.democracynow.org/2023/9/22/full_interview_colombian_president_gustavo_petro.
17. "The 25 Best Places to Travel in 2025," *BBC Travel*, January 16, 2025, https://www.bbc.com/travel/article/20250115-the-25-best-places-to-travel-in-2025.
18. Lauren Camera, "College Enrollment Declines Are Here to Stay," *U.S. News & World Report*, May 26, 2022, https://www.usnews.com/news/education-news/articles/2022-05-26/college-enrollment-declines-are-here-to-stay.
19. *Reinventing School*, "Episode 3: The Shift to Distance Learning," *web video* series, posted May 21, 2020, https://www.learningrevolution.com/reinventingschool/announcing-episode-3-the-shift-to-distance-learning.
20. "Fast Facts: Educational Institutions," Institute of Education Sciences, https://nces.ed.gov/FastFacts/display.asp?id=84.

21. Correlates of War—National Material Capabilities Version 6.0 (2021), "Military Personnel as a Share of Total Population," Our World in Data, last updated July 26, 2024, https://ourworldindata.org/grapher/military-personnel-relative-to-total-population.
22. "Employees," USAFacts, updated May 17, 2021, https://usafacts.org/annual-publications/2021/government-10-k/part-i/item-1-purpose-and-function-of-our-government-general/employees/.
23. Patricia Jennings, *Mindfulness for Teachers* (W. W. Norton, 2015), 2, 4.
24. Jennings, *Mindfulness*, 89.

About the Authors

Howard Blumenthal is a senior scholar with the University of Pennsylvania's Positive Psychology Center, and executive director of the 21st Century Learning Project at the University of Virginia's School of Education and Human Development. As founder of *Kids on Earth*, Howard has interviewed hundreds of children and teenagers all over the world. Their wisdom led to this book. Howard is best known in the US as the cocreator and producer of the Emmy and Peabody Award–winning public television series for children and teenagers, *Where in the World Is Carmen Sandiego?* He has developed and produced media productions for Food Network, the History Channel, HBO, Nickelodeon, Showtime, ITV, Merriam-Webster, and many other clients and partners. Howard led the initial MTV development team for—and helped to launch—Nickelodeon. His documentary work includes *On the Other Side of the Fence*, recognized by the United Nations with a special award for public service. Howard has served as a senior vice president for a children's media division of Hearst and for the world's largest music website for Bertelsmann. Howard is the cofounder of the National Archives of Game Show History at the Strong National Museum of Play. He is the author or coauthor of twenty-five books about creativity, media, marketing, business, US history, popular music, science, and technology. For many years, Howard was a popular syndicated columnist distributed to more than one hundred newspapers by The NY Times Syndicate and United Features. He is the recipient of an honorary doctorate of human letters from the State University of New York.

Robert C. Pianta is the Batten Bicentennial Professor of Early Childhood Education, professor of psychology, and founding director of the Center for Advanced Study of Teaching and Learning at the University of Virginia. Pianta's research and policy interests focus on the intersection of education and human development. In particular, his work has advanced the conceptualization and measurement of teacher-student relationships and documents their contributions to students' learning and development. Pianta has led research and development on measurement tools and interventions that help teachers interact with students more effectively and that are used widely in the United States and around the world. Pianta began his career as a special education teacher and joined the University of Virginia faculty in 1986. He is the past editor of the *Journal of School Psychology* and associate editor for *AERA Open*. An internationally recognized expert in both early childhood education and K–12 teaching and learning, Pianta regularly consults with federal agencies, foundations, universities, and governments. He was named a fellow of the American Education Research Association and received the Distinguished Alumni Award from the University of Minnesota in 2016. Pianta served as dean of the UVA School of Education of Human Development from 2007–2022 and remains a member of the faculty.

Index